Praise for Lisa Barnes and Petit Appetit

"This collection of more than 150 organic recipes is sensitive to children with food allergies. The book contains a nice assortment of vegetarian and vegan selections and fare that is free of added sugar, eggs, gluten, and wheat. Several recipes require no cooking at all. (Pssst! You also can use non-organic ingredients and produce yummy results.) Added bonus: Recipes the whole family can enjoy." —*Denver Post*

"Parents who don't mind taking a few extra steps in the kitchen will find that *The Petit Appetit Cookbook* offers many interesting, wholesome, and fun reasons to skip the grocery store's baby food aisle. And they just might find that their own diets improve accordingly." —*The New York Sun*

"If you've got toddlers at your table, or have a baby due soon, I urge you to get a copy of *The Petit Appetit Cookbook*." —**Lime.com**

"Little ones will love the all-organic recipes in Lisa Barnes's cookbook—they're kids-tested, healthy, and easy to prepare." —*Body & Soul*

"You'll never feed your baby or toddler food from a jar or a drive-thru ever again after seeing the delicious, nutritious, and easy recipes in this fabulous cookbook." —**Babystyle.com**

"*The Petit Appetit Cookbook* not only is an enchanting collection of wholesome recipes but also includes countless resources for nutritional information, shopping, organization, special diets, food safety and storage, and more. Barnes succeeds at encouraging seasonal, organic eating, and keeping a great variety of flavors and textures in baby's repertoire. *Mais oui! Merci!*" —**Leslie Pave, chef and writer, www.menuboom.com**

continued . . .

"When it comes to food and our children's health, Lisa Barnes may be our most accomplished and creative 'mom-to-mom' writer. To the morning question every mother has, 'What shall I feed them today?' Lisa has more answers in her books than a Chinese restaurant menu. And every one is healthy and full of nutritious good sense. If you're time-constrained with young children, like Lisa is, her hands-on experience and wisdom will be welcome relief." —**Dave Smith, author of *To Be of Use* and editor and founder of organic food team blog www.organictobe.org**

"In *The Petit Appetit Cookbook,* Lisa Barnes has produced a most creative and clever book abundant with recipes for feeding babies and toddlers. She succeeds with a wide variety of healthy, organic, and delicious recipes that suit each developmental stage. Her tips and information are the backbone for this delightful cookbook." —**Dana Laake, RDH, MS, LDN, licensed nutritionist and coauthor of *The ADHD & Autism Cookbook***

"Part of the reason [Lisa's] included in our Quest for the Best (besides her great recipes) is her delightful style: She's easy-going and totally non-judgmental. As we busy moms know, we want great ideas, not guilt!" —**Kelly Corbet, CEO of Smart Foods, Healthy Kids**

"As a registered dietitian, educator, and counselor, I'm thrilled to have this cookbook as a resource both professionally and personally." —**Melissa Halas-Liang, MA, RD CNSD, CDE, founder of SuperKids Nutrition**

"Another masterful creation by Lisa Barnes! She brings to the forefront the need and importance of reversing American families' reliance on chemical and fat-laden processed foods and empowers parents to nourish their kids with wholesome foods made from pure and natural ingredients." —**Ivy Marx, registered dietitian, Los Angeles Unified School District**

"Lisa has a talent for creating simple, delicious recipes with easy cooking techniques, manageable ingredient lists, and plenty of information about storage, variations, and nutrition. These qualities make her book a great choice for families of any background or income level. I frequently use this book at home with my family and also at work during our cooking and nutrition workshops. Even though she wrote it for parents, many of these recipes are great for 'movers and shakers' of any age!" —**Adrienne Markworth, founder of Leah's Pantry**

petit appetit

Eat, Drink, and Be Merry

Easy, Organic Snacks, Beverages, and
Party Foods for Kids of All Ages

LISA BARNES

A PERIGEE BOOK

A PERIGEE BOOK
Published by the Penguin Group
Penguin Group (USA) Inc.
375 Hudson Street, New York, New York 10014, USA

Penguin Group (Canada), 90 Eglinton Avenue East, Suite 700, Toronto, Ontario M4P 2Y3, Canada
   (a division of Pearson Penguin Canada Inc.)
Penguin Books Ltd., 80 Strand, London WC2R 0RL, England
Penguin Group Ireland, 25 St. Stephen's Green, Dublin 2, Ireland (a division of Penguin Books Ltd.)
Penguin Group (Australia), 250 Camberwell Road, Camberwell, Victoria 3124, Australia
   (a division of Pearson Australia Group Pty. Ltd.)
Penguin Books India Pvt. Ltd., 11 Community Centre, Panchsheel Park, New Delhi—110 017, India
Penguin Group (NZ), 67 Apollo Drive, Rosedale, North Shore 0632, New Zealand
   (a division of Pearson New Zealand Ltd.)
Penguin Books (South Africa) (Pty.) Ltd., 24 Sturdee Avenue, Rosebank, Johannesburg 2196, South Africa

Penguin Books Ltd., Registered Offices: 80 Strand, London WC2R 0RL, England

While the author has made every effort to provide accurate telephone numbers and Internet addresses at the time of publication, neither the publisher nor the author assumes any responsibility for errors, or for changes that occur after publication. Further, the publisher does not have any control over and does not assume any responsizbility for author or third-party websites or their content.

Copyright © 2009 by Lisa Barnes
Cover art and design by Satoko Furuta
Text design by Jill Weber

First edition: March 2009

Library of Congress Cataloging-in-Publication Data

Barnes, Lisa.
   Petit appetit : eat, drink, and be merry : easy organic snacks,
   beverages, and party foods for kids of all ages / Lisa Barnes.— 1st ed.
      p. cm.
   "A Perigee book."
   Includes bibliographical references and index.
   ISBN 978-0-399-53489-8
   1. Snack foods. 2. Natural foods. 3. Children—Nutrition. I. Title.
   TX740.B3765 2009
   641.5'3—dc22   2008039558

PRINTED IN THE UNITED STATES OF AMERICA

10 9 8 7 6 5 4 3 2 1

PUBLISHER'S NOTE: The recipes contained in this book are to be followed exactly as written. The publisher is not responsible for your specific health or allergy needs that may require medical supervision. The publisher is not responsible for any adverse reactions to the recipes contained in this book.

Most Perigee books are available at special quantity discounts for bulk purchases for sales promotions, premiums, fund-raising, or educational use. Special books, or book excerpts, can also be created to fit specific needs. For details, write: Special Markets, Penguin Group (USA) Inc., 375 Hudson Street, New York, New York 10014.

Contents

Acknowledgments

ONE OF THE BEST PARTS OF MY DAY is sharing dinner at home with my family. We have a nightly ritual where each family member (no matter how young) tells about the favorite part of his or her day and shares three things he or she is grateful for. Sometimes they're sweet (and easy) like "Mom, Dad, and brother/sister," and other times it's all about the food (instant gratification) like "bread, fish, and milk."

In the spirit of "thankfuls" (as my kids call them), I'd like to share some of mine in writing this book:

I am very lucky to have consistency and support from those who worked on my first book, *The Petit Appetit Cookbook*. I am grateful for my literary agent, Nancy Crossman, who, even though she lives in Chicago and I live in California, couldn't be more supportive, encouraging, and determined to help me spread my philosophy and recipes. Thanks to John Duff at Penguin for allowing me to do another book, and providing the perfect title. I also appreciate all the good cheer and editing efforts of the Jeanettes—Jeanette Shaw and Jeanette Egan—for making sure my ideas, recipes, and words all make sense (and don't run long). And thanks to Satoko Furuta for another great cover design.

I'm thankful to all the "experts" who contributed to the book: everyone from food bloggers, to nutritionists, to chefs, to pediatricians, to educators, to growers, and more. Thank you for the thoughtful foreword by Melissa Halas-Liang and comments by Ivy Marx—two fellow children's nutrition advocates. And to Monica Matheny for her recipe review, creative suggestions, and friendship.

Of course, the most generous contributors were children—especially those at my son's preschool in the Rabbit and Monkey classes. The honesty of a child who loves or hates your recipes is priceless. I truly enjoyed preparing food for and with them and listening to their laughter and banter. In my research (and as a mom), I've found many like-minded parents who are concerned for their child's health and nutrition and love sharing their stories, tips, and wisdom about feeding their families. Their comments and experiences are insightful, inspiring, and funny.

My family gets big thanks and hugs because they gave me the time and encouragement to write another book (while they continue to shamelessly promote the first book). (Although I think Nana, Poppa, Unc, Tee Tee, Gido, Grandma, and Grandpa liked the extra excuse for babysitting duty and recipe testing.) I'm especially thankful to my sister for her helpful aunt duties while on her "layover" (conveniently close to my deadline). My family also provided material for the reality of outside influences (good and bad) that shape my children's eating habits. Most important, I enjoyed reflecting on celebrations and recipes from my own childhood. The person who created most of my special "every days" is my mom.

I'm grateful for my helpful sous chefs (children), Jonas and Ellery, for providing me with so much inspiration, love, and laughter in the kitchen and otherwise. I look forward to creating more special "everyday" moments and celebrations for their many adventures and events to come. Thanks for their understanding and enthusiasm when they got Dad all to themselves (when Mom needed to sit at the computer).

Finally, thank you to my husband, Lee, for so much, but most important, for warming my side of the bed while I finished long nights of writing. I love you.

Thank you.

Foreword

RECENTLY, WHEN SPEAKING TO A GROUP of young mothers about baby and toddler nutrition, I recommended Lisa Barnes's first book, *The Petit Appetit Cookbook*. At the same time, I wished there was a follow-up book for older children and parents to enjoy that included helpful tips and recipes just as delicious, simple, and resourceful. So I was overjoyed when I heard she had written this book for just that very reason.

After the toddler years, it's easy for moms to get off track from healthy eating as life gets busier and kids become more independent. This book puts you back on course to continue fulfilling the healthy intentions you've had ever since you were preparing your baby's first foods. Now you have a compass to navigate the school-age years. These fun, delectable, adventurous recipes and helpful guides will help you and your children cook and live a healthy lifestyle with ease. Lisa's creativity and passion for kid-friendly cuisine shine throughout each chapter.

As a registered dietitian, educator, and counselor, I'm thrilled to be able to recommend this as a must-have resource and cookbook for clients, but especially glad to have it for myself professionally and personally. *Petit Appetit: Eat, Drink, and Be Merry* brings together the connections between food, fun, health, parent modeling, and the environment. Lisa provides practical tips so you can apply these connections to create a healthy environment for your children and family. The best news is you don't need to be a gourmet chef to enjoy making these meals with ease or become a health expert to find the way to live well. It's all here for Mom or Dad, yet so simply presented you'll wonder why you didn't think of it yourself.

As you find yourself taking on new adventures with your little chefs, whether it be in the kitchen, farmers' market, grocery stores, or garden, take pleasure in the new or enhanced perspective that this book brings: good nutrition can grow a healthy family with simplicity and enjoyment.

MELISSA HALAS-LIANG, MA, Registered Dietitian,
Certified Diabetes Educator, and Founder of SuperKids Nutrition, Inc.

Introduction

M Y FAMILY HAS ALWAYS SHARED GIGGLES, goofs, and good times together in the kitchen. As a baby, my son watched me knead dough, listened to my songs about fruits and veggies, waved a whisk, and sometimes slept, all while I tested recipes for my first book, *The Petit Appetit Cookbook.*

My daughter was six days old when she joined our family for a Sunday morning at the farmers' market. And when it was time for her first bite– look out! She wanted it all. Since then, it's seemed as though she's never put down her fork. She has a healthy and varied appetite, and like her brother, came in handy for recipe testing for my next book, Williams-Sonoma's *Cooking for Baby.*

My children have grown with my philosophy of eating healthy, fresh, organic foods from their very first bite, and I get so excited to learn from other parents that they are doing the same. Parents all over the country (and even across the globe) have told me how they, too, enjoy cooking for and with their children, and they've requested more recipes and ideas for creating healthy snacks, drinks, and party foods. I feel as if our children are growing up together and experiencing many of the same foods, flavors, and eating stages, and I want to share this book with everyone who is guiding children to healthier food and drink choices for school, play, and every day!

In writing this book I had a few kitchen tests go awry (a new microwave was necessary after a popcorn problem) and I underestimated the time necessary for testing and writing with two little ones. Sometimes I thought if people saw me cooking (and scorching, especially at midnight), they would never believe I write cookbooks. Then I realized that's exactly who should write children's food recipes: someone with real children and busy lives going to school and sports practices and dealing with the outside influences of junk foods and peer pressures (rather than a food stylist with a big staff in a large fancy kitchen with endless hours to test recipes and create magical food pyramids in silence).

I'm inspired by parents, teachers, nutritionists, chefs, and pediatricians who are making a positive impact on children's health and nutrition. With the recipes in this book and all the advocates in the community, I hope our children become confident in their food choices and rely on their good eating habits established at home when at school, playdates, soccer practice, birthday parties, and as they celebrate life's events.

It's so great to share my recipes, experiences, and traditions with other families. Of course, each child is an individual and will have her own preferences. But it's how we as parents allow them to experience foods and teach them about growing, cooking, eating, shopping, and sharing at snack time, party time, and any time that builds healthy habits and nurtures responsible eaters.

I underestimated the enthusiasm and curiosity my children would have for helping in the kitchen. They really want to be in the middle of the action. They participate in everything from stirring batters, dumping ingredients, and counting eggs, to turning on "zoom-zooms" (the stand mixer and food processor), choosing produce, and setting (and clearing) the table. There's some kitchen competition, too; it's a little like mini *Top Chef*. Brother and sister vie for position and approval of the judges (Mom and Dad). Thankfully, they also enjoy experiencing new foods (for the most part), and were both eager taste testers for this book. At publication my son's favorite food is mussels and clams and my daughter's nickname at the family table is "the mad dipper."

I hope you'll enjoy the recipes in this book with your family as much as I have enjoyed creating them with mine.

Bon Petit Appetit!

CHAPTER 1

Using This Book

SNACKS, DRINKS, AND CELEBRATIONS are a big part of our children's lives. As parents, we want our children to be happy and healthy at home, at school, and at play. Get the most out of this book by thinking outside the bag (of store-bought chips, crackers, and premade dips) and can (of soda and "vitamin" sports drinks) and learn to create and reinvent family favorites with great-tasting, healthy, organic ingredients, and have fun in the process. Take the opportunity and time to empower your children to make positive food and drink choices; participate in the shopping and preparation; and allow them to help create their own snack, drink, and party favorites. In addition to recipes, you'll find expert advice, tips, stories, and resources for reading food labels; reducing allergen risks; eliminating harmful food ingredients; and overall "greening" of snacks, drinks, and party foods for children.

When you cook at home, you're making a choice to reduce the additives, preservatives, and other potentially harmful ingredients in your child's foods. You can feel good about preparing your own foods and drinks that your children will eat, enjoy, share, and help create while putting them on a path to making healthy food choices for a lifetime. Celebrated pediatrician Dr. William Sears wrote in *The Family Nutrition Book*, "After years of observation, I became convinced that the children who ate the healthiest foods were the healthiest kids. They were sick less often, had fewer discipline problems and achieved better in school. They not only had healthier bodies, they had healthier minds."

ABOUT THE RECIPES

There's a variety of food and beverages for all ages, stages, and tastes in this book (even those who are "choosy" eaters). Because texture is such a large part of children's adversity to food, the snack section ("Eat") is based on sound and mouth feel. Recipes in the beverage chapter ("Drink") are also categorized for those who like a variety of flavors, temperatures, and textures. Finally, the "special occasion" foods ("Be Merry") are meant to be shared and appeal to a number of ages, themes, and celebrations. Many of these recipes are not set to traditional holidays or beliefs; they celebrate the everyday excitement in a child's life. The recipes can be interchanged between sections. The recipes in the "Eat" and "Drink" sections can be doubled or tripled to serve a crowd in the "Be Merry" category. And leftover "Be Merry" foods such as Pizza Pinwheels (page 164) can also be packed for lunch as an "Eat" option. So look over the entire book for recipes and ideas before planning and prepping.

Recipe Icons and Definitions

The recipes have been reviewed by parents and nutritionists to find a balance of appetizing foods that are also quick and easy to prepare; some do not even require cooking. Each recipe shows the ingredients, amounts, nutritional analysis, prep tips, and ingredient icons. If a health professional has diagnosed your child with allergies, intolerances, or other health issues, the recipe icons can help quickly identify recipes that meet dietary and cooking restrictions. For readers of *The Petit Appetit Cookbook* these icons should be familiar, with a few additions to help identify foods with nuts (a no-no at many schools) and milk (for those with casein and lactose issues). There are also indicators for best recipes for sharing and packing, and those appropriate for the youngest in the family.

 Egg-free: Recipes without eggs, especially important for those with egg allergies and adults with cholesterol concerns.

Milk-free: Recipes without cow's or goat's milk, using alternatives such as rice milk. Especially good for babies under one year and those with lactose intolerance or casein allergy.

 Gluten-free: Recipes without gluten, the elastic protein, using wheat-free alternative flours and grains. They may be convenient for those with celiac disease, although some recipes should be reviewed closely, as they may contain oats. Many recent studies indicate that the protein found in oats may not be harmful to most people with celiac disease. However, there is concern that the oats may be contaminated with wheat during the milling and processing. Please consult your physician or dietitian before adding oats to your child's diet.

 Nut-free: Recipes without peanuts or tree nuts, including almonds, Brazil nuts, cashews, chestnuts, coconuts, hazelnuts (filberts), hickory nuts, macadamia nuts, pecans, pine nuts, pistachios, and walnuts, plus marzipan, nut butters, nut paste, nougat, and nut extracts. This is helpful for those under two years and those with nut allergies. Pack for lunch at nut-free schools and occasions where there could be people with allergies.

 Cook with Kids: Recipes with simple tasks for children to help prepare. Good for children's cooking parties and gatherings.

 Good for Groups/Party Pleasers: Recipes that make a large quantity and are appropriate for a variety of ages, palates, and venues.

 Perfect for Packing: Foods that are easy to pack for school and day trips.

 No Cook: Simple recipes that do not need to be cooked, even in a microwave.

 No Sugar Added: Recipes without added sugar or sweetener such as brown rice syrup and molasses.

Wheat-free: Recipes without wheat, especially for babies with wheat allergies.

Vegetarian: Recipes without animal meats, including poultry and fish, but may include eggs or milk products.

Vegan: Recipes without any animal products, including honey, eggs, and dairy products.

Baby/Beginner: Recipes appropriate for even the youngest children, with suggestions for serving (bottle, cup, and straw).

Go Green: Tips for how to improve the preparation, presentation, and storage to make the recipe more earth-friendly.

Kids Korner: Boxes at the bottom corner of many recipes to share tips, suggestions, and stories about including children in the kitchen, where all the action (and laughter) happens!

Nutritional Analysis

The analyses of the recipes were performed by CompuFood Analysis, Inc. (www.compufoodanalysis.com). Some things to note:

- When the ingredient, sauce, or serving suggestion is optional or not included in the main recipe, it is not included in the nutritional analysis.

- The serving sizes are based on the Food and Drug Administration portions for adults for many of the recipes (especially in the "Drink" and "Be Merry" sections). However, some in the "Eat" section are based on an average child's portion.

Ingredients

Please note that the recipes will sometimes list organically grown and raised produce, fish, poultry, and meats, as well as other foods. This is not meant to be exclusionary; conventionally grown and raised ingredients and products will work as well, though I suggest using as many fresh, locally grown, organic ingredients as possible in order to yield the most nutrition and flavor. The ingredients specified as "organic" are those that have been identified as the most contaminated and potentially harmful to your family. See Dirty Dozen (page 15) and Other Potentially Harmful Foods (pages 16–19). Many grocery stores are expanding their inventory of natural and organic foods; however, some ingredients may not be readily available at your local supermarket, or are too cost-prohibitive for your budget. You can check local specialty stores, health food stores, farmers' markets, online (see the store and website resources on pages 256–259), or substitute with another item. Recipes make note of such ingredients and substitutions.

> The information contained in this publication should not be used as a substitute for the medical care and nutritional advice of your pediatrician. There may be variations in treatment and diet that your pediatrician may recommend based upon your child's individual facts, health, and circumstances.

CHAPTER 2

Do You Know What They're Eating?

Fake food—I mean those patented substances chemically flavored and mechanically bulked out to kill the appetite and deceive the gut—is unnatural, almost immoral, a bane to good eating and good cooking.

JULIA CHILD

You need the whole food. Processing removes nutrients.

MARION NESTLE, author and professor of nutrition
and public health at New York University

THE HIDDEN TRUTHS OF PROCESSED FOODS

When children are hungry (or as they sometimes say, "starving"), it's easy to reach for a bag of processed snacks to calm them. This is only a quick fix. That bag may contain additives, preservatives, trans fats, and high-fructose corn syrup, all of which may disrupt and harm their growing bodies and minds in the long term. Even in the short term we see the effects of these foods on children's moods and activity level. A research study published online by the British medical journal *The Lancet* concluded that common food additives and colorings found in many children's foods can increase hyperactive behavior in a broad range of children. The finding lends strong support for the case that food additives exacerbate hyperactive behaviors (inattention, impulsivity, and overactivity) at least into middle childhood.

As a parent, it is hard to compete with food manufacturers that spend more than one billion dollars annually encouraging your child to eat this or drink that. Besides outside influences, our own lives are hectic and busier than ever. We want convenience, and kids expect something that tastes good. "We have turned over the nutrition education of our children to the food industry," warns Kelly Brownell, director of the Rudd Center for Food Policy at Yale. Food manufacturers rely on additives, preservatives, fillers, and low-quality ingredients to keep down costs, increase shelf life, ship longer distances, and increase profits. Of course these goals do not benefit the health and nutrition of our families. Shopping with children is hard enough, and supermarkets aren't helping parents by placing all the highly processed, overly packaged, and fanciful food items at your child's eye level and reach.

The ingredients below are found in a staggering number of processed snacks, beverages, and condiments. Eating whole foods and making your own snacks and drinks will help you eliminate or at least reduce consumption of the following:

High-Fructose Corn Syrup

High-fructose corn syrup (HFCS) can be six times as sweet as cane sugar and is cheaper to produce because it's made from corn, a heavily subsidized crop. It makes up nearly half of the sweeteners used in processed foods and is found in everything from sodas and fruit juice to cereal and crackers. According to the April 2004 issue of *The American Journal of Clinical Nutrition*, high-fructose corn syrup is utilized differently from other sugars by the body, as it is processed in the liver and triggers the release of triglycerides, which puts people at higher risk for heart disease, stroke, and weight gain. This sweetener does not send the same "full" signal to the brain as sugar does. Thus, people overeat items containing HFCS. In a 2001 study published in *The Lancet*, researchers found children who drank one soft drink per day had a 60 percent greater chance of becoming obese, which increases chances of developing type 2 diabetes, heart disease, stroke, respiratory problems, and some cancers.

If nutritional hazards aren't concerning enough, consider that the corn used to make this sweetener is almost always genetically modified, thus exposed to more herbicides and pesticides than regular crops.

Trans Fats

Trans fats are produced from vegetable oil that is converted from unsaturated fatty acids into saturated ones. In processed foods they are used to replace naturally occurring solid fats such as butter and liquid oils, which are more expensive. Trans fats allow packaged cookies, cakes, crackers, and other baked goods to have a longer shelf life. Unfortunately, according to the American Heart Association, these trans fats lower our "good" cholesterol and increase the "bad," which increases insulin resistance and elevates the risk of type 2 diabetes and heart disease.

Refined Sugar and Carbohydrates

Medical experts caution about added sugars in today's food, especially food aimed at children. Christine Gerbstadt, MD, RD, tells parents to give children natural sources of sugar such as fruits, vegetables, whole grains, and milk whenever possible. This is a challenge for families who already are used to overly sweet flavors and foods. Roberta Anding, RD, and spokesperson for the American Dietetic Association, suggests "focusing on reducing rather than trying to eliminate sugar altogether."

Allergen Risks

Based on information from the Food and Drug Administration (FDA), it is estimated that 2 percent of adults and about 5 percent of infants and young children in the United States suffer from food allergies. About 30,000 consumers require emergency room treatment and 150 Americans die each year because of allergic reactions to food, according to a December 21, 2005, FDA release.

There is an abundance of processed foods that are manufactured and transported with other foods that may routinely cause allergies. "The eight major food allergens account for 90 percent of all documented food allergic reactions, and some reactions may be severe or life-threatening," said Robert E. Brackett, PhD, director of the FDA's Center for Food Safety and Applied Nutrition. Effective 2006, the FDA implemented the Food Allergen Labeling and Consumer Protection Act to require food labels to clearly state if food products contain any ingredients that are derived from protein from the eight major allergenic foods:

Crustacean shellfish

Eggs

Fish

Milk

Peanuts

Soybeans

Tree nuts

Wheat

The food label must list these ingredients and indicate the name of the source of the food allergen, or explain that the food is "made in a facility that also processes" a source of allergen.

According to the FDA, this labeling is meant to be especially helpful to families with children who must learn to recognize the presence of substances they must avoid. For example, if a product contains the milk-derived protein casein, the product's label will have to include a milk warning in addition to the ingredient name "casein" so that those with milk allergies can clearly understand the presence of the allergen they need to avoid.

If your family has such allergies, consult the packages and read the warnings. Many foods that you would not suspect, such as condiments (ketchup, soy sauce), snack foods (chips, crackers), and even toothpaste are potentially harmful to those with allergies. While peanut is the most common allergen, it is difficult to identify which products have trace amounts. Cross-contamination is likely when nut parts or dust contaminate other foods during manufacturing. Depending on the allergy and sensitivity, even trace amounts may cause a reaction.

> "Lanie's food needs became a real bonding experience for our family. We still love to make meals with spelt pasta." Lanie outgrew her wheat and grain allergies and now eats pretty much everything, according to dad, Rick Bayless (Chef and owner, Frontera Grill and Topolobampo, in Chicago), and daughter, Lanie, now fifteen, authors of *Rick and Lanie's Excellent Kitchen Adventures.*

You should know if your child is allergic to any of the following foods and ingredients derived from them. This list is courtesy of Dana Laake, RDH, MS, LDN, co-author of *The Kid-Friendly ADHD & Autism Cookbook*.

◆ **Corn:** Cornstarch, cornmeal, popcorn, maize, corn oil, corn syrup, dextrin, glucose, fruit pectin, fructose, high-fructose corn syrup, lecithin, malt dextrin, monosodium glutamate (MSG), salt, thickeners, and vegetable starch

◆ **Eggs:** Egg powder, albumen globulin, vitelin livetin, ovoglobulin, ovamucin, ovamucoid, ovovitellin, ovovitelia, and lysozyme

◆ **Gluten:** Wheat, semolina, bulgur, couscous, wheat berries, graham flour, whole meal flour, groats, malt, oats, barley, rye, triticale, spelt, and kamut

◆ **Milk:** Casein, calcium, caseinate, galactose, milk protein, lactalbumin, lactate, lactic acid, lactoblobulin, lactose, magnesium caseinate, and potassium caseinate

◆ **Nuts:** Peanuts and tree nuts (see list on page 3)

◆ **Soy:** Edamame, miso, natto, tofu, soy sprouts, tamari, tempeh, tempura, and yuba

STOCKING THE KITCHEN FOR QUICK AND EASY SNACKS AND DRINKS

Having the right food items in your pantry will enable you to make quick bites, drinks, and party foods that don't even require a recipe or measurement. Here are some staple items for your pantry and refrigerator to make a quick and healthy snack for your child, or an impromptu nutritious spread for the whole team. Some of these items can be eaten alone, too.

◆ **Beans:** Canned beans are great for quick spreads (hummus and black bean) for sandwiches, crackers, and wraps. Some children even like the beans rinsed and eaten cold right out of the can.

◆ **Cheeses, Hard:** (Cheddar, mozzarella, jack) Shredded in everything from quesadillas and wraps to melted on toast or topping a quick flatbread.

- **Cheeses, Soft:** (goat, Brie, cream, ricotta, cottage) Spread on lavosh or crackers or mixed into pasta noodles. Cottage and ricotta cheeses can be mixed with fruit chunks or spread on veggies.

- **Condiments:** Organic ketchup, mustard, and low-fat dressings are great on everything from cooked meats to sandwiches and dipping veggies. Some children (my daughter) will eat anything if it has a dip.

- **Eggs:** Enjoy scrambled, fried, and hard-cooked. Make a quick omelet or breakfast burrito combined with cheese and veggies.

- **Fruits, Dried and Freeze-Dried:** Great alone or combined with cereals for trail mixes. Also as a topping for yogurt and mixed into muffin, scone, and cookie batters.

- **Fruit, Frozen:** Added to smoothies, shakes, yogurt, and oatmeal. Some children enjoy it plain, right out of the freezer.

- **Fruit Butters and Spreads:** Topping on bagel, crackers, toast, pancakes, and waffles. Mixed into yogurt and cottage cheese.

- **Nuts and Seeds:** Alone or combined with cereals, dried fruits, trail mix, or in muffins and cookies.

- **Nut, Seed, and Soy Butters:** Peanut, cashew, almond, sunflower, tahini, soy, and more. Spread on sandwiches and the favorite all-time snack, apple slices.

- **Pasta:** Lots of shapes and colors for eating plain as finger foods, skewered with dipping sauce, or topped with cheese and veggies.

- **Vegetables, Frozen:** Add to pastas, wraps, and omelets. Some children enjoy frozen. When my son discovered frozen peas at age three, he ate them as dessert for a month straight.

- **Whole Grains:** Crackers, breads, lavosh, tortillas, and bagels can be the foundation for nut and seed butters, cottage cheese, cream cheese, hummus, melted cheese, and cooked meats and veggies.

- **Yogurts:** For quick smoothies and parfaits and low-calorie dressings and dips for fruits and veggies. Enjoy plain or frozen for pops.

PROCESSED FOODS VS. HOMEMADE

When you look at food, you should see nature. The stem of an apple recalls its attachment to a tree. The rough brown flakes in a cracker recall the rippling fields of wheat. The neon orange of an artificial cheese puff recalls clown wigs, costume jewelry, and Rit dye.

KAREN W. CULLEN, pediatrician

When considering the advantages of homemade food over store-bought, the difference is the use of whole food ingredients versus the additives, preservatives, and numbered ingredients for color and flavor you find in a ready-made supermarket product. Here are a few comparisons of grocery store items and some of the homemade food and drink recipes featured in this book:

Eat

I found a popular prepackaged item by Oscar Mayer called Lunchables Cracker Stackers in the grocery store, which I had seen advertised in magazines and in a few kids' picnic bags at the playground. The package said it contained turkey, cheese, crackers (not whole wheat), and a cookie sandwich. It didn't sound too bad; however, those four simple items have more than sixty ingredients listed, containing 390 calories, 19 grams of fat, 1 gram trans fat, 870 milligrams of sodium, and 18 grams of sugar.

Compare that with Jonas's Turkey Roll-Up (page 82), with only three ingredients containing 300 calories, 12 grams of fat, 0 trans fat, 600 milligrams of sodium, and 2 grams of sugar. You can even add Chocolatey Sliced Cookies (page 216) for 80 calories and still never have any trans fat, plus less overall fat (14 grams) and sugar (9 grams combined) and only add 10 ingredients (for a total of 13), without additives, preservatives, and wasteful packaging. Plus, the homemade version is higher in protein, fiber, whole grains, and other nutrients.

Drink

Let's take a look at soda. To compare apples to apples, I chose ginger ale. Canada Dry ginger ale has 120 calories and 33 grams of sugar and six ingredients, with the second greatest being high-fructose corn syrup (the first is water). The diet version has 0 calories and 0 sugars, but is made with aspartame, which contains phenylalanine and carries a warning for those with PKU (the inability to metabolize phenylalanine) and pregnant women.

Compare that with Ginger Soda (page 129), which has 35 calories and only 10 grams of sugar. And no warnings are necessary.

Be Merry

There are many options for birthday cakes and cupcakes, whether you decide to make yours from scratch or from a mix, or just to pick one up from the bakery. Looking at the basic box of chocolate fudge cake mix from Betty Crocker, the label lists more than thirty ingredients (before you add the water, oil, and egg), containing 270 calories, 1 gram trans fat and 18 grams of sugar. Of course you'll want to add frosting, too. The brand's vanilla frosting contains 140 calories, 1.5 grams trans fat, with 22 grams of sugar and more than twenty-seven ingredients, including partially hydrogenated oil, yellow #5, red #40, and other "artificial colors and flavors." Added together, that makes 410 calories, 9 grams of fat, 2.5 grams trans fat, 40 grams of sugar, and more than 57 ingredients—for one serving.

Compare that with our homemade Little Devil's Cake (page 160), with 260 calories, 9 grams of fat, 0 trans fat, and 30 grams of sugar. That's even better news considering that the homemade cake's serving size is bigger—the store-bought cake yields 12 servings per 8-inch cake, while the homemade cake yields 8. More cake for less calories!

CHAPTER 3

Choosing Organic: Why, When, and How

It's bizarre that the produce manager is more important to my children's health than the pediatrician.

MERYL STREEP

ACCORDING TO THE DEPARTMENT OF HEALTH and Human Services, the greatest exposure to pesticides and chemicals occurs in a child's first four years. This is why many advocate for providing organic foods for children whenever possible. Sometimes organic is more costly than conventional foods, due to the higher cost of growing methods, land conversion, and raising practices. But you also want to consider the cost of your family's health and well-being, as well as a decision to support the environment by preserving water resources and preventing agriculture-related problems. The extra monetary cost may be outweighed by concern over the possibility of harming your child's health and development. For more information regarding how you benefit your children, the community, and the environment by choosing organic foods, see *The Petit Appetit Cookbook*.

Results of a four-year European Union study on the benefits of organic food published in *Medical News Today* in 2008 suggest that organically grown fruit, vegetables, and milk are more nutritious than nonorganically produced food and may contain higher concentrations of cancer-fighting and heart-beneficial antioxidants.

> *There's so much out there that I can't protect them from. At least their home and the food they eat should be as safe as I can make it.*
>
> EIGHT-YEAR-OLD CASEY'S and TEN-YEAR-OLD CAMERON'S mom

DIRTY DOZEN

Most Contaminated, Buy Organic

If you can't always buy organic, you can lower your family's exposure to pesticides by up to 90 percent if you avoid the twelve most contaminated conventionally grown fruit and vegetables. Here's what the Environmental Working Group calls the Dirty Dozen:

Apples	Nectarines
Bell peppers*	Peaches
Celery	Pears
Cherries	Potatoes
Grapes (imported)*	Spinach
Lettuce	Strawberries*

*NOTE: You may want to be especially wary of imported produce, including grapes, strawberries, tomatoes, and bell peppers, which average nearly three times higher organophosphate pesticide residues (chemicals linked to decreased intelligence and increased attention problems in children) than domestic varieties.

Least Contaminated, Can Buy Conventional

The next list, also from the Environmental Working Group, names those produce items that have the least amount of contaminants; thus, they're the safest to buy if grown and purchased conventionally:

Asparagus	Eggplant
Avocados	Kiwifruit
Bananas	Mangoes
Broccoli	Onions
Cabbage	Peas (frozen)
Corn (frozen)	Pineapples

Besides buying organically grown and raised foods, the Environmental Protection Agency (EPA) offers these tips to reduce consumption of pesticides on foods:

- ◆ **Wash and scrub** all fresh fruits and vegetables under running water. (Soaking produce isn't the same. It doesn't have the abrasive effect of running water.)

- ◆ **Peel** fruits and vegetables, when possible.

- ◆ **Discard** the outer leaves of leafy vegetables.

- ◆ **Trim** fat from meat and skin from poultry because some pesticide residues collect in fat.

- ◆ **Eat** a variety of foods from a variety of sources. Doing so will provide a better mix of nutrients and reduce the likelihood of exposure to a single pesticide.

OTHER POTENTIALLY HARMFUL FOODS

If we are what we eat, with all the genetically modified and imitation foods we now eat, what the heck are we?

ANONYMOUS

In addition to produce, there are other foods that have potential risk when buying conventionally produced and raised items.

Peanuts

Peanuts rank among the top ten foods contaminated with persistent organic pollutants, according to the Pesticide Action Network. These chemicals linger in the environment for years and can also build up in the body's fatty tissues. Americans eat about 2.4 billion pounds of peanuts every year, about half in peanut butter.

Soybeans, Corn, and Cotton

In the United States, 89 percent of the 2006 soybean crop was genetically modified (GM), and that percentage is growing. Experts warn against buying GM foods because their effects haven't been adequately studied. These are also banned in many other countries. The same warning goes for corn, as nearly half of all corn planted in America in 2004 was GM.

One problem for Americans is the pervasive use of soy in products we may not even be aware of. From 2000 to 2005, more than 2,100 new foods containing soy hit the U.S. market. Most of the U.S. soy crop is crushed into soybean oil, which is then hydrogenated and makes its way as trans fat into chips, cookies, crackers, and more.

In 2000, 61 percent of the 15.5 million acres of cotton grown in the United States was genetically engineered. Every year, half a million tons of cottonseed oil makes its way into salad dressings, baked goods, and snack foods. About 1.4 million tons of cottonseed meal is fed to livestock annually.

Beef

Conventional farmers often give their cows hormones to enhance growth. While the FDA deems them safe, the European Union disagrees and has banned their use. Farmers also give cows antibiotics even when they're not sick, contributing to antibiotic resistance. Finally, the "food" conventional cows eat may contain manure and other animal products, which can lead to bacteria and *E. coli* contamination. Organically raised cows eat only organic feed and grass.

Initial research suggests that eating grass-fed beef may be healthier than conventional beef because it's generally leaner and is a richer source of omega-3 fatty acids.

Dairy

Recombinant bovine growth hormone (rBGH) is a synthetic drug given to cows to increase milk production. Milk from these cows contains higher levels of a natural growth factor called Insulin-Like Growth Factor (IGF-1). Some experts link excess levels of IGF-1 in humans to breast and prostate cancers. Although the FDA says it's safe, the European Union has banned the drug. Use of rBGH also increases infections in cows, prompting farmers to administer even more antibiotics. This is especially worrisome, as children drink so much milk. Look for organic options or rBGH free–labeled milk, yogurt, and cheese.

According to the *Journal of Dairy Science,* initial research has found that on average organic milk contains more omega-3 fatty acids (essential for heart, brain, and cardiovascular health) when compared to conventional milk.

Pork, Poultry, and Eggs

Farmers use antibiotics on these animals in the same preventive way as with cattle, again contributing to the rise of resistant bacteria and potentially harming local ecosystems. In a 2006 study by the Institute for Agriculture and Trade Policy (IATP) of supermarket chicken products, more than half of the samples tested positive for arsenic from antibiotic use. One of the IATP's recommendations is to buy organic.

As far back as 1999, research sponsored by the Department of Agriculture found that free-range poultry has less saturated fat and more nutrients than the confined factory-raised chickens.

Seafood

Fish is a high-protein, low-fat food that provides a range of health benefits. White-fleshed fish in particular is lower in fat than any other source of animal protein, and oily fish are high in omega-3 fatty acids, also known as the "good" fats. Despite their valuable qualities, some fish can pose health risks to children, pregnant women, and the elderly when contaminated with substances such as metals (e.g., mercury and lead), industrial chemicals (e.g., PCBs), and pesticides (e.g., DDT and dieldrin), which, according to the Environmental Defense Fund, can cause development problems and diseases such as cancer. There are also environmental dangers to oceans and fish around the world because of overfishing and unsafe fishing practices.

As of April 4, 2004, supermarkets are required to label unprocessed seafood to identify where it is from and whether it is farm-raised or wild-caught. If such information is not available in a store or on a restaurant menu, be sure to ask. Check consumption recommendations for those fish with the highest contaminant levels, including large bluefin tuna, shark, swordfish, shrimp, and salmon. For a current list of the least contaminated and most sustainable fish in your area, go to www.seafoodwatch.com.

Chocolate

Both chocolate and coffee crops naturally grow in the shade. But to meet increasing demand, farmers favor sun-loving varieties, resulting in clear-cutting and heavy pesticide use. Cacao, which is used to make chocolate, is one of the world's most heavily sprayed crops, according to the United Kingdom's Soil Association.

ORGANIC LABEL CONSIDERATIONS

Food labels have become very confusing over the last few years as food manufacturers use clever marketing tactics and "creative" phrasing to get you to buy their foods. Words like *natural*, *organic*, and *healthy* used to mean more than just a slogan without any credentials to back it up. The best advice when shopping is to not only read labels but learn to decipher them. This is especially important when buying processed foods.

Just because a processed food product is labeled *organic* doesn't necessarily mean it is healthier than the nonorganic version. Researchers say marketers are cashing in on what they call an "organic halo," because the majority of households with young children believe that if something is labeled "organic," it is automatically better for their children. Take for example a cheese puff. It doesn't matter if the cheese puff is organic or not; it still has little or no real cheese or whole food ingredients, and is lacking in any nutritional value. In addition, watch out for food products marketed for children. The organic label does not necessarily mean the product is good or appropriate for them. That's your job; you'll need to read the labels closely to make wise choices.

I hear many parents' frustrations and concerns with having to scrutinize labels when shopping. I understand the task may already be long and tiring (especially with hungry children in tow). Besides health concerns, the ease of choosing unprocessed foods with a very short (or no ingredient) label may be another compelling reason to buy whole foods.

When switching to organic processed foods such as peanut butter, breads, and cereal, children may have to get used to a new brand, flavor, or texture. It may be difficult at first to substitute a familiar favorite with a new "organic" or healthier version. For instance, a peanut butter made with partially hydrogenated oils and additives will appear different from all-natural peanut butter (which only contains peanuts and possibly salt, but needs a stir to combine the oil). Decide where it will make the biggest impact on your child's health to favor organic over nonorganic foods. Keep in mind another added benefit of some organic foods is that they contain no additives, coloring, trans fats, or preservatives.

Those small numbered stickers on fruit mean something, too.

A four-digit number means it's conventionally grown.

A five-digit number beginning with nine means it's organic.

A five-digit number beginning with eight means it's genetically modified (GM).

According to the Center for Food Safety, GM foods have been in stores only since the 1990s, so we don't know the long-term health risks, and in a 1998 EPA sampling, 29 percent of the foods tested contained detectable pesticides.

Here's a reminder of the organic labels on multiple-ingredient foods:

100 percent organic: All ingredients are organic.

Organic: At least 95 percent of ingredients are organic.

Made with organic ingredients: At least 70 percent of ingredients are organic.

If less than 70 percent of the ingredients are organic, the word *organic* can be mentioned on the information panel, but not on the front of the package.

IS BUYING ORGANIC ENOUGH?

For the freshest, healthiest, and most environmentally friendly foods we must look beyond the organic label and turn toward foods that are sustainable, local, and in season. But what does that all mean?

Sustainable

Sustainable agriculture refers to the ability of a farm to produce food indefinitely without causing irreversible damage to ecosystem health. This involves food production methods that are healthy, do not harm the environment, respect workers, are humane to animals, provide fair wages to farmers, and support farming communities. To find markets, stores, restaurants, and farms offering sustainable foods in your area see Resources (pages 255–262).

Local

Locally grown produce does not travel as far to get to your table. According to the Center for Urban Education about Sustainable Agriculture, the average American meal travels about 1,500 miles from farm to plate. With local produce, the difference in mileage saves fossil fuels, allows farmers to pick produce at the peak of flavor, preserves the nutritional content of fresh produce, and strengthens local economies. The actual distance and definition of "local" is not a standard and can be considered within "food miles," single city, or ecoregion.

Fair Trade

Not everything we eat and drink can be grown locally. Fair trade is a market-based approach to alleviating global poverty and promoting sustainability. The movement ensures that foods (and other material goods) are produced under conditions that are most beneficial to workers. Most people in developed countries take these principles for granted, such as: protection of workers to exposure to high levels of chemicals and pesticides, payment of fair wages, good living conditions, clean water, welfare, education, and medical aid. Fair trade practices focus in particular on exports from developing countries to developed countries, most notably coffee, cocoa, sugar, tea, bananas, and honey, among others. According to Fair Trade Labeling Organizations International, in 2006 fair trade certified sales amounted to approximately $2.3 billion worldwide, which was a 41 percent year-to-year increase.

Seasonality

Seasonality of food refers to the times of the year when a given type of food is at its peak, either in terms of harvest or flavor. This is usually the time when the item is the most abundant, least expensive, and freshest on the market. As consumers, we have become accustomed to getting what we want when we want, so out-of-season produce can still be found at supermarkets (mostly grown in other countries) but at higher cost, less flavor, and fewer quality standards.

For instance, if you buy a pear out of season, even though it may be grown organically, the pear has to travel thousands of miles from a country in the Southern Hemisphere to reach your supermarket. Thus the "organic" label isn't enough; locally grown and in season is important, too. On the other hand, you may choose to buy a fruit that's in season at a farm, like a blackberry. You can ask the farmer about his farming practices, and while he may not be "certified" organic (because it is too expensive or he is still going through the process), he may use organic, sustainable practices. So even though the blackberry isn't certified organic, it is a good, healthy, and tasty choice.

GETTING GREENER

Besides the many organic choices for buying and eating foods to limit your family's exposure to pesticides and potentially harmful chemicals, there are also "green" ways to serve and store foods. Green used to be just a color; today it is much more. By choosing greener products and practices, you can make a positive impact on your family, your community, and the environment. Everyone benefits.

Each of the following chapters recommends child- and environmentally safe choices for storing, packing, and serving foods. In the beginning you may need to make an investment of money and time, such as purchasing glass baking and storage dishes, and taking extra shopping minutes to read food labels; however, you'll be saving expenses and resources in the long term. You don't need to do everything overnight, but perhaps take one suggestion at a time and see how it works for your lifestyle. With my own family I was buying organic foods, but I realized I was not as diligent on other "green" practices. I introduced one or two new practices a month, to concentrate on a single change at a time and get into a habit before trying the next. I found it helps to get kids involved, especially if they can be in charge of something or it's a change that will impact them. They are great little reminders of what you're doing wrong, and like to point out how things should be done. For instance, I bring my own bags when food shopping. My son has become the "bag king." He likes the job of reminding me and carrying the bags into the store.

COOL NEWS

COOL, as in "country of origin labeling," is giving consumers more information about where food comes from by placing a label or stamp on the food or a sign near food products. This was enacted into law by Congress in 2002, but implementation was delayed until September 30, 2008. By July 2008, more than 60 percent of produce sold by U.S. retailers met COOL standards, according to Robert Guenter of the United Fresh Produce Association. COOL labeling will also be found on items such as beef and peanuts.

CHAPTER 4

Instilling Good Eating Habits at Home and Away

Good habits formed while young make all the difference.

ARISTOTLE

WHEN CHILDREN ARE IN YOUR CARE and under your control, your job is easier. However, when children are faced with out-side choices, freedom, and independence, your job becomes much harder (whether it's food or anything else). Instilling healthy eating habits early on at home will hopefully give your children the confidence to make similar choices when away from home as well. For instance, my son always chooses a bran muffin when at a café or farmers' market. He is familiar with a "brown"-colored muffin because that's what we bake at home (using whole grain wheat flours). However, he will eat a piece of cake (no matter what kind or color) at a friend's birthday party, because the choice is limited to cake or no cake. That choice is a given.

FREEDOM OF CHOICE

Elementary school cafeterias require students as young as five to navigate entirely new options, none of them controlled by their moms or dads. The U.S. Department of Agriculture mandates schools must include milk, protein, fruits or vegetables, grains or breads on their lunch menus, and no more than 30 percent of their calories may be from fat. In addition to the lunch option, many schools offer additional snacks, sweets, and drink items for sale. The newfound freedom and numerous choices can be overwhelming to a child.

In the past few years, parents have been the changing force behind the push toward healthier foods in many schools. Some schools themselves are making a positive step by taking the children out of the lunchrooms and teaching them how to plant, grow, nurture, choose, and cook their own food. This growing movement, driven by celebrated chef and author Alice Waters through her Edible Schoolyard Program, is a way to teach "the connection of farms to communities, meals to culture, and health to environment." Teachers at all grade levels are incorporating food lessons into the curriculum and agree that cooking is a great way to learn about subjects such as math and science, as well as experience different cultures. Ivy Marx, registered dietitian at the Los Angeles Unified School District (LAUSD), which serves more than 690,000 meals a day, has helped set up more than sixty salad bars in Los Angeles public schools. Ms. Marx said, "I had a kid at one school where we had a salad bar come up to me and say, 'This is the best day of my life,' all because of the salad bar!"

Lead by Example

I had a very fraught relationship with my mother. But the greatest thing I inherited from her was that she made us cook.

NIGELLA LAWSON

Our children are influenced by things we have little control over, such as television and print ads, supermarket food placement, number of fast-food chains near school, etc. Leading by example is the most useful way to lessen the impact of outside influences. Your child becomes confident in his food choices because healthy foods are familiar and part of his everyday routine. Kids who see Dad enjoy a fresh-picked peach are more likely to want to make the same food choice.

In addition to watching you, as children get older they know what their friends, their siblings, and their cousins are eating. Some children are good role models for others, while some older siblings can sabotage efforts to keep unhealthy items away from younger children. My son loves nuts. He didn't have them until after age two, due to the potential for allergy and choking. However, he managed to slip his sister a cashew at age thirteen months "to see if she liked them." (Luckily, there were no problems and I kept a closer watch at snack time after that.)

> *Children follow what you do, not what you say.*
> STEPHEN T. SINATRA, MD, cardiologist and author of *Sugar Shock!*

You can help shape how your child perceives food temptations and choices away from home by doing the following:

- **Educate** your children about the benefits of healthy foods (they help you have more energy, grow stronger, run faster).

- **Teach** your children how to tune in to their bodies' signals if they are not feeling well due to too many sweets or junk foods.

- **Show** them where food comes from (look to nature vs. the supermarket).

- **Explain** that the goal of some manufacturers, restaurants, and sports venues that sell low-quality foods is to make money and they do not have your best interests and health in mind (like Mom and Dad).

- **Bring** along homemade snack favorites to share at school, parks, events, and playdates.

- **Shop** at local farmers' markets and natural stores instead of big-box grocery chains.

NAME IT!

Before having a toddler of my own, I underestimated the importance of what food is called. I would hesitate anytime we went out to dinner or to a friend's house before answering my son's question "What d'at?" The wrong name could send him away to play with his cars; the right name and he was ready to sit and eat it.

Big food companies have spent a fortune on marketing and researching what kids like and react positively to. Use the names and get inspiration for your own healthy versions. The words *pizza, chicken nuggets,* and *fries* can have good connotations if they are homemade and healthy versions. Cut something in a strip and call it a "fry" and your kids just may try it. Chef and mother Suzanne Goin of Lucques and A.O.C. in Los Angeles says she "sells" nutrition-packed pomegranate seeds to children as "little rubies." Chef and father Michael Anthony of Gramercy Tavern in New York calls squash croquettes "Daddy Nuggets" at home.

Create names that your child identifies with. If a child likes cars, hummus can be called Speedy Sauce. If it's princesses, edamame can turn into "Princess Peas." You'll see on page 62 that guacamole became Oscar Dip after the color of Oscar the Grouch on *Sesame Street.*

> We make your jambalaya recipe all the time. We call it pirate stew and it's become my son's favorite meal.
>
> THREE-YEAR-OLD DARBY'S mom

MAKE IT!

As a cooking teacher for four years, I always had picky eaters in my class. Most of them would announce they would not be eating the food. But once they were involved in preparing the food, they most always ate it and loved it.

LESLIE PAVE, private chef and food writer

Children are much more invested in something if they participated in creating it. Whenever my son wants to try something that's prepackaged in the store, he asks, "Mommy, can we make that?" Usually the answer is yes. I, too, like to make (and eat) cookies with him. He's learned that the experience is part of the enjoyment and it's going to be healthier for him than opening a bag. Where's the fun in that?

Sarah Lindsay Warden Wong of Sarah Lindsay Cakes in San Francisco loves teaching cake classes to six- to fourteen-year-olds because they are so enthusiastic and proud of their cakes. She shared with me that "one mother even emailed me that her daughter was going to freeze her cake so her grandparents from Hong Kong could see it a few weeks later on their visit."

WRAP IT!

Kids are very visual, and a lunch or snack packed in a fun container is always more exciting (and safer) than a plain paper bag. I suggest allowing your child to choose his lunchbox or snack bag. Children like to make decisions and feel in control. Ask them about wrappings and containers. Several years ago, my college roommate told me about her four-year-old son's preference for sandwiches in a plastic bag "top side in." "Top side in," she explained, is when the rounded top of the bread goes in the bag first and the sandwich is packed vertically. Apparently it led to a few melt-downs before she got it right. Basically he didn't want to get messy hands, so he wanted to reach in for crust, instead of the cut side where sandwich elements can leak out. Whew! Glad she figured that one out.

SERVE IT!

Making home-cooked food look more appetizing than store-bought food can some-times be tricky. Children are very visual and are drawn to colors, fun shapes, and individual portions (because they don't feel they have to share and can eat it all). However, you can let children decide how your homemade food should be served. What dishes? How would they like things cut? How should it be arranged on the plate? I've heard some children even make their own artwork for homemade paper snack wrappers.

> To keep my son interested in his lunch I use my apple slicer to make flower shapes out of his sandwiches. The slicer cuts the sandwiches into perfect bite-size pieces.
>
> THREE-YEAR-OLD JESSIE'S mom

INSPIRE IT!

You don't have to avoid all your children's favorites. You may want to choose foods your child already enjoys such as pizza, but make changes they may not notice—less cheese, more veggies, and a wheat crust. You can get inspiration from store-bought, processed, and restaurant foods to create better-tasting and healthier versions at home. And great ideas and recipes can come from discovering an unfamiliar fruit or vegetable your child sees at the farmers' market.

> *We like to discover new fruits and vegetables. Leah picked out pomelos and artichokes at the farmers' market. I'm not sure I'd ever had a pomelo before.*
>
> FOUR-YEAR-OLD LEAH'S mom

Out of ideas? I bet your child has some. Ask him to create his own food or snack. You never know what he'll come up with. Let him mix two or three things together and see what happens. There are many combinations that may seem odd, but are quite good; think of apples dipped in peanut butter—which, by the way, was the clear winner at my son's preschool when I asked the class for their favorite snack.

CHAPTER 5

Having Fun with Food and Family

The highlight of my childhood was making my brother laugh so hard that food came out of his nose.

GARRISON KEILLOR

YOU MAY BE WONDERING AFTER READING LABELS, shopping with kids, and getting home before dark to actually cook the food—where's the fun (and reality) in that? I agree it can be daunting and at first may seem like a lot of work, but finding food that eliminates unhealthy ingredients can be fun, too.

HAVING FUN WHILE SHOPPING HEALTHY

Starting a garden is key. Any kind of garden on any kind of plot will get kids connected to where their food comes from.

GREG CHRISTIAN, founder and chairman, the Organic School Project, Chicago

- ◆ **Shop** farmers' markets (see Resources, page 257, to find one in your area). It's hard to choose unwisely at a farmers' market and there are few labels to read.

- **Join** a food co-op. Pick up or have a "mystery" box of fresh, seasonal produce delivered, and discover a new fruit or veggie.

- **Shop** online. If you want to shop during your child's naps and late at night, do all your homework on the computer and have it delivered to your door. This also avoids store tantrums.

- **Grow** a community (or home or school) garden. This won't take care of all your shopping, but it will teach your child about agriculture and allow her to get her hands dirty.

- **Visit** farms. This is a great hands-on experience for children, and engages a child's five senses: touching the plants, smelling the soil, tasting the ripe fruit and veggies, seeing how things grow, and hearing the sounds of animals and machinery.

Can't avoid the grocery store? Here are some tips for making the trip easier:

- **Give children tasks and responsibilities.** Older ones can hand you needed items. Younger ones can look for certain colors or shapes on food items. Think of a treasure hunt or I Spy.

- **Go at the right times** for you and your kids. Heading in during nap time is a recipe for disaster. For a faster trip, try to go when the store is the least crowded.

- **Give a healthy snack.** Bring something from home or open a banana or bag of whole wheat crackers before your child melts down for something he sees in the snack or candy aisle.

- **Make a list.** Having all your ingredients on paper will make for a quicker and more organized trip. And hopefully you won't have to make another trip back because you forgot milk.

- **Stick to the perimeter of the store.** Most of the whole foods (produce, dairy, meats, fish) are located there. The inner aisles are where the majority of processed foods are found.

- **Set guidelines.** Tell your children what they can and can't do before you get to the store—such as what they're allowed to touch and sample and whether they will walk or sit in the cart.

- **Provide time for fun.** If your child likes to watch the "rainstorm" in the produce department, stand and enjoy it. There're also always children gathered around to greet the live crabs and lobsters in the fish section.

> When my kids were little, I remember going down the middle of the aisles as fast as I could. My kids would have a bagel in their hands to keep them occupied rather than grabbing from the shelves.
>
> NANCY, mother of two teenagers

KIDS IN THE KITCHEN

Cooking with your family doesn't just get food on the table; it lays the groundwork for the lifetime of your relationship.

—ALTON BROWN, author, television chef, and dad

No matter your child's age, he wants to "help" and participate in everything you do—and that includes shopping, cooking, eating, and assisting. At eighteen months old, my daughter's favorite word was *See!* She yelled it whenever she was curious about something in the kitchen that she couldn't see and wanted a closer look. It may not always be convenient to have them in the kitchen or when food shopping, and you'll need extra patience, but you're making an investment of your time for their health and happiness.

KITCHEN SAFETY FOR ALL AGES

The kitchen is a natural gathering spot. Rather than have the kitchen off limits for children, take the time to teach them how they can safely contribute to preparing, cooking, and sharing foods. Remember that kitchens are designed for grown-ups. This means tall counters, sinks, and islands. Be sure your child has a safe spot from which to watch and help.

Amanda Moore is a mother and the owner of re:place, a holistic interior design studio in New York. She advises incorporating Montessori principles, which encourage parents to foster a kid's independence, involving them in household tasks and putting useful everyday (but age-appropriate) items within their reach.

Six tips for making children feel welcome and safe in the kitchen:

1. Bring the action to the child's level. This is especially necessary if they will be helping rather than just watching. Just about every activity needs to be modified for a child's eye level, as it focuses their attention and allows them to participate and reach things more easily (and safely).

2. A small table and chairs or child-size picnic table is perfect for the kitchen if you have the room. An instant cooking party or playdate starts with a small table in the kitchen.

3. When preparing a family meal, seat children at the regular dining or kitchen table where everyone is used to their own spot (baby in high chair, toddler in booster) and bring the prep and cook work to the table.

4. Ask parents of child guests to bring their own chairs for every child's comfort and safety.

5. Child-proof accessible cabinets and drawers containing breakable and unsafe cooking and cleaning products.

6. Reserve an unlocked cabinet to house healthy snacks and kitchen accessories such as bowls and measuring cups for children.

Age-Appropriate Cooking Skills

As a children's cooking teacher and founder of What's Cooking, a children's cooking school in San Rafael, California, Michelle Stern is always asked by parents about what their kids can really do in the kitchen. Michelle says, "Parents find it hard to believe that their toddler can actually help, without causing chaos." Here Michelle highlights some age-appropriate cooking skills for children. You know your child best, and need to use your discretion about how this list applies to your own family.

Keep in mind, even adults make a mess when they are creating in the kitchen, so expect children to have even more mishaps and build in enough time for mistakes and cleanup. Remember to remain calm and have a sense of adventure and humor!

2- TO 3-YEAR-OLDS CAN:	4- TO 6-YEAR-OLDS CAN:	7- TO 12-YEAR-OLDS CAN:
Rinse vegetables or fruits.	Pour.	Write your shopping list and read it to you at the store.
Tear large pieces of lettuce.	Mix.	Help select which recipes the family will share at meal-time.
Stir.	Count and do simple measurements.	
Pour with assistance.	Cut with a plastic or butter knife.	Read and follow recipes.
Select which ingredients they want to taste or use.	Crack eggs.	Work with a heat source (supervised).
Recognize changes to ingredients during the cooking process.	Start to follow recipe cards and symbols.	Cut with a sharper knife (with instruction).
Sort ingredients.	Create their own recipes, and draw them on cards.	Create their own recipes and write the steps.
Help identify ingredients in the grocery store.	Identify images or diagrams of ingredients on your grocery list.	Help wash dishes.
Group utensils when setting the table.	Set the table.	Do tasks listed at left.
	Do tasks listed previously.	

Helpful Tools

There are many stores that market cooking equipment and essentials to kids. While some are useful in the kitchen, such as small-size whisks, others are simply cute but impractical. Items such as a mini oven mitt are fine for a pretend play kitchen; however, I would never recommend a preschooler put his hands in a real oven or carry something hot enough to need an oven mitt. While it is certainly not necessary to go out and buy the following items, you may find a few that are helpful to have for child-friendly tasks. You may even have some of these items already in your kitchen.

- **Cookie cutters.** Great for making shapes in sandwiches, cookies, fruit slices, cheeses, and deli meats.

- **Egg slicer.** Allows children to slice cooked eggs, mushrooms, strawberries, and kiwifruit with a quick and safe push (with adult supervision).

- **Hand juice squeezer.** Metal handles allow children to help squeeze juice (and less likely to squirt eyes).

- **Melon baller.** Make shapes of fruit or for scooping cookie dough.

- **Mini rolling pin.** Roll bread and pizza dough.

- **Muffin pans.** Hold seeds, raisins, and colored sugars, when decorating cookies, breads, and muffins.

- **Paper muffin cups.** Line muffin cups with decorations and allow for easy cleanup and sharing.

- **Pastry bags.** Fill with frosting, cream cheese, or dips (hummus, guacamole) for decorating and topping. (A plastic freezer bag with a hole cut in the corner will work, too.)

- **Ramekins.** Hold everything from spreads and dips to small ingredients. Also allows for easy mixing for little ones. Great for serving food as well.

- **Rotary grater.** Good for grating cheeses while protecting little knuckles.

- **Rubber spatulas.** Help with mixing, spreading, and leveling.

- **Small spreaders.** Allow small hands to do-it-themselves for making sandwiches (cream cheese, nut butters), pizza (sauce), and cupcakes (frosting).

- **Spice shakers.** Hold cinnamon, sugar, and cocoa powder for easy sprinkling without mess.

- **Splat mat.** Protection for tables and floors and makes for easy cleanup. Can be a tablecloth, craft mat, old sheet, or simply newspapers.

- **Squeeze bottles.** Little hands can squeeze condiments and toppings such as sour cream, yogurt, and syrup and use with icing for decorating cakes and cookies.

- **Tartlet pans.** Can use for small ingredients and spices for sharing and decorating (see muffin pans above).

CHAPTER 6

Eat: Snacks

Humans are the only animal that eats set meals because we are social and lead busy lives. All other animals snack or graze throughout the day.
DR. BROCK BERNSTEN, pediatrician, Town and Country Pediatrics, San Francisco

So WHAT'S WRONG WITH SNACKING? Nothing, actually. Amy Jamieson-Petonic, RD, and spokesperson for the American Dietetic Association, tells parents not to "demonize snacking, because kids' bellies are smaller than adults', they can't eat nearly as much in one sitting and need regular refueling throughout the day." Most pediatricians and nutritionists, such as Ellyn Satter, international expert on eating and feeding and author of *Child of Mine: Feeding with Love and Good Sense,* advises feeding children three meals and two snacks daily at regular times to establish healthy eating habits. It's the snack food *choices* that are the problem.

Unfortunately, people think snacks mean something that comes in a shiny wrapper, or a colorful individual serving with preservatives, additives, high-fructose corn syrup, and trans fats. Even worse, families lead such hurried lives that foods are eaten quickly on the go (that's why we have "fast" foods everywhere), rather than enjoyed at a more leisurely pace. Sara Duskin, International Board Certified Lactation Consultant at DayOne parenting resource in San Francisco, reminds moms in her workshops to "Sit down!" She advises parents to "take time to enjoy meals with their children whenever possible." Even if you are out and about, your child's snack food is more satisfying and enjoyable (and safer, with less mess) when eaten while sitting on a public bench, rather than consumed while walking to the park.

This section will give you ideas for healthy bites for your growing child to eat while sitting at home, picnicking at the park, and traveling on a plane and other places life takes him. These healthy foods will provide the necessary fuel for his development and activity level throughout the day, instead of the processed food offerings devoid of valuable vitamins, nutrients, fiber, and protein.

When your child was a baby, getting him to eat whole fruits and vegetables was easy. He probably didn't know much else. However, as he grows, makes friends, attends school, participates in sports, and views advertisements he's influenced and tempted by an overwhelming number of processed foods marketed as "snack" items. Your child is no longer under your watchful eye and his diet is monitored by someone else. Different families have different ideas about what's acceptable, and may even make decisions about daycare, schools, and afterschool programs based upon food offerings.

> I'm looking for a preschool that only allows healthy foods. At home, we eat mostly organic, and we read labels carefully. I don't want someone just slapping down any old processed food in front of my son.
>
> SARAH GILBERT, mom of a three-year-old son, Portland, Oregon

Respect Children's Preferences, But Keep Trying

> If my sister and I whined about the food my mother offered, we would hear, "Like it or lump it."
> Author and mother of JONAS, AGE FOUR AND A HALF, and ELLERY, AGE TWENTY MONTHS

Many parents quickly dismiss a food because their child spits it out, makes a face, or returns it uneaten in her lunch bag. Paying attention to your child's reaction and reasons for eating (or not eating) is important when trying to discover her likes and dislikes. A baby who spits out a carrot may be rejecting it for a variety of reasons, such as texture, color, flavor, smell, or temperature. It could also be things that are not as easy for a child to communicate, such as unfamiliarity. According to Ellyn

Satter, you may have to introduce the same food to a child up to twelve times before she accepts it.

An older child may reject foods, including past favorites. Ask questions and listen to the answers. She may not like the way it feels in her mouth (texture). Or maybe the food is too warm (temperature). She also may tell you it isn't cut correctly (appearance). The next time you make the food, try it cooked a different way (or not cooked at all, such as a raw carrot), or serve it with a favorite dip or present it whole (such as an apple) instead of sliced. Getting your child's preferences, even her "instructions" first can cut down on a lot of frustration for everyone.

Tuning in to your child's eating habits is another good reason to sit together for meals and snacks whenever possible. Most adults don't care if their carrots are cut into coins or sticks, so try making them the way your child suggests so it will be eaten by the whole family. This becomes a problem when one child wants coins and the other wants sticks. Then you may want to trade off; your daughter picks one afternoon and your son picks another. Choosy or picky eaters become decision makers when given a choice and can participate in the meal, but it is up to you to present healthy choices for your children.

This section of the book is divided by texture, since many children (and adults, too) have a real preference, so you can easily choose which recipes to make. Feel free to combine as well. My daughter loves to dip her food and my son likes crunchy foods. If I make the bagel chips for texture (son), I'll also make the black bean hummus for dipping (daughter). Just be sure with texture that your child is developmentally ready and able to eat them safely, especially with those in the crunchy and chewy sections. Ingredients such as nuts, dried fruits, and raisins can be choking hazards for any age.

CREATE IT!

You need to be creative. Your food needs to be tasty and look special to go up against some of the other mass-produced food and beverage offerings. One thing that's on your side is you know your child better than the advertisers. You know his likes and dislikes. And you can empower him to choose and help make his own foods that he can look forward to at school, at home, and at play.

The recipes here are organized by texture and flavor. So if you know your son likes crunchy foods, start with that section. If your daughter is a dipper (like mine), head to the creamy section for healthful dips, sauces, and spreads. While some recipes in this chapter are complete snacks, others are meant to be combined to create a complete mini meal that is going to give your child the energy and fuel required to maintain his activity levels and development, as well as satisfy his hunger and palate. For instance, yogurt with fruit is a good snack, but can be made even healthier by adding a sprinkle of nuts and trail mix. For children to feel satisfied and energized, your snack or mini meal should include a combination of protein, carbohydrates, and fat.

PLAN AHEAD

I receive many emails with questions about appropriate snacks to pack for school, outings, and travel. Parents often think planning is looking over recipes, making lists, and working in the kitchen. Planning for children's snacks simply means to think ahead and have something in case someone is hungry. It could be as simple as always having a container of whole wheat crackers, a banana, and a bottle of water in your bag. It could also mean determining the length of a car trip and stocking a small ice chest with sandwich roll-ups, fruit and veggie slices, and milk. The thing to avoid is thirst and hunger. Children are not happy, patient, understanding, quiet, or respectful if they are hungry, thirsty, or tired. We as parents will do anything to fix the situation, which may mean running into a convenience store or grabbing fast food. If you have something on hand, you can ward off a potential problem and carry on with your travels or at least wait until there are healthier food options such as arriving home, going into a natural food store, or sitting down at a restaurant.

Time-Saving Tips When Packing a Lunch or Snack

- ◆ **Ask.** Get your child's opinion in advance of shopping about what he'd like for snacks, foods, and drinks to avoid unwelcome surprises or meltdowns when the bag is opened. Children like to feel in control and that their choices matter and will be heard. Give your child healthy, simple options so you're both happy with his choice. Then you can make a list and buy ingredients for meals and snacks and think about leftovers for the week.

- **Prepack.** When cleaning and cutting raw veggies, prep extra and pack in individual containers to store in the refrigerator for grabbing quickly.

> *I make individual snack packs for my son. Each container contains two or three different cereals, raisins, and crackers that he likes. I already have the portion and he knows he only gets one per day."*
>
> TWO-AND-A-HALF-YEAR-OLD MILES'S mom

- **Organize.** If you have a crowded and messy refrigerator and pantry, it is harder to pack and make convenient snacks. Have room in the refrigerator designated for lunch and snacks items so you can grab, pack, and go.

- **Reinvent.** Dinner's leftovers are perfect for packing in a school lunch. Pack it when cleaning up the night before so it's ready in the morning. Try putting a new twist or spin to make it appealing. Tortellini from dinner can be put on skewers and packed with dipping sauce, or wrap grilled veggies into a tortilla.

SNACKS FOR TRAVELING

Opposite is a chart of snack suggestions for venues and travel and best ways to pack and carry. There are also things to keep in mind when packing and eating on the go. For instance, if your child asks for a snack while you are driving, it is easier to pass back something long and dry such as a breadstick vs. small and slippery like fruit chunks. (For safety's sake, it's best to pull over before handing any food to your child.) Also keep in mind when traveling, you and your child may not be able to get out of your car or airplane seat for a period of time, so pack wipes and bags for cleanup and waste.

SNACK PACKING AND STORING

The New York State Department of Environmental Conservation estimates that one student taking a disposable lunch to school each day will create forty-five to ninety pounds of garbage per year.

PLACE	FOOD AND DRINK	PACKING	KEEP IN MIND
DAYCARE	Dry low-sugar cereal, egg pieces, beans, hard-cooked egg, steamed veggie chunks, cut cheese bites, milk, formula, or water	PVC- and lead-free insulated bag with ice pack and Bisphenol-free bottle or spillproof cup	Pack things child can eat himself in case care provider is busy with another child.
SCHOOL	Sandwich, cut fruit, veggies with dip, bagel with healthy spread, granola bar, yogurt, milk, water, or diluted juice	PVC- and lead-free lunch box or lunch box/bento box system with ice pack and aluminum canister	Child should be independent when opening containers.
GRANDMA'S or FRIEND'S HOUSE	Trail mix, cheese and whole wheat crackers, granola bar, berries, milk, water, or tea	PVC- and lead-free insulated bag with ice pack and aluminum canister	Bring enough to share with other children, if any.
CAR RIDE	Bread sticks, crackers, raisins, cut apple slices, cheese sticks, raw or steamed veggies, water	PVC- and lead-free insulated bag or mini ice chest with aluminum canister, Bisphenol-free bottle and sippy cup, or thermos, plus reusable bag for trash	Choose things that won't crumble or get stuck in seat. Do not give something that could be a choking threat.
PLANE TRIP	Trail mix, bread sticks, veggie rolls, banana, raw or steamed veggies	PVC- and lead-free insulated bag with ice pack, empty drink containers, plus reusable bag for trash	Take into account security checkpoint lines in airport (check with airline for latest restrictions). Be courteous of passengers next to your child with regard to spillproof containers and foods with strong odors.

Eat: Snacks

In an effort to teach children about the environmental impact of their food and beverage choices, and focus on reducing, recycling, and reusing to avoid waste, many schools are committed to reducing waste on campus. One method is to encourage parents to pack a "waste-free" lunch. This means everything in your child's lunch box is reusable or consumable. Schools such as Marin Primary School in Marin, California, are not only recycling and composting, but they have done away with plastic utensils, cups, and plates by washing reusable plates that the children have made themselves. Children's cloth napkin company Fabkins (see page 258) is working with schools to provide children's-size napkins for fundraisers, classroom party baskets, and lunchrooms throughout the country.

The number of children's product recalls due to lead paint, poor plastics, and polyvinyl chlorides (PVC) has increased dramatically. Luckily, there is a big "green" market to fill the void of safe products, when it comes to lunch boxes and food storage. There are many fun and colorful lead-free, old-fashioned metal lunch boxes as well as soft PVC- and lead-free lunch totes that children can choose from. Allowing your child to choose is important so that he's proud of his lunchbox and excited to see and eat what's inside.

A new way to eliminate the waste of plastic bags, sandwich wrap, and waxed paper is with a lunch box system. These are composed of a set of safe plastic boxes arranged in a larger box, like that of a traditional Japanese bento box. For disposable options, bamboo is a great renewable resource now used for making utensils and plates. Even corn is being made into plastic for cups, straws, and biodegradable utensils for use at restaurants and sports venues.

Preschool teacher Joanne Haight advises parents to pack foods for school in containers that keep food fresh and safe but are also child-friendly to open. She says at this preschool age, self-help is just as important as what they are eating. These green on-the-go tips work for all ages and venues, whether they're headed to school, daycare, or a family outing.

- **Keep perishables** cold in insulated lunch bags. There are many PVC- and lead-free choices. Rather than using an ice pack you can freeze items such as yogurt or water, which will thaw and be ready by mealtime.

- **Pack drinks** in reusable nonplastic bottles and drink holders. Thermos containers made from stainless steel and aluminum reduce waste and concern of leaching of toxins such as Bisphenol A, which is linked to birth defects, miscarriage, and prostate cancer.

- **Wrap sandwiches** in foil over plastic wrap and baggies. Unlike waxed paper and plastic wrap, aluminum foil is available in 100 percent recycled form, is recyclable in most areas, withstands heat and cold, and works better than plastic and waxed paper at keeping moisture in. Aluminum is also oil-free and is not made from petroleum, the way that wax and plastic are. You can also reduce landfill waste by eliminating plastic bag use, as they can last up to one thousand years.

- **Provide metal or ceramic utensils,** which can be used and washed. Just remind your child to bring them home. Or provide bamboo renewable and biodegradable forks and spoons, rather than plastic.

See Resources (pages 258–259) for stores and online retailers of "green" packing options.

NUTRITIOUS SNACKS: TIME-SAVING TIPS

Keep it simple. To cook well you need the freshest ingredients.
—BRADLEY OGDEN, Chef, cofounder, Lark Creek Restaurant Group

There are many foods and snacks that we make up as we go. Certainly any whole food is good on its own— bananas, apples, edamame, carrot sticks, etc. However, when you want to dress it up, or increase the nutritional value and your child's interest, the following ideas don't require a recipe, just fresh high-quality ingredients and a little creativity. Children are great at coming up with their own concoctions of ingredients. My son likes to ask, "What would happen . . . ?" quite a bit in the kitchen. As in "What would happen if we squeezed an orange in my milk?" A few more ingredients (honey, yogurt) and you could make a shake. My daughter doesn't ask first. She just does: dunking turkey in her water glass and dipping raisins into mustard. I'm sure that's how some of the great pairings got started.

Here are some suggestions to jump-start you and your children's creativity for quick, easy, and healthy snacks that do not require a formal recipe.

TAG-ALONGS

Organic natural nut and seed butters (peanut, almond, sunflower, tahini) are a good source of protein and go well with these suggestions.	Chunks of apple, jicama, and celery Spread on toast with slice of cheese Sandwiched between two waffles or pancakes Spread on wheat tortilla, topped with banana, and rolled
Veggies and fruits make their own snacks with a little extra effort to make them special and appealing for children.	Celery stick spread with cream cheese and sprinkled with raisins Zucchini cut in half lengthwise, spread with bean dip then put back together A cored apple stuffed with granola or cereal Spinach and lettuce leaves stuffed with favorite spread (egg, tuna, hummus) and vegetable sticks and rolled
Variety trail mixes are an easy "to go" snack. Besides the trail mix (page 53), here are some other suggestions.	Handful of toasted oats cereal mixed with raisins and shredded unsweetened coconut Handful of granola mixed with dried apricots and cranberries Handful of dried fruit chunks mixed with wheat pretzels Handful of raw almonds and walnuts mixed with goji berries and cacao nibs
Pita bread makes a handy and healthy pocket with which to stuff your child's favorite fillings.	Stuffed with lettuce, avocado, and cheese sticks Stuffed with spinach and hummus Stuffed with ricotta cheese and herbs Stuffed with leftover meats
Lavosh or flatbread and tortillas make a neat roll-up for little hands. These rolls can also be cut for a special, colorful presentation, kind of like sushi. Besides the recipes on pages 81–83, here are some other options.	Spread with roasted red pepper sauce and vegetable sticks and rolled Spread with black bean dip and sprinkled with jack cheese Spread with hummus and cooked chicken

Bagels make a good platform for lots of spreads and fillings. You can even cut in half and remove some of the bread, so filling stays in better and bagel is not so filling for little tummies. Here are a few options.	Spread with marinara, sprinkled with mozzarella, like a pizza Stuffed with cottage cheese and sliced strawberries Stuffed with omelet pieces Spread with nectarine or other fruit butters
Waffles and pancakes can be good for making fun sandwiches and rolls.	Spread pancakes with cream cheese and any fruit puree and roll up Spread peanut butter and all-fruit spread between two waffles Layer scrambled eggs between waffles for a breakfast sandwich

This next list is dedicated to my dipper daughter, who loves any dip, sauce, or spread and comes up with some strange combinations on her own. Again, these are fun and easy and can be whipped up without measuring at a moment's notice.

DIPPITY DOO-DA, DIPPITY YEAH!	
Yogurt	Serve alongside angel food cake pieces, toast points, waffles, pancakes, and fruit and vegetable slices
Natural nut, soy, and seed butters	Spread on fruit slices (apples, of course), bagels, rice cakes, waffles, pancakes
Fruit purees	Dunk pieces of pancakes, waffles, cooked meats, noodles
Vegetable purees	Dip pita points, tortilla chips, and vegetable spears. Also good as a pasta topping.
Soft cheeses such as goat and Brie	Spread on whole wheat crackers, raw veggie sticks, and sandwich wraps

Eat: Snacks

45

Organic ketchup	Have on hand for leftover cooked meats and vegetables, potato crisps
Mustards	There are a variety of mustard options. Mustard and honey (see Note, below) is of course a favorite for chicken, meatloaf, broccoli, and cauliflower trees. For an Asian flair, your child may enjoy mustard with soy sauce for dipping noodles, vegetables, and tofu sticks.
Cream cheese and ricotta	Dip raw vegetables such as carrots and celery as well as fruit slices of apples and pears. Also a versatile spread on sandwiches, wraps, and whole grain crackers.
Low-fat dressings and soy-based mayonnaise	Mix with herbs for dipping veggies and greens
Salsas and chutneys	These can be spicy, such as tomato-roasted chilies, or sweet, such as mango or apple. Good for tortilla chips, rice, and cooked meats.

NOTE: Do not give honey or agave nectar to children under one year of age because of the danger of botulism.

Crunchy: Crackers, Crisps, Sticks, Veggies, Granola, and Bites

Apple Crisps

An alternative to boring potato chips, this simple treat satisfies a child's need for crunch. Using a mandoline provides convenience and accurate cuts for even baking. However, a careful, steady knife works as well. The apples crisp in the low heat, which dries out the moisture. Once in the oven, these need no attention (just remember to turn off the oven overnight), until it's time to pack them (or eat) them in the morning.

MAKES ABOUT 48 APPLE CRISPS; 4 (12-CHIP) SERVINGS

2 tablespoons evaporated cane juice
1 teaspoon ground cinnamon
½ teaspoon freshly grated nutmeg
2 large organic apples such as Fuji or Braeburn

Preheat oven to 200°F. Line 2 baking sheets with parchment paper and set aside.

Stir together evaporated cane juice, cinnamon, and nutmeg in a small bowl.

Using a mandoline or a steady hand and a knife, cut the apple vertically into ⅛-inch-thick rounds. You do not need to core or peel the apple. The seeds will fall out or can easily be removed from apple slices after cutting.

Place apple slices on prepared baking sheets in a single layer and sprinkle with cinnamon mixture. Bake in the middle of the oven for

1½ hours. Rotate pans and cook for 1 hour more. Turn off heat and leave in the oven overnight if apples are not dry and crisp. Loosen chips with a spatula to remove from parchment paper.

KIDS KORNER

Shake It Up! The easiest way to lightly and evenly sprinkle sugars and spices is to transfer them to a spice shaker. Having a specially marked shaker for cinnamon and sugar saves time when making other snacks such as cinnamon toast or spicing up plain yogurt. This is also a "neat" way to get children to help with decorating and flavoring tasks.

Bread Sticks

This is a quick and tasty way to make crunchy bread sticks for a crowd. They look extra special served in a tall glass or vase. They also work well for passing to your children in the backseat when they want a snack. Shorter sticks fit well in lunch bags.

MAKES 36 TO 40 (8-INCH STICKS) OR 24 (15-INCH) STICKS

1 cup whole wheat flour
1 cup unbleached all-purpose flour
1½ teaspoons baking powder
1½ teaspoons kosher salt
3 tablespoons organic unsalted butter, chilled
¾ cup iced water
1 tablespoon extra-virgin olive oil

Preheat oven to 350°F. Line 2 baking sheets with parchment paper and set aside. In the bowl of a food processor, pulse flours, baking powder, and ½ teaspoon of the salt to combine. Add butter and pulse until dough is crumbly. With motor running, gradually add iced water and process just until dough comes together, about 1 minute.

Carefully transfer the dough (may stick to blade) to a lightly floured surface and press to flatten with your fingers into a rectangle shape. Roll out dough with a rolling pin to an 8 × 10-inch rectangle, about ¼ inch thick. Cut the dough lengthwise into ¼- to ½-inch strips.

Using your hands, gently roll each strip into a stick; as you roll, the sticks will get longer. Cut into smaller sticks if desired. For twisted sticks, grab each end of dough strip with fingers and stretch and twist in the opposite direction.

Arrange sticks on prepared baking sheets. They do not need to be spread out, but they should not be touching. Brush each stick lightly with olive oil, then sprinkle with remaining salt. Press ends of sticks to sheet to remain straight during baking.

Bake for 15 to 18 minutes, until firm and cooked through.

KIDS KORNER
These sticks don't need to be perfect. Let your child roll and twist the sticks into desired lengths or even create fun shapes. Just be sure to cook similar lengths together, for even cooking time.

NUTRITION FACTS

Serving Size 1 (8-inch)
bread stick (14g)
Calories 35
Calories from Fat 15
Total Fat 1.5g
Saturated Fat 0.5g
Trans Fat 0g
Cholesterol 5mg
Sodium 95mg
Total Carbohydrate 5g
Dietary Fiber 1g
Sugars 0g
Protein 1g

Eat: Snacks

Veggie Platter

Show your child how exciting and beautiful a vegetable platter can be with a rainbow of colors and flavors, served along with Yogurt-Herb Dip (page 61) or Spinach Hummus (page 187). You can make this simple with two or three veggies for a quick snack, or more elaborate with multiple dips and veggies for a crowd. Feel free to skip the step for steaming carrots and beans for older children who want maximum crunch. Nutritionists recommend having cut-up veggies on hand to put on the table when you're preparing dinner. If kids are hungry, they'll eat them; and if they spoil their dinner with veggies, that's not so bad.

MAKES ABOUT 4 CUPS VEGETABLES; 8 SERVINGS

½ small jicama, peeled
½ small cucumber, peeled
1 large organic carrot, peeled, or 12 baby organic bagged carrots
4 ounces organic wax or Blue Lake green beans, trimmed
10 organic cherry tomatoes

Bring a medium pot of water to a boil.

Cut jicama, cucumber, and carrot (if whole) into stick shapes or similar size.

Add beans and carrots to boiling water and blanch about 1 minute. Remove vegetables from water with a slotted spoon and place in a bowl of cold water to stop cooking.

Pat vegetables dry. Arrange all vegetables in various glasses, ramekins, and bowls for vegetables to stand up. Create small arrangements of color and sizes for little hands to grab and dip.

TIP

Tender. Blanched hard and fibrous vegetables such as beans and carrots are easier for small children to eat and enjoy, and reduce choking hazard. You can also partially steam vegetables in a microwave rather than turning on the stove. Raw is quicker, easier, and crunchier if you're serving older children.

Energy Bark

Inspired by a 2006 *Parents* magazine recipe, this snack gives a boost of fuel to keep up with busy children. This is a favorite around my house because of the great crunchy texture and sweet flavor. Feel free to omit or substitute your favorite crunchy cereal for the almonds if you want to avoid nuts.

MAKES ABOUT 3 CUPS; 14 SERVINGS

1 cup rolled oats
1 cup slivered almonds
½ cup unsweetened coconut flakes
¼ cup toasted wheat germ
2 tablespoons whole wheat flour
¼ teaspoon ground cinnamon
¼ cup packed brown sugar
3 tablespoons organic unsalted butter
2 tablespoons honey or agave nectar (see Note, page 46)

Preheat oven to 325°F. Line a baking sheet with aluminum foil and set aside. In a large bowl, mix together the oats, almonds, coconut, wheat germ, flour, and cinnamon.

In a small saucepan, combine the brown sugar, butter, and honey. Bring to a boil over medium heat and cook until thick and bubbly, 30 seconds. Pour the sugar mixture over oat mixture and stir with a rubber spatula to combine and coat all dry ingredients.

Spread on prepared baking sheet and bake for 20 minutes. Remove pan from oven and let cool completely on baking sheet. Break into pieces.

KIDS KORNER
Kids love to break things. Once thoroughly cooled, allow children to help break apart pieces into desired sizes.

NUTRITION FACTS
Serving Size about
¼ cup (30g)
Calories 140
Calories from Fat 80
Total Fat 9g
Saturated Fat 3.5g
Trans Fat 0g
Cholesterol 5mg
Sodium 0mg
Total Carbohydrate 15g
Dietary Fiber 2g
Sugars 7g
Protein 3g

Eat: Snacks

Baked "Zuke" Sticks

Zucchini is a tough word to pronounce for little ones; *zuke* sounds much more fun. These are a good snack food, side dish, or party food to serve with other veggie sticks. A side of marinara sauce or Tot's Tomato Sauce (page 63) is good for these little dippers.

MAKES ABOUT 50 STICKS; ABOUT 6 SERVINGS

¾ cup dried bread crumbs
¼ teaspoon kosher salt
⅛ teaspoon freshly ground black pepper
½ cup unbleached all-purpose flour
⅓ cup organic milk
3 medium zucchini, cut lengthwise into 3 × ½-inch pieces
    (peel if desired)

Preheat oven to 350°F. Line a jelly-roll pan with parchment paper and set aside.

In a medium bowl, combine bread crumbs, salt, and pepper. Place the flour on a plate. Pour milk into a shallow bowl.

Dip each zucchini stick in flour until lightly coated. Then dip in milk. Finally, roll in bread crumb mixture until covered, pressing so mixture adheres to zucchini.

Transfer zucchini sticks to prepared pan and bake for 22 to 24 minutes, until zucchini is tender and coating is crisp and brown.

KIDS KORNER

Enlist older children to help by rolling sticks in flour, milk, and bread crumbs. This may become a messy job, as mixture can stick to fingers. A child who does not like messy hands will pass on this task.

NUTRITION FACTS

Serving Size 8 sticks (128g)
Calories 110
Calories from Fat 10
Total Fat 1.5g
Saturated Fat 0g
Trans Fat 0g
Cholesterol 0mg
Sodium 180mg
Total Carbohydrate 20g
Dietary Fiber 2g
Sugars 3g
Protein 4g

petit
appetit

EAT, DRINK,
AND
BE MERRY

No-Nuts Trail Mix

This mix is nut-free for taking to school as well as on-the-go snacks. This is so easy; just choose your child's favorite ingredients and the entire mix will be eaten. Dried fruits have just as much fiber and nutrients as fresh fruits. In fact, dried fruits such as prunes and raisins have an even higher nutrient concentration than fresh fruit. Check the ingredients in dried fruits, as some such as pineapple and banana chips have added sugars and fats.

MAKES 3 CUPS; 10 SERVINGS

1 cup toasted oats or favorite cereal
½ cup chopped unsweetened dried pineapple
½ cup dried cranberries
½ cup dried unsweetened banana chips
¼ cup unsweetened shredded coconut
¼ cup sunflower seeds

Mix all ingredients in a bowl. Store in an airtight container for up to 2 weeks.

TIP
Always watch children when they're eating nuts and raisins, as both are potential choking hazards.

NUTRITION FACTS

Serving Size about
½ cup (28g)
Calories 120
Calories from Fat 45
Total Fat 5g
Saturated Fat 3g
Trans Fat 0g
Cholesterol 0mg
Sodium 70mg
Total Carbohydrate 19g
Dietary Fiber 4g
Sugars 11g
Protein 1g

Eat: Snacks

Bagel Bites

This is a fun way to turn a thick, soft bagel into a kid's crunchy snack for at home or on the go. These can be made with any flavor bagel such as wheat, cinnamon raisin, or poppy—or go crazy with an everything bagel. There're also large as well as mini-bagel options. They can have just about any topping: butter, cinnamon sugar, or cheese. Once cooled, add any spread or dip, such as yogurt, fruit puree, or Pumpkin Butter (page 65). Let your child's imagination be your guide. Just make sure the adults do the bagel slicing.

MAKES 4 SERVINGS

1 large whole wheat bagel (1½ to 2 inches thick)
2 teaspoons organic unsalted butter, melted
⅛ teaspoon ground cinnamon

Preheat oven to 375°F. Line a baking sheet with aluminum foil or parchment paper and set aside.

Using a serrated knife, carefully slice bagel lengthwise so you have 4 to 5 (¼-inch to ⅓-inch) slices. A bagel slicer or mandoline makes for a safer and cleaner cut if you have one. Lay bagel slices on baking sheet.

Brush bagel pieces with butter and sprinkle with cinnamon. Bake for 10 minutes, until crisp. (If using mini-bagels, cook for 8 minutes.) Let cool on pan for maximum crispness.

VARIATION

Use grated Parmesan cheese on whole wheat, rye, or plain bagels and ground cinnamon and nutmeg on cinnamon raisin bagels.

TIP

Storage. If you want to keep these crisp, store wrapped in foil or in an airtight container. They may lose crispness if stored in plastic bags.

NUTRITION FACTS

Serving Size 1 oz (28g)
Calories 90
Calories from Fat 20
Total Fat 2.5g
Saturated Fat 1.5g
Trans Fat 0g
Cholesterol 5mg
Sodium 120mg
Total Carbohydrate 14g
Dietary Fiber 2g
Sugars 2g
Protein 3g

petit
appetit

EAT, DRINK,
AND
BE MERRY

Cherry-Almond Granola

This recipe comes from my "healthy baking" friend and food blogger, Amy Andrews. Once I tested and tasted this, I knew I was hooked, as was my son. It's become one of his favorite breakfast foods to eat dry with a glass of milk on the side. To create more variety, substitute other dried fruits such as cranberries, raisins, or blueberries for the cherries. This crunchy treat packs and travels well for an on-the-go snack, and can be gifted to teachers and neighbors in a glass mason jar.

MAKES ABOUT 13 SERVINGS

2 cups rolled oats (see gluten-free icon, page 3)
1 cup sliced almonds
½ cup unsweetened grated coconut
3 tablespoons flax meal
¼ cup cacao nibs (optional)

Granola Syrup
2 tablespoons expeller-pressed canola oil
3 tablespoons agave nectar (see Note, page 46)
3 tablespoons maple syrup
½ teaspoon pure vanilla extract
½ teaspoon salt

1 cup dried cherries, chopped

Preheat oven to 250°F. Line a baking sheet with parchment paper and set aside.

In a large bowl, combine oats, almonds, coconut, flax meal, and cacao nibs (if using).

Make the Granola Syrup: In a small bowl, whisk together canola oil, agave nectar, and maple syrup. Add the vanilla and salt. Pour over oat mixture and stir with a wooden spoon to combine.

Pour the granola mixture onto the prepared baking sheet and spread to an even layer. Bake for 1 hour and 15 minutes, until golden in color, stirring twice during the baking.

NUTRITION FACTS

Serving Size 2 oz (57g)
Calories 250
Calories from Fat 120
Total Fat 14g
Saturated Fat 6g
Trans Fat 0g
Cholesterol 0mg
Sodium 95mg
Total Carbohydrate 27g
Dietary Fiber 5g
Sugars 13g
Protein 5g

Eat: Snacks

Remove pan from oven and add the dried cherries. Stir to combine and let cool. Enjoy as a topping to organic yogurt or as a cereal with your favorite milk or nut milk. Store in an airtight container at room temperature.

TIP

Flax facts. Flaxseed is a great source of heart-protective alpha-linoleic acid. Besides using the whole seed for this granola, buy ground flaxseed for sprinkling on yogurt, pancakes, and mixing into smoothies.

Mozzarella and Tomato Flatbread

This is a simple snack for every age and appetite. Having lavosh on hand means you can make this (as well as roll-up sandwiches or cracker cut-outs) in no time.

MAKES 6 (4-INCH) SQUARES

1 piece lavosh (11 x 9 inches)
⅓ cup tomato sauce or Tot's Tomato Sauce (page 63)
½ cup shredded Cheddar or mozzarella cheese (rBGH-free)
¼ teaspoon dried oregano

Preheat oven to 350°F. Place lavosh on a baking sheet. Spread lavosh with sauce, and sprinkle with cheese and oregano.

Bake for 10 minutes, until cheese has melted and lavosh is crispy on edges.

NUTRITION FACTS

Serving Size 1 piece (24g)
Calories 50
Calories from Fat 30
Total Fat 3g
Saturated Fat 2g
Trans Fat 0g
Cholesterol 10mg
Sodium 130mg
Total Carbohydrate 2g
Dietary Fiber 1g
Sugars 1g
Protein 3g

Eat: Snacks

Parmesan-Walnut Flatbread

I like to make this for a quick playdate snack, or in the morning to cool and pack for taking to school or on a day trip. It even works as an appetizer.

MAKES 6 (4-INCH) SQUARES

1 piece lavosh (11 x 9 inches)
¾ cup shredded parmesan cheese (rBGH-free)
½ cup coarsely chopped walnut pieces
1 tablespoon honey (see Note, page 46)

Preheat oven to 350°F. Place lavosh on a baking sheet. Sprinkle lavosh with cheese and walnuts and drizzle honey over the top.

Bake for 10 minutes, until cheese has melted and lavosh is crispy on edges.

petit
appetit

EAT, DRINK,
AND
BE MERRY

Creamy: Dips, Spreads, Sauces, Yogurts, and Soup

Black Bean Hummus

Hummus is a versatile dip for veggies and pita as well as a spread for tortillas and sandwiches. This version uses antioxidant- and folate-rich black beans in place of the ordinary garbanzo beans. Pack in a small airtight container for dipping at school or play. Surprise kids and adults with an assortment of hummus flavors and colors for healthy dipping at a gathering.

MAKES 1½ CUPS; 16 SERVINGS

1 (15-ounce) can black beans, rinsed and drained
1 clove garlic, chopped
2 tablespoons organic firm tofu
2 tablespoons tahini (sesame paste)
½ teaspoon ground cumin
1 tablespoon extra-virgin olive oil, plus additional as needed
2 tablespoons freshly squeezed lime juice (about 1 lime),
    plus additional as needed
⅛ teaspoon freshly ground black pepper
⅛ teaspoon salt

Combine all ingredients in a food processor fitted with the steel blade. Process until smooth and creamy. Add additional olive oil or lime juice to thin, if necessary.

EGG FREE
MILK FREE
GLUTEN FREE
NUT FREE
GROUP PLEASERS
PERFECT FOR PACKING
SUGAR FREE
NO COOK
WHEAT FREE
VEGAN

NUTRITION FACTS

Serving Size about
2 tablespoons (28g)
Calories 50
Calories from Fat 20
Total Fat 2g
Saturated Fat 0g
Trans Fat 0g
Cholesterol 0mg
Sodium 20mg
Total Carbohydrate 6g
Dietary Fiber 2g
Sugars 0g
Protein 2g

Eat: Snacks

petit
appetit

EAT, DRINK,
AND
BE MERRY

Yogurt Mix-Ins

So many parents automatically buy yogurt marketed for babies, cute little single-serving containers in "natural" flavors. Then later it's natural to give in to "tubes" of yogurt out of convenience. However, they're chock-full of additives, sugars, and colorings. How about making the real deal with your child's custom flavorings, and eliminating the additives and reducing the sugars? They can even mix in the flavorings themselves. For on the go, pack the yogurt in single-serving reusable plastic containers. Below are a few options to try.

MAKES 1 (½-CUP) SERVING

Maple Yogurt

½ cup organic plain low-fat yogurt
¼ teaspoon ground cinnamon
1 teaspoon pure maple syrup

Mix all ingredients together.

Variations

ALL-FRUIT YOGURT
½ cup plain low-fat organic yogurt
Substitute 1 tablespoon all-fruit spread for the cinnamon and maple syrup.

FRUITY SORBET YOGURT
Substitute 1 tablespoon fruit sorbet (see Cherry Sorbet, page 221) for the cinnamon and maple syrup.

SAUCY YOGURT
Substitute 1 tablespoon organic applesauce, store-bought or homemade (page 68), for the cinnamon and maple syrup.

Go Green! For on-the-go convenience, pack yogurt in single-serving reusable plastic containers. According to teachers polled in *Parents* magazine, they dislike parents packing yogurt "tubes" because of the mess and waste. One teacher in Colorado noted, "[It] lands on their toes, not in their mouths."

Yogurt-Herb Dip

This is a creamy alternative to dips and dressing full of fats and sugars found in the supermarket aisle. It is a good base for just about any herbs in your cupboard or fresh from your garden. Serve as a dip for Veggie Platter (page 50), as a dressing for mixed greens or alongside Potato Chips (page 93).

MAKES ABOUT ½ CUP; ABOUT 4 SERVINGS

½ cup organic plain low-fat yogurt
1 tablespoon organic buttermilk
½ teaspoon dried thyme
½ teaspoon dried dill
⅛ teaspoon salt
Freshly ground black pepper, to taste

    Place the ingredients in a medium bowl and stir well to combine. Serve immediately or store in the refrigerator for up to 2 days.

NUTRITION FACTS

Serving Size
2 tablespoons (28g)
Calories 15
Calories from Fat 5
Total Fat 0g
Saturated Fat 0g
Trans Fat 0g
Cholesterol 0mg
Sodium 80mg
Total Carbohydrate 2g
Dietary Fiber 0g
Sugars 2g
Protein 1g

Eat: Snacks

Oscar Dip (aka Guacamole)

The lime juice and cilantro give this salsa a sweet, instead of spicy, flavor. Increase the onion for those who enjoy more spice. Serve with Tortilla Cut-Outs (page 89), or layer in a wrap or roll-up sandwich to go.

MAKES 4 SERVINGS

1 avocado
1 tablespoon freshly squeezed organic lime juice
1 tablespoon minced fresh cilantro
1 teaspoon minced organic green onion
½ teaspoon salt

Mash avocado with the back of a fork in a small bowl. Add remaining ingredients and stir to combine.

KIDS KORNER

As "guacamole," my son wasn't interested; however, once we called it Oscar Dip after the green lovable monster from *Sesame Street*, he was hooked.

NUTRITION FACTS

Serving Size 2 tablespoons
Calories 60
Calories from Fat 50
Total Fat 6g
Saturated Fat 0.5g
Trans Fat 0g
Cholesterol 0mg
Sodium 290mg
Total Carbohydrate 4g
Dietary Fiber 1g
Sugars 0g
Protein 1g

petit
appetit

EAT, DRINK,
AND
BE MERRY

Tot's Tomato Sauce

This is a simple, bright red sauce that goes with everything from pastas and pizzas to dips for veggies and Bread Sticks (page 49), with a lot less sugar and additives than the jarred versions.

MAKES ABOUT 15 SERVINGS

1 pound vine-ripened tomatoes or 1 (16-ounce) container
   Pomi tomatoes
1 tablespoon extra-virgin olive oil
2 cloves garlic, minced
½ teaspoon fine-grain sea salt
1 teaspoon honey (see Note, page 46)

If using fresh tomatoes, preheat oven to broil. Pierce each tomato with a small knife and place tomatoes in a glass baking dish. Broil tomatoes for 15 minutes, turning halfway through cooking, until skins are split and begin to turn brown. Once cool, peel off tomato skins and puree tomatoes in a food processor. If using Pomi tomatoes, simply puree.

Combine olive oil, garlic, and salt in a medium saucepan over medium heat. Sauté until garlic starts to turn golden, 2 to 3 minutes. Stir in tomatoes and bring to a simmer. Add honey and cook for 5 minutes. Remove from heat.

NOTE: Pomi tomatoes are garden-ripe tomatoes grown in Italy and packed in cartons. You can find them in the grocery aisle with the canned tomato products. These tomatoes have no seeds, no skins, no stems, and no preservatives or citric acid. No kidding!

Serving Size
2 tablespoons (28g)
Calories 15
Calories from Fat 10
Total Fat 1g
Saturated Fat 0g
Trans Fat 0g
Cholesterol 0mg
Sodium 70mg
Total Carbohydrate 1g
Dietary Fiber 0g
Sugars 1g
Protein 0g

Eat: Snacks

Lemony Snicket Sauce

This is a quick snack in lieu of a presweetened yogurt. It is also a simple dip for fresh fruit kebobs or a sauce for drizzling over fruit salad. Try this with any yogurt version to create variety (nonfat, whole milk, Greek, or European style). Agave nectar is a natural sweetener that comes from the heart of the blue agave plant. It mixes well with the yogurt for sweetness, with a lower glycemic index than sugar. Alternatively, honey can be used.

MAKES ABOUT 6 SERVINGS

1 (6-ounce) container organic plain whole-milk yogurt
½ teaspoon grated fresh organic lemon zest (see Go Green! below)
1 teaspoon freshly squeezed lemon juice
1 teaspoon agave nectar (see Note, page 46)

In a small bowl, whisk together all ingredients until blended.

Go Green! While lemons (and limes) are not on the Dirty Dozen list as potentially harmful, organic is suggested because you'll be using the zest (the outside peel, where pesticides can be heavy).

NUTRITION FACTS

Serving Size
2 tablespoons (28g)

Calories 20
Calories from Fat 5
Total Fat 0g
Saturated Fat 0g
Trans Fat 0g
Cholesterol 0mg
Sodium 15mg
Total Carbohydrate 3g
Dietary Fiber 0g
Sugars 2g
Protein 1g

petit
appetit

EAT, DRINK,
AND
BE MERRY

Pumpkin Butter

In the fall I always look forward to a few prepared foods from local purveyors, and pumpkin butter is one of them. Then I wondered why not make it myself so I can have it year-round? I discovered it is easy to make and can be frozen for any time you want to dress up toast, bagels, or banana bread, or even use it as a dip for Pretzels (page 90), one of my daughter's favorites.

MAKES ¾ CUP; 8 SERVINGS

½ cup canned pumpkin
⅓ cup organic unfiltered apple juice
1 tablespoon pure maple syrup
1 teaspoon honey (see Note, page 46)
½ teaspoon ground cinnamon
¼ teaspoon freshly grated nutmeg
⅛ teaspoon ground ginger

Add all ingredients to a medium saucepan. Cook over medium-low heat until hot and bubbling, 5 to 7 minutes. Pumpkin Butter will last up to 1 week in the fridge and 3 to 4 weeks in the freezer.

NUTRITION FACTS

Serving Size
2 tablespoons (28g)
Calories 20
Calories from Fat 0
Total Fat 0g
Saturated Fat 0g
Trans Fat 0g
Cholesterol 0mg
Sodium 0mg
Total Carbohydrate 5g
Dietary Fiber 1g
Sugars 4g
Protein 0g

Eat: Snacks

Mustard-Honey Sauce

This is a versatile dip, sauce, and spread that perks up everything from vegetable sticks to Baked Chicken and Apple Bites (page 226) to sandwiches. For some children, Dijon mustard is too spicy; feel free to substitute yellow mustard instead.

MAKES 4 SERVINGS

¼ cup Dijon mustard
2 tablespoons honey (see Note, page 46)

Combine mustard and honey in a small bowl and whisk to blend and smooth together.

TIP
Coat the inside of the measuring cup with cooking spray before measuring sticky ingredients such as honey and nut butters to minimize sticking, ease release, and help cleanup.

KIDS KORNER
Don't be surprised if your little one licks the dip and leaves the food behind. My daughter at eighteen months loved saying, "Dip, dip." Little magicians sometimes make the dip disappear while the dippers (chicken and carrots) remain the same size.

petit
appetit

EAT, DRINK,
AND
BE MERRY

White Bean Spread

For kids who love to spread and dip their foods, this is a versatile, high-protein recipe that works as a spread on sandwiches or a dip for vegetables. Adjust the garlic to suit your family's tastes, or add it to the garlic lover's portion only.

MAKES 18 SERVINGS

1 (16-ounce) can cannellini beans
1 clove garlic, minced
3 tablespoons freshly squeezed lemon juice
3 tablespoons extra-virgin olive oil
¼ teaspoon white pepper (optional)

Empty beans into strainer and rinse with water until liquid is removed and water is clear. This eliminates any salt or canned taste. Put beans, garlic, lemon juice, oil, and pepper (if using) into a food processor or blender. Process mixture until smooth and creamy, about 20 seconds. For a smoother consistency, add more lemon juice or oil to suit your taste.

TIP

Quick adult fix. For an easy hors d'ouevre, spread bean mixture on toasted baguette slices and garnish with sun-dried tomatoes or sliced kalamata olives.

NUTRITION FACTS
Serving Size
2 tablespoons (30g)
Calories 40
Calories from Fat 20
Total Fat 2.5g
Saturated Fat 0g
Cholesterol 0mg
Sodium 90mg
Total Carbohydrate 4g
Dietary Fiber 1g
Sugars 0g
Protein 1g

Eat: Snacks

Applesauce

The sweetest fruit will yield the sweetest sauce. This applesauce has flavor, but no sweetener. For those who like it sweetened, try date sugar, honey, or agave nectar (see Note, page 46), which are not as processed as refined sugars. This also works great to sweeten baked goods and as a dip for pancakes, muffins, and toast.

MAKES ABOUT 2 CUPS; 4 SERVINGS

6 medium organic apples, washed, quartered, and cored just before cooking
¼ teaspoon pure vanilla extract
½ teaspoon ground cinnamon

Place apples in a steamer basket set in a pot with about 1 to 2 inches of lightly boiling water (make sure water does not touch basket). Cover tightly for best nutrient retention and steam until apples are tender, 10 to 12 minutes. Apples should pierce easily with a toothpick. Set apples aside to cool.

Scrape flesh from apple skins. Pulse in a food processor for smoother texture or put through a ricer or mash with a potato masher for a chunkier texture. Stir in vanilla and cinnamon.

Go Green! Pack applesauce in individual reusable containers in the fridge so they are ready to go for snacking, anywhere, at any time. Just remember to bring a spoon!

petit
appetit

EAT, DRINK,
AND
BE MERRY

Ellery's Minestrone

Minestrone soup is a great way to use an abundance from your garden (if you're lucky enough to have one) or community-supported agriculture (CSA) box, and also get your family to eat a healthy dose of vegetables.

MAKES ABOUT 5 CUPS; 5 SERVINGS

2 tablespoons extra-virgin olive oil

⅓ cup sliced leek (about ½ large)

1 medium organic carrot, chopped (about ⅓ cup)

1 medium zucchini, chopped (about ¾ cup)

2 ounces green beans, chopped (about ⅓ cup)

¼ cup chopped organic celery

1 teaspoon dried oregano

¼ teaspoon salt

¼ teaspoon freshly ground black pepper

1 quart organic low-sodium vegetable stock

3 medium vine-ripened tomatoes, chopped (about 2 cups)

2 tablespoons tomato paste

1 tablespoon fresh thyme

1 cup canned cannellini beans, rinsed and drained

¼ cup elbow macaroni (use egg-free for vegans)

Heat olive oil in a large saucepan over medium-high heat. Add leek, carrot, zucchini, green beans, celery, oregano, salt, and pepper and cook until veggies start to soften, 5 to 7 minutes. Cover, reduce heat to low, and cook for 15 minutes, stirring occasionally.

Stir in stock, tomatoes, tomato paste, and thyme, and bring to a boil. Cover, reduce heat to low, and simmer gently for 20 minutes.

Add cannellini beans and macaroni and simmer for 10 minutes or until pasta is al dente. Adjust seasonings to taste.

KIDS KORNER

This recipe is named after my daughter because at seventeen months we discovered how much she enjoyed soup while having dinner with my family at an Italian family-style restaurant. She soaked her clothes, but was happy as can be slurping her minestrone. At home she wears only a diaper to enjoy soup, usually followed by a bath.

NUTRITION FACTS

Serving Size 1 cup (227g)
Calories 100
Calories from Fat 30
Total Fat 3.5g
Saturated Fat 0g
Trans Fat 0g
Cholesterol 0mg
Sodium 220mg
Total Carbohydrate 15g
Dietary Fiber 3g
Sugars 4g
Protein 3g

Eat: Snacks

Butternut-Apple Soup

This is a sweet and aromatic soup that can be enjoyed in mini ramekins for little mouths to simply sip. This makes a comforting and nutritious playdate snack on a chilly autumn day after playing outdoors.

MAKES 7 CUPS; 7 SERVINGS

1 tablespoon expeller-pressed canola oil or other vegetable oil
⅓ cup chopped onion
1 pound peeled and cut squash (can buy prepackaged in produce section) or 2 pounds whole butternut squash, peeled and cut into 1-inch pieces
2 medium organic Fuji apples, peeled, cored, and coarsely chopped
1 (14-ounce) can organic low-sodium vegetable broth
1 cup water
1 teaspoon fresh thyme or ¼ teaspoon dried thyme
½ teaspoon salt
⅛ teaspoon freshly ground black pepper
1 cup organic milk

In large saucepan, heat oil over medium heat. Add onion and cook until tender and golden, about 10 minutes. Stir in squash, apples, broth, water, thyme, salt, and pepper. Heat over high heat until boiling. Reduce heat, cover, and simmer, stirring often until squash and apples are tender, 10 to 15 minutes. (If not using prepackaged squash, you'll need to increase cooking time by 15 to 20 minutes.)

Spoon one-third of squash mixture into a blender or food processor and puree until smooth. Be careful: Mixture is hot and steam can burn when processing. Pour puree into bowl and continue processing remainder of squash mixture. (Soup can be prepared to this point and refrigerated overnight.)

When ready to eat, return puree to saucepan and stir in milk. Heat through over medium heat until hot.

TIP

Babes and soup. Just remember, many children do not like foods too warm, so serve at room temperature for the youngest. Because this recipe has cow's milk, it should not be served to those under one year old.

petit
appetit

EAT, DRINK,
AND
BE MERRY

Tuna Waldorf Salad

Adapted from Lucie Costa, chef of North Plank Road Tavern in New York, and printed in *The Yale Guide to Children's Nutrition*, this tuna salad is sweet and appealing to children, and certainly a healthier version than tuna salads made with plain mayonnaise. To serve, stuff salad into pita bread or spread on crackers or toast.

MAKES 1 CUP

1 (6-ounce) can chunk light albacore tuna packed in water
2 tablespoons organic Neufchâtel cheese
½ cup organic golden raisins, chopped
1 tablespoon organic unfiltered apple juice

Drain tuna and flake with fork into a medium bowl. Add cream cheese, raisins, and juice and mix until well blended. (You can also put the mixture into a food processor and cream together for a smoother texture.)

Go Green! Remember to choose chunk light (skipjack and yellowfin) tuna over all-white or chunk white (albacore), as the mercury is lower. Children and pregnant women should eat no more than 6 ounces of canned tuna per week, due to mercury exposure.

NUTRITION FACTS

Serving Size ½ cup
Calories 50
Calories from Fat 5
Total Fat 0.5g
Saturated Fat 0g
Trans Fat 0g
Cholesterol 5mg
Sodium 70mg
Total Carbohydrate 6g
Dietary Fiber 0g
Sugars 6g
Protein 5g

Eat: Snacks

Sunny Tofu Salad

This was inspired by a sandwich I had from Whole Foods Market. It's the same idea as egg salad but uses tofu in place of egg. The mustard still gives the sunny color of egg yolks. Stuffed into pita bread or rolled into lettuce leaves, this is a tasty vegetarian option for those not eating eggs. It is also a nice addition to a party platter.

MAKES ABOUT 1 ⅓ CUPS

8 ounces organic extra-firm tofu, drained
1 tablespoon organic whole-milk yogurt
1 tablespoon chopped green onion (optional)
1½ teaspoons prepared mustard
1 teaspoon freshly squeezed lemon juice
1 teaspoon chopped fresh dill or ¼ teaspoon dried
⅛ teaspoon salt

Place tofu on a cutting board lined with a kitchen towel or paper towels. Gently squeeze tofu between towels to remove excess liquid.

Put tofu in a medium bowl and crumble apart using a fork. Add yogurt, green onion (if using), mustard, lemon juice, dill, and salt and mix to combine.

Go Green! Be sure to buy organic tofu. Non-organic tofu is more than 84 percent likely to be genetically modified.

NUTRITION FACTS

Serving Size about
⅓ cup (65g)
Calories 35
Calories from Fat 10
Total Fat 1g
Saturated Fat 0g
Trans Fat 0g
Cholesterol 0mg
Sodium 160mg
Total Carbohydrate 2g
Dietary Fiber 0g
Sugars 1g
Protein 4g

petit
appetit

EAT, DRINK,
AND
BE MERRY

Chewy: Bars, Wraps, Roll-Ups, and Quesadillas

Chewy Granola Bars

Who needs prepackaged granola bars from a box at the grocery or convenience store when you can make these chewy favorites? Let your child choose his favorite crunchy ingredients for new flavor combinations. For those who can eat nuts, feel free to add toasted walnuts for more crunch and omega-3s.

MAKES 16 (2-INCH) BARS

1 ⅓ cups rolled oats (see gluten-free icon, page 3)
½ cup raw sunflower seeds
½ cup oat bran
1½ cups crisp brown rice cereal
1 cup dried cranberries
2 tablespoons crystallized ginger, chopped
½ cup brown rice syrup
¼ cup turbinado sugar
1 teaspoon pure vanilla extract
½ teaspoon fine-grain sea salt

    Grease an 8-inch-square glass baking dish and set aside.

    Mix oats, seeds, oat bran, cereal, cranberries, and ginger in a large bowl.

    In a small saucepan, combine rice syrup, sugar, vanilla, and salt. Cook over medium heat, stirring constantly until the mixture comes to a boil and starts to thicken, about 3 to 5 minutes. Pour over oat mixture

NUTRITION FACTS

Serving Size 1 bar (42g)
Calories 150
Calories from Fat 25
Total Fat 3g
Saturated Fat 0g
Trans Fat 0g
Cholesterol 0mg
Sodium 100mg
Total Carbohydrate 30g
Dietary Fiber 2g
Sugars 19g
Protein 3g

Eat: Snacks

and stir with rubber spatula until all is moist and coated. Spread mixture into prepared dish and cool to room temperature. Cut into pieces.

Go Green! Wrap granola bars in aluminum foil, since it is available in 100 percent recycled form, is recyclable in most areas, withstands heat and cold, and works better than plastic wrap and waxed paper at keeping moisture in. It is also oil free and is not made from petroleum, the way that waxed paper and plastic wrap are.

Parmesan O's

Anelletti is pasta shaped like little O's. It makes a good finger food for older babies and an easy way for little forks to grab these cheesy rings. Feel free to substitute other small pasta shapes as well.

MAKES ABOUT 4 CUPS

1 cup anelletti pasta
⅓ cup freshly shredded Parmesan cheese (rBGH-free)
1 tablespoon organic unsalted butter
1 tablespoon freshly squeezed lemon juice (from about ½ Meyer or
    other lemon)
¼ teaspoon salt
Fresh basil, minced (optional)

    Boil noodles according to manufacturer's directions. Reserve about 1 tablespoon pasta cooking water. Drain noodles and put back in cooking pot.

    While noodles are hot, add cheese, butter, juice, salt, and reserved water and stir until combined and cheese is melted. Sprinkle with basil (if using).

KIDS KORNER

One day my son put the O over a skinny mini carrot and was very proud of his invention. It looked like a little ring toss game. Now I serve the rings with zucchini and carrot matchsticks for the kids to thread and eat every time.

NUTRITION FACTS

Serving Size ½ cup (84g)
Calories 160
Calories from Fat 45
Total Fat 5g
Saturated Fat 3g
Trans Fat 0g
Cholesterol 10mg
Sodium 260mg
Total Carbohydrate 22g
Dietary Fiber 1g
Sugars 0g
Protein 7g

Eat: Snacks

Pear and Brie Slice

In San Francisco I lived one block from Food Inc., a wonderful gourmet deli and Italian foods shop. They made a delicious pear and Brie sandwich on walnut bread. Whenever my mom would visit, we'd always head there for her "fix." I realized I could make it at home with little effort, and a few high-quality ingredients. Though we no longer live in the neighborhood, we can still enjoy this pairing any time.

MAKES 1 (5-INCH-OVAL) OPEN-FACED SANDWICH

1 ounce Brie cheese
1 oval slice walnut bread
½ organic pear, sliced thinly

Spread Brie on bread. Layer pear over Brie.

Serve at room temperature or toast quickly in a toaster oven or in a 300°F oven for 2 to 3 minutes.

TIP

Cheese, please. My son liked all cheeses from a very early age. At two he'd ask for Brie and blue cheese whenever there was a cheese plate. Now at 4½, he enjoys choosing a new cheese whenever we head to the store.

NUTRITION FACTS

Serving Size 1 sandwich
(91g)
Calories 180
Calories from Fat 80
Total Fat 9g
Saturated Fat 5g
Trans Fat 0g
Cholesterol 30mg
Sodium 250mg
Total Carbohydrate 21g
Dietary Fiber 6g
Sugars 4g
Protein 9g

petit
appetit

EAT, DRINK,
AND
BE MERRY

Seed Tuilles

I saw some very expensive sesame cookies in a gourmet grocery store and decided to try to make my own. This was actually very different from my inspiration, but surprisingly better. They are fragile and thin like a typical tuille cookie, but with new ingredients to provide the crackle, crunch, and chew. For children who can't enjoy nuts, the texture and flavor is quite satisfying. Although this tuille may look like bird food, it's a lovely, sticky, and chewy treat. Be patient and wait for the tuilles to cool completely so they'll harden and peel easily off the baking sheets.

MAKES ABOUT 25 (3-INCH) TUILLES

½ cup white sesame seeds
½ cup sunflower seeds
2 tablespoons toasted flaxseeds
¼ cup unsweetened carob chips (vegan)
¼ cup dried currants
½ teaspoon baking soda
¼ cup brown rice syrup
¼ cup honey (see Note, page 46)
2 teaspoons expeller-pressed canola oil

Preheat oven to 300°F. Line a baking sheet with parchment paper and set aside.

In a medium bowl, combine all seeds, carob chips, currants, and baking soda. In a small bowl, whisk together brown rice syrup, honey, and oil. Pour syrup mixture over seeds and stir together with a rubber spatula until combined.

Scoop out rounded teaspoonfuls using a melon baller or teaspoon and place on prepared baking sheet. Bake for 8 to 10 minutes, until tuilles have spread and are golden brown.

These will be very gooey when they come out of the oven. Be patient and allow them to cool (and harden) completely, 20 to 30 minutes, before carefully pulling away from the parchment paper.

TIP

Sticky situation! Be sure to stack these individually between sheets of waxed paper in an airtight container for storage. Otherwise, they will all stick together like one big happy family.

NUTRITION FACTS

Serving Size 1 tuille (18g)
Calories 80
Calories from Fat 35
Total Fat 4g
Saturated Fat 1g
Trans Fat 0g
Cholesterol 0mg
Sodium 45mg
Total Carbohydrate 10g
Dietary Fiber 1g
Sugars 7g
Protein 2g

Eat: Snacks

petit
appetit

EAT, DRINK,
AND
BE MERRY

Baked Sweet Potato Chips

Here's a Petit Appetit class favorite. Unlike commercially processed potato chips, these chips require very little oil and no frying, which make them a good choice for all ages. You can bake them plain or, for variety, sprinkle with herbs and spices. They are also good dipped in yogurt or Silly Salsa (page 88).

MAKES 18 CHIPS; ABOUT 8 SERVINGS

1 large organic sweet potato (8 to 9 ounces), thinly sliced
2 tablespoons extra-virgin olive oil
Sea salt, freshly ground black pepper or other dried herbs,
    to taste (optional)

Preheat oven to 425°F. Line a baking sheet with foil. Grease foil, and set baking sheet aside.

Thinly slice potato into ⅛-inch slices, using a mandolin or steady, sharp knife. Put potato slices in a resealable plastic bag. Drizzle potatoes with oil. Move plastic bag around potatoes to coat all sides (without getting messy).

Place individual potato slices in a single layer on prepared baking sheet. Sprinkle with salt and pepper or herbs, if desired. Bake in oven for 15 to 20 minutes. (To move these into the "crunchy" section, turn down heat to 325°F and cook an additional 5 to 10 minutes until crisp). Remove potato slices and place on rack to cool.

KIDS KORNER

It's in the bag! Let kids coat the potato slices with oil. Since it's in the bag, there's no oily mess. They'll also appreciate sprinkling the spices on top.

Oatcakes

Here's a quick way to get your toddler to eat his oatmeal without sitting down to a bowl. You'll feel good about sharing this quick breakfast with your little one, as it does not have the high sugars, additives, and preservatives as some prepackaged breakfast bars.

MAKES 15 TO 18 (2-INCH) ROUNDS

2 cups rolled oats (see gluten-free icon, page 3)
½ teaspoon ground cinnamon
½ teaspoon baking soda
⅛ teaspoon salt
2 tablespoons organic butter
1 tablespoon honey (see Note, page 46)
3 tablespoons finely chopped unsweetened dried apricots
2 tablespoons unsweetened finely shredded coconut
1 cup water

Preheat oven to 400°F. Line a baking sheet with aluminum foil. Grease foil, and set baking sheet aside.

Put oats, cinnamon, baking soda, and salt into a mixing bowl. Make a well in the center and add the butter and honey. Combine with rubber spatula until oats are coated. Mix in apricots and coconut. Heat 1 cup water in a saucepan until very hot (but not boiling). Stir in water by tablespoonfuls until mixture becomes a sticky dough.

Using 2 large spoons, scoop and drop dough on prepared baking sheet. With wet fingertips, shape dough into 2-inch rounded, flat oatcakes. Bake for 15 minutes, or until the edges turn golden brown and the oatcakes are firm and not sticky. (They'll crisp when cooling.) Remove to a wire rack to cool.

NUTRITION FACTS

Serving Size 1 oatcake (31g)
Calories 60
Calories from Fat 15
Total Fat 1.5g
Saturated Fat 0.5g
Trans Fat 0g
Cholesterol 0mg
Sodium 65mg
Total Carbohydrate 10g
Dietary Fiber 1g
Sugars 2g
Protein 2g

Eat: Snacks

Cheese and Egg Roll

Not your typical "egg roll," but simply a rolled-up egg omelet—perfect for little hands to hold and eat themselves. I discovered this when my daughter wanted an egg, but we were getting ready to head out the door. The egg cooks in only a few minutes, but we didn't have time for her to sit at the table to enjoy it. Voilà. Simply cook and roll. You can even get creative and stuff with cooked meats or veggies.

MAKES 1 SERVING

1 large cage-free organic egg
1 teaspoon organic milk
2 tablespoons grated Cheddar cheese (rBGH-free)

In a small bowl, whisk together the egg and milk.

Heat a 6- or 8-inch skillet over medium heat. Coat the skillet with cooking spray.

Pour egg mixture into skillet. Let egg cook, undisturbed, until egg is no longer runny, 2 to 3 minutes. Carefully flip egg with a rubber spatula. Sprinkle cheese on top of egg and cook until cheese is melted and egg is completely cooked, about 1 minute.

Slide egg onto plate. Eat with fork or knife like a pancake, or carefully roll egg around melted cheese and eat with hands or pack in foil.

petit
appetit

EAT, DRINK,
AND
BE MERRY

Hummus and Veggie Wraps

This is a favorite of the children at Leah's Pantry, where families living in transitional housing are educated and empowered to make healthy food choices. Kids love to create their own wraps and layer just about anything. This hummus is a convenient and easy recipe, and does not require a run to the store for the usual tahini (sesame) paste. For younger kids, use smaller-size tortillas for smaller hands and mouths.

MAKES 4 (10-INCH) TORTILLA WRAPS; ABOUT 1¾ CUPS

Hummus
1 (16 ounce) can garbanzo beans, rinsed and drained
½ cup plain organic nonfat yogurt
1 teaspoon minced garlic
1 tablespoon freshly squeezed lemon juice
1 teaspoon ground cumin

4 (10-inch) whole wheat tortillas
1 organic red bell pepper, sliced
1 tomato, sliced
1 cup alfalfa sprouts

Prepare hummus: Puree all ingredients in a food processor or blender. Refrigerate until ready to use.

To assemble, spread hummus on tortillas, layer with vegetables, and roll.

NUTRITION FACTS

Serving Size 1 wrap (205g)
Calories 340
Calories from Fat 60
Total Fat 7g
Saturated Fat 0g
Trans Fat 0g
Cholesterol 0mg
Sodium 280mg
Total Carbohydrate 56g
Dietary Fiber 9g
Sugars 7g
Protein 14g

Eat: Snacks

Jonas's Turkey Roll-Up

At the time of this writing my son requests this be packed for school almost every day. The best part is it is simple and can be done in only a few minutes. If my son ever gets out of this rut, he'll realize how versatile this can be, too; prosciutto or roast beef slices can be substituted for the turkey. For a veggie option, see the opposite page. I usually make one whole lavosh roll-up for the day—half for my son's lunchbox and half for my daughter's on-the-go snack.

MAKES 1 ROLL; 2 SERVINGS

1 piece lavosh (about 13 x 9 inches)
2 ounces organic Neufchâtel cheese
2 ounces thinly sliced organic cooked turkey

Spread lavosh with a layer of cheese. Layer turkey in single layer on cheese.

Starting from narrow side, roll lavosh until you reach the end. You may want to add a small spread of cream cheese to secure roll. Using a sharp knife, make a quick cut in the center of roll. Cut each half in half again. Then cut each quarter in half, so you have 8 pieces.

KIDS KORNER

Need more glue? My son likes these rolled tightly and packed in his bento-style container. He likes to be sure I spread enough "glue," aka cream cheese, to keep them together without unraveling.

petit
appetit

EAT, DRINK,
AND
BE MERRY

Veggie Cheese Roll-Up, Please

Here's a vegetarian version of my son's favorite lunchtime food or snack. You can grate just about any vegetable to sprinkle on the cheese. Even leftover cooked and chopped vegetables such as asparagus, broccoli, or carrots will work here. The trick is to cut small enough pieces to roll up neatly, without any hidden choking chunks.

MAKES 1 ROLL

1 piece lavosh (about 13 × 9 inches)
2 ounces organic Neufchâtel cheese
⅓ cup grated organic carrots, zucchini, or red bell pepper, or combination
⅓ cup grated mozzarella cheese (rBGH free)

Spread lavosh with a layer of Neufchâtel cheese. Sprinkle with vegetables and mozzarella cheese over cream cheese.

Starting from narrow side, roll the lavosh until you reach the end. Push down to secure. You may want to add a small spread of cream cheese to be sure end will stick. Using a sharp knife, make a quick cut in the center of roll. Cut each half in half again. Then cut each quarter in half, so you have 8 pieces.

NUTRITION FACTS

Serving Size ½ roll (64g)
Calories 110
Calories from Fat 40
Total Fat 4.5g
Saturated Fat 3g
Trans Fat 0g
Cholesterol 15mg
Sodium 300mg
Total Carbohydrate 9g
Dietary Fiber 1g
Sugars 3g
Protein 7g

Eat: Snacks

GROUP PLEASERS

Chicken and Mango Quesadillas

A simple quesadilla is a great way to make a tasty snack out of leftover chicken, beef, or pork. You can alter the color and flavor of these quesadillas by choosing from a variety of flavored tortillas; spinach, corn, and tomato are a few of many options available. Baking quesadillas in the oven rather than on the stovetop allows for two or more to be ready at once, without dirtying multiple pans and allowing everyone to sit and eat together.

MAKES 2 QUESADILLAS; 4 SERVINGS

4 (8-inch) whole wheat tortillas
Vegetable oil
1½ cups grated Cheddar cheese (rBGH-free)
1½ cups cooked organic free-range chicken, shredded
1 mango, peeled, pitted, and sliced
¼ cup chopped fresh cilantro

Preheat oven to 375°F. Brush 2 tortillas with oil. Place tortillas, oil side down, on a baking sheet. Sprinkle each with half of the cheese, half of the chicken, half of the mango, and half of the cilantro. Top each with 1 tortilla, pressing to adhere; brush top with oil.

Bake quesadillas for about 10 minutes, until filling is heated through and edges begin to crisp. Using a large metal spatula, carefully turn each over and bake for an additional 5 minutes, until bottom is crisp.

Transfer quesadillas to plates. Cut into wedges with a pizza cutter. Let cheese cool sufficiently to prevent burning little tongues before serving.

NUTRITION FACTS

Serving Size ½ quesadilla
(134g)
Calories 330
Calories from Fat 120
Total Fat 14g
Saturated Fat 6g
Trans Fat 0g
Cholesterol 60mg
Sodium 380mg
Total Carbohydrate 27g
Dietary Fiber 2g
Sugars 4g
Protein 22g

petit
appetit

EAT, DRINK,
AND
BE MERRY

Salty and Spicy: Chips, Pretzels, Popcorn, and Nuts

Curry Chickpeas

Aromatic, spicy, and crunchy all in one, it's surprising how many children like and accept the taste of curry. If they like crunch, too, this should become an instant favorite.

MAKES 1½ CUPS

1 (16-ounce) can chickpeas, drained and rinsed (about 1½ cups if cooking fresh)
¼ teaspoon curry powder
¼ teaspoon ground cinnamon
⅛ teaspoon salt

Place chickpeas in a strainer and rinse with water. Drain and blot excess water with paper towels or kitchen towel. Add chickpeas to a small, dry skillet. Season with curry powder, cinnamon, and salt.

Stove-top method: Cook over medium heat about 35 to 40 minutes, stirring every 5 minutes with a rubber spatula so they cook evenly but don't stick to pan. Chickpeas will be deep golden brown in color and crispy.

Oven method: Preheat oven to 400°F. Roast on baking sheet about 35 to 40 minutes, stirring every 10 minutes with a rubber spatula so they cook evenly but don't stick to pan. Chickpeas will be deep golden brown in color and crispy.

Let cool.

TIP
Perfect for packing and sharing. I took these to the park for my children to eat, and found we were sharing them with lots of other curious and interested children.

NUTRITION FACTS

Serving Size about ¼ cup (41g)
Calories 70
Calories from Fat 10
Total Fat 1g
Saturated Fat 0g
Trans Fat 0g
Cholesterol 0mg
Sodium 50mg
Total Carbohydrate 11g
Dietary Fiber 3g
Sugars 2g
Protein 4g

Eat: Snacks

MILK FREE

GLUTEN FREE

GROUP PLEASERS

PERFECT FOR PACKING

WHEAT FREE

VEGETARIAN

petit
appetit

EAT, DRINK,
AND
BE MERRY

Sugar, Nuts, Spice, and Everything Nice

Skip the "whatever's on sale" nut mix can or jar full of preservatives, oils, and salt. This is simple to make with your child's favorite nuts to substitute for the pecans. There are many variations of spiced nuts. This one is special because the raisins give an added crunch, sweetness, and chew to the mix.

MAKES 2½ CUPS

1 tablespoon plus 1 teaspoon evaporated cane juice
¼ teaspoon salt
½ teaspoon ground cinnamon
⅛ teaspoon ground cloves
1 large cage-free organic egg white
1½ cups organic pecan halves
1 cup organic golden raisins

Heat oven to 375°F. Line a baking sheet with aluminum foil. Lightly grease foil, and set baking sheet aside.

In a small bowl, combine evaporated cane juice, salt, cinnamon, and cloves.

In another small bowl, beat egg white until frothy, about 30 seconds with an electric mixer. Add spice mixture to egg and stir with a rubber spatula to combine. Stir in pecans and raisins and toss until evenly coated.

Spread pecan mixture on baking sheet in a single layer. Bake for 15 minutes, until nuts and raisins are browned, but not burned, stirring and rotating pan one-quarter turn every 5 minutes. Cool completely before eating.

Toasted Pita Wedges

My mother made these all the time when I was growing up. This version substitutes whole wheat pitas for regular pitas to eliminate the white flour and add some fiber. They're so easy, you don't really need a recipe to make them—but you'll wonder why you haven't made them before. Serve with Black Bean Hummus (page 59) or Spinach Hummus (page 187) and vegetable sticks for a quick snack.

MAKES 16 WEDGES

2 whole wheat pita bread rounds
1 tablespoon extra-virgin olive oil
¼ teaspoon sweet paprika
Salt, to taste (optional)

Preheat oven to 375°F. Cut each pita round into 8 wedges, like a pie. Brush the wedges with olive oil and put on a baking sheet. Sprinkle with paprika and salt (if using). Bake for about 10 minutes, until crisp.

KIDS KORNER
Older kids can practice their scissor skills by using food shears to make wedges. Then give them a pastry brush for "painting" on the oil.

NUTRITION FACTS

Serving Size 4 wedges (36g)
Calories 120
Calories from Fat 40
Total Fat 4.5g
Saturated Fat 0.5g
Trans Fat 0g
Cholesterol 0mg
Sodium 170mg
Total Carbohydrate 18g
Dietary Fiber 2g
Sugars 0g
Protein 3g

Eat: Snacks

Silly Salsa

This is a simple and versatile salsa to top quesadillas or to dip Tortilla Cut-Outs (opposite page) and veggie sticks. If your child does not like a chunky texture, use the blender or food processor to make smoother.

MAKES ABOUT 1 ½ CUPS

3 vine-ripened tomatoes, chopped (about 1½ cups)
¼ cup chopped green onions (about 4)
2 tablespoons minced fresh cilantro
1 teaspoon freshly squeezed lime juice
¼ teaspoon salt

Combine all ingredients in a medium bowl and mash with the back of a fork to release more of the tomatoes' juices.

KIDS KORNER
My daughter loves tomatoes, or as she calls them "may mays." For her this is "may may" dip.

Go Green! Organic tomatoes have more lycopene than conventionally grown. You'll also avoid genetically modified produce.

Tortilla Cut-Outs

These are a fun and healthy alternative to processed, store-bought chips. The variety of colors and shapes are endless and perfect for a children's party or playgroup. Choose any soft tortilla such as wheat, flour, spinach, or tomato, or make a variety. Try to keep sizes the same, so chips cook evenly. Serve with Oscar Dip (page 62).

MAKES ABOUT 40 (2-INCH) CHIPS; 8 SERVINGS

5 (9-inch) whole wheat tortillas
Olive oil spray

Preheat oven to 375°F. Line a baking sheet with foil. Grease foil, and set baking sheet aside.

Using cookie cutters, cut tortillas into desired shapes. Place tortilla shapes in a single layer on prepared baking sheet. Spray with olive oil spray. Bake for 5 to 7 minutes, until crisp.

KIDS KORNER
Older children can help choose shapes and cut the tortillas. Even "scraps" from shapes can make their own funny images, so don't waste them.

NUTRITION FACTS

Serving Size 5 chips (28g)
Calories 90
Calories from Fat 20
Total Fat 2g
Saturated Fat 0g
Trans Fat 0g
Cholesterol 0mg
Sodium 135mg
Total Carbohydrate 16g
Dietary Fiber 1g
Sugars 0g
Protein 2g

Eat: Snacks

Soft Pretzels

Sing "Take Me Out to the Ball Game" while enjoying these do-it-yourself pretzels at home in front of the game. It's the best seat for your child to see the action, and you won't have to take him to the bathroom when the bases are loaded.

MAKES 48 (2- TO 3-INCH) PRETZELS; 24 SERVINGS

1½ cups warm water
2 packages active dry yeast
2 tablespoons sugar
1 teaspoon salt
2 cage-free organic eggs
2 cups whole wheat pastry flour
2 cups unbleached all-purpose flour
Coarse salt, poppy seeds, and sesame seeds, for sprinkling

Preheat oven to 425°F. Line a baking sheet with parchment paper and set aside.

Combine water and yeast in a large bowl and stir until yeast is dissolved. Add sugar, salt, 1 egg, and flours. Transfer dough to a floured surface. Knead dough until elastic, about 3 minutes. Pull off small pieces and roll into different shapes (circles, hearts, and twists), and place 2 inches apart on a prepared baking sheet. Beat the remaining egg. Brush the pretzels with beaten egg and sprinkle with coarse salt or seeds as desired.

Bake for 12 minutes, until golden. Serve with Mustard-Honey Sauce (page 66).

KIDS KORNER

This recipe has it all for kids. First there's shaping, playing with, molding, and rolling the dough. Next is painting on the egg. Then there's sprinkling the salt. And finally there's dipping in the mustard.

NUTRITION FACTS

Serving Size 2 pretzels (41g)
Calories 80
Calories from Fat 5
Total Fat 0.5g
Saturated Fat 0g
Trans Fat 0g
Cholesterol 20mg
Sodium 105mg
Total Carbohydrate 17g
Dietary Fiber 2g
Sugars 1g
Protein 3g

petit
appetit

EAT, DRINK,
AND
BE MERRY

POPPED CORN POSSIBILITIES

Parmesan Popped Corn

I brought this to share with friends at the beach. Who knew it would be such a hit with all ages! Grapeseed oil makes a good choice, as it is good for high-heat cooking and will not smoke while popping.

MAKES ABOUT 7 (1-CUP) SERVINGS

½ cup organic popcorn
¼ cup grapeseed oil
2 tablespoons organic unsalted butter, melted
¼ cup freshly shredded Parmesan cheese (rBGH-free)
¼ teaspoon salt

Pop the popcorn using a large 10-inch heavy pot with a tight-fitting lid or a popcorn maker. If using the pot, coat the bottom of the pot with oil and heat over medium heat. Drop in 1 kernel of corn. Wait until it pops then add the remaining kernels. Cover and shake pan. Continue to shake pan until all the corn has popped, being careful not to burn, about 3 minutes. (You may want to slightly lift lid every minute or two so steam can escape.)

Place the popped popcorn in a large bowl. Drizzle with the butter and sprinkle with the cheese and salt. Toss gently to combine and serve immediately.

KIDS KORNER
It's fun for older kids to watch the popping action if you have a glass cover for your pot. If they can't see, they can at least hear the sounds of popping kernels. Just be sure they are at a safe viewpoint.

NUTRITION FACTS

Serving Size about 1 cup (31g)
Calories 170
Calories from Fat 110
Total Fat 12g
Saturated Fat 3.5g
Trans Fat 0g
Cholesterol 10mg
Sodium 135mg
Total Carbohydrate 12g
Dietary Fiber 2g
Sugars 0g
Protein 3g

Eat: Snacks

Kettle Corn

Kettle corn is a perfect mix of salt, sugar, and crunch that both kids and adults find addictive. Be careful and patient when popping on the stove, as moving the lid may cause hot popcorn to escape. Have children listen from a safe distance.

MAKES ABOUT 7 CUPS

½ cup organic popcorn
¼ cup grapeseed oil
¼ cup evaporated cane juice
1 teaspoon coarse salt

Pop the popcorn using a large 10-inch heavy pot with a tight-fitting lid or a popcorn maker. If using the pot, coat the bottom of the pot with oil and heat over medium heat. Drop in 1 kernel of corn. Wait until it pops then add the remaining kernels. Sprinkle the cane juice over the kernels. Cover and shake pan. Continue to shake pan until all the corn has popped, being careful not to burn, about 3 minutes. (You may want to slightly lift lid every minute or two so steam can escape.)

Place the popped popcorn in a large bowl. Sprinkle with the salt. Toss gently to combine and serve immediately.

Go Green! Buy organic corn kernels since more than half of America's corn crops are genetically modified.

petit
appetit

EAT, DRINK,
AND
BE MERRY

Potato Chips

This recipe was inspired by my son's favorite book, *The Greatest Potatoes* by Penelope Stowell. In the story, U.S. tycoon Cornelius Vanderbilt spans the globe trying to find the greatest potato dish. He is persnickety and ornery and turns his nose up to all, until he meets George Crum, fry cook at Cary Moon's Lake House Restaurant in Saratoga Springs, New York, and tastes his new invention, the potato chip. This is a bit of a variation on the book's actual recipe, but I'm sure it will please any little persnickety gourmands in your house.

MAKES 20 TO 30 CHIPS PER POTATO; 4 TO 6 SERVINGS

Organic russet potatoes (12 ounces each)
Salt, to taste (optional)

Preheat oven to 350°F. Line 2 baking sheets with aluminum foil. Grease foil, and set baking sheet aside.

Using a mandoline set on ⅛ inch, the long edge of a box grater, or a sharp knife, cut potatoes evenly into paper-thin slices. Place potato slices in a large bowl and cover with cold water. Let soak for 10 to 15 minutes. Drain and rinse until water runs clear.

Dry potato slices by spinning in a salad spinner. Kids love to help with this step. Place potato slices in a single layer on prepared baking sheets. Bake for 25 to 30 minutes, turning carefully with tongs about every 7 minutes. As the chips brown, remove from baking sheet, one by one, until the batch is complete and crunchy. Sprinkle with salt (if using).

KIDS KORNER
The salad spinner brings out the competitive nature in children. They want to spin it faster than Mom, Dad, and Sister (at least at my house). My son even wants to measure how much water he is able to remove from the potatoes.

NUTRITION FACTS

Serving Size 5 chips (28g)
Calories 20
Calories from Fat 0
Total Fat 0g
Saturated Fat 0g
Trans Fat 0g
Cholesterol 0mg
Sodium 0mg
Total Carbohydrate 5g
Dietary Fiber 0g
Sugars 0g
Protein 1g

Eat: Snacks

Sweet: Fruit, Cookies, Muffins, and Ice Pops

Fruit Kebobs

It's so much fun to go to my son's school and make or bring a snack. The reactions are unexpected and fun. This was the biggest hit. I made enough for the students to have two kebobs each, and they were begging for more. You can put a variety of fruit on these sticks. Those that are denser will stay on better. The melon baller keeps everything the same size with little effort; however, you can cut same-size chunks, too. For an added treat, serve with Lemon Snickety Sauce (page 64).

MAKES 24 KEBOBS

1 cantaloupe
1 honeydew
½ watermelon
½ pineapple

Using a melon baller, create as many balls of cantaloupe, honeydew, and watermelon as possible. Cut pineapple into 1-inch chunks.

Carefully thread each fruit ball on a flat wooden stick, making sure each one has all four kinds.

KIDS KORNER
This is a great recipe to involve the kids. Some can make balls with the melon baller, some can count and line up the wooden sticks, and others can thread them.

Go Green! Be sure to wash and recycle wooden sticks for gluing, building, and creating all kinds of art projects with your children.

NUTRITION FACTS
Serving Size 2 kebobs (82g)
Calories 30
Calories from Fat 0
Total Fat 0g
Saturated Fat 0g
Trans Fat 0g
Cholesterol 0mg
Sodium 10mg
Total Carbohydrate 8g
Dietary Fiber 1g
Sugars 6g
Protein 1g

petit
appetit

EAT, DRINK,
AND
BE MERRY

Pumpkin-Ginger Muffins

Because of the use of pumpkin, this recipe makes a perfect autumn treat for large and small hands alike. These muffins are both sweet and savory, which makes them a good accompaniment for soups and salads as well as alone for breakfast or a snack. There's no need to worry about nuts or frosting, so you can safely make a double batch to present at playdates or share at school. These muffins can also be made in mini muffin trays—but reduce baking time and check doneness frequently.

MAKES 10 MUFFINS

1 cup unbleached all-purpose flour
¾ cup whole wheat flour
⅓ cup evaporated cane juice
2 teaspoons baking powder
¼ teaspoon salt
½ teaspoon ground cinnamon
¼ teaspoon freshly grated nutmeg
1 large cage-free organic egg, lightly beaten
¾ cup organic whole milk
½ cup canned pumpkin
¼ cup expeller-pressed canola oil
½ teaspoon grated fresh ginger

Topping (optional)
½ teaspoon ground cinnamon
½ teaspoon evaporated cane juice

Preheat oven to 400°F. Lightly grease 10 muffin cups; set pan aside.
In a large bowl, combine flours, evaporated cane juice, baking powder, salt, cinnamon, and nutmeg. Make a well in the center. In a medium bowl, combine egg, milk, pumpkin, oil, and ginger until smooth. Pour wet ingredients into well in dry ingredients. Stir just until combined and dry ingredients are moistened. Fill prepared muffin cups one-half to two-thirds full.

NUTRITION FACTS

Serving Size 1 muffin (73g)
Calories 180
Calories from Fat 60
Total Fat 7g
Saturated Fat 1g
Trans Fat 0g
Cholesterol 25mg
Sodium 150mg
Total Carbohydrate 27g
Dietary Fiber 2g
Sugars 10g
Protein 4g

Eat: Snacks

In a small bowl, combine cinnamon and sugar for topping (if using). Sprinkle each muffin with topping. Bake 15 to 18 minutes, until golden. Remove muffins from pan and serve warm.

TIP

I can? Pumpkin is one of the few ingredients that is better from a can. There is actually more flavor and nutrients in the canned version than the fresh, and certainly less work is required. Be sure to buy canned pumpkin, and not pumpkin pie filling. The filling is loaded with sugars and spice.

Choco-Fruit Flax Biscuits

I started to make a chocolate chip cookie and ended up with a great chocolate chip biscuit instead. These are drop biscuits, so they're not perfectly shaped, but they are tasty and have an added helping of protein with flax meal. If you'd rather have something prettier, you can roll out dough on a floured surface, then cut with a biscuit cutter.

MAKES 36 TO 40 (2-INCH) BISCUITS

2½ cups unbleached all-purpose flour
1 cup plus 2 tablespoons flax meal
1 teaspoon coarse salt
½ teaspoon baking soda
½ cup organic unsalted butter, at room temperature
½ cup packed brown sugar
½ cup organic apple puree or sauce
2 large cage-free organic eggs
2 teaspoons pure vanilla extract
3 tablespoons organic plain whole-milk yogurt
1¼ cups organic semisweet chocolate chips

Preheat oven to 350°F. Line a large baking sheet with parchment paper and set aside.

In a large bowl, whisk together flour, flax meal, salt, and baking soda. In a medium mixing bowl, beat butter and sugar on medium-high speed until creamy, about 3 minutes. Add apple puree. Beat in eggs and vanilla. Reduce speed to low and add half of the flour mixture. Blend in yogurt and beat in remaining flour until combined. Stir in chocolate chips. Cover and freeze dough for 10 minutes.

Drop rounded tablespoons of dough about 2 inches apart on prepared baking sheet. Flatten slightly and bake about 12 to 14 minutes, until centers are set and biscuits turn pale brown on bottom.

NUTRITION FACTS

Serving Size 1 biscuit (35g)
Calories 130
Calories from Fat 60
Total Fat 7g
Saturated Fat 3g
Trans Fat 0g
Cholesterol 20mg
Sodium 75mg
Total Carbohydrate 16g
Dietary Fiber 2g
Sugars 8g
Protein 2g

Eat: Snacks

Any Juice Pops

Look beyond the boxed pops in the freezer section of the grocery store. There's no telling how many combinations and variations you and your children can make by having an ice pop mold on hand. These are nice and icy on a hot day and can be made with any juice you have in the fridge. Adding water dilutes the juice and sugar a bit and also lends a more "icy" texture.

MAKES 8 (¼-CUP) POPS

1½ cups fresh organic fruit juice such as unfiltered apple juice
½ cup water

Shake juice container to mix contents before measuring and pour into pitcher. Add water to juice and stir. Pour liquid into ice pop molds. Put the tops on and transfer to the freezer on a flat shelf to freeze until solid, about 1 hour.

To remove the pops from the mold, stand the mold in a bowl of cold water (or run water under 1, to release only 1 pop) for 1 to 2 minutes until the pops lift out.

KIDS KORNER
Mix It Up! There's no need to stop at one juice for these pops. Ask your child for flavor combinations. Combine orange and apple or pear and pomegranate. Once you get the hang of it, you'll be making lots of colors and flavors of frozen treats.

NUTRITION FACTS

Serving Size 1 pop (59g)
Calories 20
Calories from Fat 0
Total Fat 0g
Saturated Fat 0g
Trans Fat 0g
Cholesterol 0mg
Sodium 0mg
Total Carbohydrate 5g
Dietary Fiber 0g
Sugars 5g
Protein 0g

petit
appetit

EAT, DRINK,
AND
BE MERRY

Crispy Cupcakes

This is the answer to standard marshmallow-and-cereal crispy treats. These are crunchy, tasty, and very pretty served in cupcake cups on a celebration table. They are also handy to have on hand in the freezer any time the kids are looking for a sweet and crunchy snack.

MAKES 10 CUPCAKES

5 tablespoons organic unsalted butter

¼ cup honey (see Note, page 46)

1½ cups rolled oats (see gluten-free icon, page 3)

1½ cups puffed brown rice cereal

2 teaspoons sesame seeds

½ cup unsweetened organic dried fruit pieces, such as cranberries and raisins

Melt butter and honey in a small saucepan over low heat.

Mix oats, rice cereal, sesame seeds, and dried fruit in a medium bowl. Add butter and honey mixture and stir to combine.

Spoon into muffin cup papers and press down to shape and hold together. Let chill in the freezer for 1 hour before serving. Store leftovers in freezer or refrigerator for these to hold their shape and crunch.

NUTRITION FACTS

Serving Size 1 cupcake
(37g)
Calories 160
Calories from Fat 60
Total Fat 7g
Saturated Fat 3.5g
Trans Fat 0g
Cholesterol 15mg
Sodium 0mg
Total Carbohydrate 22g
Dietary Fiber 2g
Sugars 12g
Protein 2g

Eat: Snacks

Juice Jiggles

My son came up with this name, which seemed very appropriate. It's a very simple way for kids to eat their juice without spills. These make a fun party tray with different shapes and sizes of molds and various colors and flavors of juices to please everyone. These can be eaten from individual tartlet molds or popped out for cool and jiggly finger foods.

12 (2- TO 3-INCH) JIGGLES

1 cup pure organic fruit juice or nectar
1 (1-ounce) envelope plain gelatin

Lightly coat 16 tartlet molds or mini muffin cups with cooking oil and set aside. Place ¼ cup of the juice in a medium bowl and sprinkle gelatin on top. Let sit for 1 minute. In a small pan over medium heat, bring remaining ¾ cup juice to a boil. Add to gelatin mixture and stir until gelatin is dissolved.

Spoon mixture into molds/cups. Chill in the refrigerator until set, about 1 hour. Pop tartlets out by going around edge with sharp knife, and invert on a plate.

KIDS KORNER
My seventeen-month-old wanted to play with her jiggles like blocks, stacking and restacking them on her plate. My four-year-old ate his with a spoon for fear of getting something on his hands (which he does not find acceptable).

NUTRITION FACTS

Serving Size 1 jiggle (23g)
Calories 15
Calories from Fat 0
Total Fat 0g
Saturated Fat 0g
Trans Fat 0g
Cholesterol 0mg
Sodium 0mg
Total Carbohydrate 2g
Dietary Fiber 0g
Sugars 2g
Protein 2g

petit
appetit

EAT, DRINK,
AND
BE MERRY

CHAPTER 7

Drink: Beverages

*E*VERY CHILD EVENTUALLY LEARNS there's more to drinks than milk and water. If you think outside the bottle, can, or juice box, there are some great options for making drinks at home. Here you'll find ideas for dressing up plain and sparkling waters into special "mocktails" for holidays and gatherings for all ages. The recipes for shakes and smoothies will find you getting out your blender or juicer. There are also broths for boosting energy and nutrients when your child is ill. And what child doesn't enjoy a hot (or warm) cider or hot cocoa on a chilly afternoon?

Making your own drinks gives you and your children the freedom to choose: sparkling or non-sparkling, with fresh fruit or a fancy-shaped ice cube, frozen or warm, and on and on. Children like to make choices, so let their creative juices (pun intended) run wild. Once they start concocting their own waters, juices, shakes, slurpies, and cocoas, there's no telling what combinations they'll come up with. Making festive drinks to go with a party theme can be fun. How about tropical frappes for a pool party, or hot chocolate for a winter wonderland?

BENEFITS OF HOMEMADE DRINKS

Save Money

Making your own drinks at home costs pennies instead of dollars at a restaurant or convenience store. And remember, water is free from your filter at home!

More Nutritious

Many sodas and juice blends are high in sugars, corn syrup, and preservatives and low on nutrients. In addition, these drinks fill children up so they are not hungry for healthier drinks and foods.

> Dentists also caution that drinking of sodas, sugary drinks, and juices increases the likelihood of cavities in young children. Dr. Ladan Vakili, DMD, believes children should keep themselves hydrated but have drinks such as fizzy waters and juices in moderation, as they have "high levels of sodium, sugar, caffeine, and preservatives which can erode teeth's enamel."

Make and Invent Your Own Flavors

Allow children to come up with their own flavors and do not limit them to what's on the shelf.

Choose and Pack Your Own Container

Your son can pick his favorite cup to hold (or you can choose a safe and leakproof option), instead of a heavy glass or oversized one.

Control Portions

Make and pack as much as you want, without having to waste drinks or tempt your child to overdo on large portions. Studies have shown that children who consume

petit
appetit

EAT, DRINK,
AND
BE MERRY

102

sodas, juices, and flavored drinks are at a higher risk for being overweight. Juice boxes marketed to young children are usually found in 6- to 8-ounce servings, which is more than the American Academy of Pediatrics recommendations of no more than 4 ounces of juice per day.

Nutritionist Sanna Delmonico, MS, RD, says the portions on bottled drinks are way too large. "No one needs that much of anything except water, and the bottles [sometimes 20 or even 24 ounces] are especially ridiculous for children."

Avoid Additives, Sugars, and Other "Fake Stuff"

Your drinks will only have ingredients you choose without the need to maintain shelf life or boost unnatural colors.

According to a 2001 study in the *Journal of Nutrition,* the choices a mother makes—from beverages she drinks to where she keeps the family snacks—dramatically affect childrens' nutrition and health risks. Children of women who often consume soft drinks typically drink more soda and less milk than children of women who don't regularly consume sugared drinks.

THE POWER OF THE BOTTLE

Your baby loved his "ba ba" and didn't want to give it up. Your toddler is always spilling and you love the "sippy" (leakproof) option. Here are the options for and issues with children's beverage containers, and the health and environmental impacts of both reusable and disposable bottles, which are leading to alternative ways to enjoy beverages. Also included are the best options for children and the environment.

DRINK PACKING AND STORAGE

A large cause for alarm with respect to babies in the past year was the studies of Bisphenol-A (BPA), the key building block of hard, clear, polycarbonate plastics (usually a number "7" on the bottom of containers) found in baby bottles and sippy cups. This chemical has been banned in Europe but still continues to be found in American baby products. At high enough quantities, BPA can disrupt hormone function and lead to certain cancers, reproductive problems, and other health issues, according to Dr. David Wallinga, director of the Institute for Agriculture and Trade Policy in Minneapolis.

There are an increasing number of brands without Bisphenol-A. Check the packaging for BPA-free bottles, as well as glass (see below) options.

Spillproof and Training Cups

"Sippy" cups are the spillproof (hopefully!) answer to giving your child a beverage that he can use independently. However, like bottles, these are also made from plastics that may leach harmful chemicals into the drink. Opt for BPA-free plastic cups. Some of the same brand of bottles and training cups come in BPA versions. Also see stainless steel and aluminum options (below) in training cup styles.

Besides the plastic concern, according to James Boylan, DDS, "There are two consequences of the use of sippy cups. The first is what fluid is in the cup and the second is when the child is allowed to drink it." He cautions against putting juice or sweetened beverages in a sippy cup. "Carrying around a sippy cup of even milk will increase the chance that cavities will be encouraged due to prolonged exposure to sugars."

Glass

The best option for reducing the possibility of chemical leaching and exposure as well as aid a child's development is an open glass. According to Ellyn Satter, a child benefits from using a sturdy glass that both hands can fit easily around. Glass is leach-free, reusable, and recyclable. This of course works for eating at home at the table and storing and pouring for a crowd. However, there's the safety concern with breakage and the inconvenience of spilling when out and about. Another benefit of glass is that it lasts forever (unless broken) and is thus a less expensive option. There are protective soft carriers for baby bottles and other drinking sizes to make glass more child-friendly.

Disposable

It is estimated that Americans go through 70 million disposable bottles daily (with almost 90 percent of them ending up in landfills). Most disposable bottles are made

petit
appetit
EAT, DRINK,
AND
BE MERRY

104

from polyethylene terephthalate (PET) plastic and believed to leach carcinogen when refilled. Juice boxes and "pouches" are marketed heavily to children; however, they are prone to leaks and spills and cannot be resealed.

Stainless Steel/Aluminum

Reusable bottles and thermoses that are coated with a protective seal from leaching now come in a variety of tops for children of different ages and stages. This is another fun way your child can make a choice with a container that fits his personality. Large thermos pitcher containers are good for outdoor entertaining, such as picnics and barbecues. They also keep soups and beverages such as Calientito (page 137) warm for camping and sporting events.

See Resources (page 258) for more information on brands and resources.

FREEDOM OF CHOICE AWAY FROM HOME

Children face drink options at home, at school, in vending machines, at restaurants, and at friends' and families' houses. Unfortunately, too many are choosing sodas and other high-calorie, high-sugar drinks with little nutritional value, which fill kids up and leave little room for nutritious foods and beverages.

Due to the increase of childhood obesity and adult-onset diabetes in children, thankfully some schools are removing or enforcing new guidelines for what is offered in school vending machines. However, in many restaurants kids are lured to sodas and sugary drinks with "children's meal" menus. Not only is there pressure to purchase sodas, but restaurants encourage drinking multiple servings with the offer of giant sizes or free refills. What child (or adult, for that matter) can resist these temptations?

In an effort to compete with drinks high in sugars, calories and colorings and low in nutrients, here are some ideas for making your own beverages for your children.

CREATE IT!

There are so many combinations of fruits, vegetables, liquids, and yogurts that can be used to make a tasty, healthy, and naturally colorful drink. Once you get started using your blender, juicer, or pitcher at home and stop grabbing for a prepackaged bottle, can, or juice box, you'll appreciate the great flavors and beverages you can easily make at home—and for less than the store brands. To serve as a guide for healthy creations at home, here are some of the vitamins and nutrients in the fruits and vegetables your children will be getting. Pair them together with the protein options and mix and match for the healthiest and tastiest options for smoothies, juices, and shakes.

VITAMINS/NUTRIENTS	FRUITS/VEGETABLES
Antioxidants	Blueberry, red grape
A	Apple, celery, cabbage, cantaloupe, carrot, mango, spinach, sweet potato
B	Beet, broccoli, cabbage, carrot, celery, spinach
C	Apple, carrot, orange, papaya, red pepper, strawberry, tomato, watermelon
D	Milk
E	Apple, mango, pear
Calcium	Milk, kale, soymilk, spinach, tofu, yogurt
Iron	Apricot, beet, carrot, cabbage, green
Protein	Milk, tofu, yogurt

INSPIRE IT!

Just like with food choices, look to your child's favorite ingredients, tastes, and textures to come up with drinks he will enjoy. If he sees someone with a fancy smoothie at school, re-create it at home using his favorite organic fruits and creamy yogurt (see Smoothies, page 113).

Let the weather and the activity inspire a drink. If he's cold and needs a warm treat, make a batch of Hot Cocoa (page 135), wrap him in his favorite blanket, and

petit
appetit

EAT, DRINK,
AND
BE MERRY

106

read a story. Maybe it's a hot day and he needs something to quench his thirst and cool his body, so pick Frozen Lemonade (page 110).

THE POWER OF LEMONADE

Who didn't grow up having a lemonade stand? The positive power of one child and a refreshing drink created a unique foundation that evolved from a young cancer patient's front-yard lemonade stand to a nationwide fund-raising movement to find a cure for pediatric cancer. Since Alexandra "Alex" Scott (1996–2004) set up her front-yard stand at the age of four, more than $17 million has been raised toward fulfilling her dream of finding a cure for all children with cancer.

DECORATE IT!

Sometimes the glass your child gets to use is almost as important (if not more) than what's in it. A favorite blue cup or a grown-up glass goes a long way to even enjoying milk or water. And why not garnish a drink with a slice of lemon or lime, or even an umbrella? I remember thinking that was very special when I was young and out to dinner with my parents. Your child likes you to make some effort and make things special. Of course, you don't need to do this every day. But if you're entertaining and the adults are having a special glass, put some effort into the child's drinks as well. Some of these fancy and tasty drinks will also appeal to the adults (especially considerate as a nonalcoholic option).

Juicy: Juices and Ades

Citrus Hints

There are a few drinks on the market that are basically flavored waters. But they're so much simpler and cheaper to do at home. If you have a hand citrus juicer, your little ones will enjoy doing this themselves. This is the answer to the question, "What can I have besides water?" For added sweet on a hot day, add juice cubes (page 142).

MAKES ABOUT 1 CUP

1 cup water
2 teaspoons freshly squeezed orange, lemon, or lime juice
   (or combination)

Put water in glass. Squeeze citrus fruit into glass and stir to combine.

KIDS KORNER

If you have a hand citrus juicer, your little ones will easily enjoy making this drink themselves. If no juicer is available, they'll just need some more muscle power (or adult help).

NUTRITION FACTS

Serving Size 1 cup
Calories 5
Calories from Fat 0
Total Fat 0g
Saturated Fat 0g
Trans Fat 0g
Cholesterol 0mg
Sodium 5mg
Total Carbohydrate 1g
Dietary Fiber 0g
Sugars 0g
Protein 0g

petit
appetit

EAT, DRINK,
AND
BE MERRY

Red-y Set Veggie! Juice

This one's a great red-colored vegetable juice that appeals to children and adults. It packs a punch of lycopene and vitamin C with the tomatoes and peppers. You'll need an electric juice extractor for this.

MAKES 1½ CUPS

2 (5-ounce) vine-ripened tomatoes
½ organic red bell pepper (about 4 ounces), seeds, core, and stem removed
1 (about 5-ounce) organic apple, seeds, core, and stem removed
2 teaspoons freshly squeezed lime juice

Process all ingredients through a juice extractor, and chill.

Go Green! When juicing, be sure to wash fruits and vegetables thoroughly, since you'll be using the peels. Also choose fresh, ripe, seasonal fruit and veggies for the healthiest and tastiest drink.

NUTRITION FACTS

Serving Size ¾ cup (278g)
Calories 80
Calories from Fat 5
Total Fat 0.5g
Saturated Fat 0g
Trans Fat 0g
Cholesterol 0mg
Sodium 10mg
Total Carbohydrate 20g
Dietary Fiber 5g
Sugars 14g
Protein 2g

Drink:
Beverages

Frozen Lemonade

This is the perfect lemonade for sipping on a hot afternoon. It is really great whipped in the blender, but if you don't want to bother, you can skip the last step and just pour over ice. Please note the color of this will be golden rather than bright yellow due to the use of raw sugar. You can always substitute white if you prefer.

MAKES ABOUT 3 ½ CUPS

Simple Syrup
½ cup turbinado sugar
½ cup water

½ cup freshly squeezed lemon juice (juice from about 4 lemons)
1 cup water
2 cups ice cubes, broken into chunks if large

Prepare Simple Syrup: Heat sugar and water in a small saucepan over medium heat. Stir until sugar has dissolved and mixture has thickened, 2 to 3 minutes. Cool to room temperature.

Combine lemon juice, syrup, and water in a blender with ice cubes and blend until slushy. Add more ice as desired.

KIDS KORNER
Be sure to call the kids for their big muscles to help squeeze the lemons.

petit
appetit

EAT, DRINK,
AND
BE MERRY

Small Shed's Fresh-Squeezed Maple Lemonade

I have always found foods to be most enjoyable when prepared simple, and nothing is more simple than our housemade lemonade. Frequently our customers will bring a box of Meyer lemons in from their yards and trade us for a flatbread pizza!

GED ROBERTSON, chef/owner at Small Shed Pizza

MAKES 2 ¼ CUPS

Juice from 1 lemon (about ¼ cup)
1 to 2 tablespoons pure maple syrup, or to taste
16 ounces sparkling water

Place all ingredients into a pitcher and stir with a spoon. Pour over ice and serve.

VARIATIONS

You can substitute still water for sparkling, and honey (see Note, page 46) for maple syrup. This lemonade tastes great made with hot water, too!

TIP

Roll lemons, pressing between your hand and the countertop. This will make them easier to squeeze and yield more juice.

Sparkling Limeade

The sour lime and sparkling water make this a refreshing combination. Because limes are always in season, your family can enjoy this year-round. Good-quality limes will be medium to large in size, smooth-skinned, light to deep green in color, and firm but not too hard.

MAKES 2 (1-CUP) SERVINGS

1½ cups sparkling water
¼ cup freshly squeezed lime juice (about 1 large lime)
¼ cup Simple Syrup (page 110)

Combine ingredients, stir, and serve over ice.

Growing up, I remember the flavor of limeade on sunny afternoons. I "made it" by opening the container of frozen concentrate and adding water. It was always hard to stir and wait for the frozen lump to combine with the water.

SIX-YEAR-OLD SARAH'S mom

NUTRITION FACTS

Serving Size 1 cup (213g)
Calories 25
Calories from Fat 0
Total Fat 0g
Saturated Fat 0g
Trans Fat 0g
Cholesterol 0mg
Sodium 0mg
Total Carbohydrate 7g
Dietary Fiber 0g
Sugars 5g
Protein 0g

petit
appetit

EAT, DRINK,
AND
BE MERRY

Frosty: Smoothies, Slurpies, and Shakes

Fruity Smoothies

This smoothie can be made with just about any single fruit or combination. Think mango or papaya, or a combo of raspberries and blueberries. The frozen banana gives this smoothie its creaminess. The use of frozen fruit rather than fresh or thawed means there's no need for ice, which can be too cold and a choking hazard for young children.

MAKES ABOUT 2½ CUPS

1 medium banana, frozen, cut into 2-inch chunks
1 cup frozen or fresh organic peaches, peeled, cut into chunks
½ cup organic plain whole-milk yogurt
1 tablespoon flax meal

Place all ingredients in a blender and blend until smooth.

TIP
Frozen bananas. To freeze bananas: Peel bananas, wrap in waxed paper, and store in freezer bags in the freezer for up to 1 month.

Tropical Fruit Frappe

Here's the piña colada taste in a cold and frozen treat for children. Coconut milk adds natural sweetness, healthy fats, and proteins.

MAKES 1 (1¼-CUP) SERVING

¼ cup canned light coconut milk
½ cup frozen pineapple chunks
1 cup frozen mango chunks

Place all ingredients into a blender and blend until smooth.

TIP

Cold convenience. No time to cut and freeze pineapple and mango chunks? Buy them pre-cut in the frozen food section for a faster frappe.

NUTRITION FACTS

Serving Size 1¼ cups
Calories 270
Calories from Fat 110
Total Fat 13g
Saturated Fat 11g
Trans Fat 0g
Cholesterol 0mg
Sodium 10mg
Total Carbohydrate 44g
Dietary Fiber 5g
Sugars 37g
Protein 2g

petit
appetit

EAT, DRINK,
AND
BE MERRY

Tofu Berry Smoothie

This recipe is courtesy of Leah's Pantry, which teaches parents and children living in transitional housing how to make healthy food choices and prepare fresh foods for their families. This is one of the kids' favorite recipes to help make and of course eat (or is that slurp?) together.

MAKES 2½ CUPS (WITHOUT ICE)

½ cup organic unfiltered apple juice
½ cup organic vanilla low-fat yogurt
½ cup (4 ounces) organic soft tofu, drained
1 cup organic strawberries, fresh or frozen (if you use frozen berries, you may not need ice cubes)
1 banana, cut into chunks
4 ice cubes (optional)

Place the apple juice, yogurt, tofu, strawberries, and banana in a blender. Cover and process until smooth.

Drop ice cubes (if using) into the blender one at a time. Process until smooth.

Go Green! Commercially grown strawberries are high in nitrites, as well as pesticides. Choose bright red, firm organic berries for the best flavor with reduced chemical exposure.

NUTRITION FACTS

Serving Size about 1¼ cups
Calories 210
Calories from Fat 35
Total Fat 3.5g
Saturated Fat 0.5g
Trans Fat 0g
Cholesterol 5mg
Sodium 45mg
Total Carbohydrate 39g
Dietary Fiber 3g
Sugars 29g
Protein 8g

Drink:
Beverages

Mango-Carrot Smoothie

Having fresh-cut fruit in your freezer will make smoothies and blended drinks a snap to make anytime. If you're short on time to cut and freeze, simply buy frozen mango chunks in the grocery freezer section. This is a bright orange pick-me-up for breakfast or a cooling afternoon snack.

MAKES ABOUT 1 CUP

1 cup frozen mango chunks
½ cup organic carrot juice
¼ cup freshly squeezed orange juice

Combine ingredients in a blender. Blend on medium speed for 30 to 60 seconds, until smooth.

Go Green! Due to high levels of nitrites in carrots, buy organic carrots and carrot juices, and eat them fresh without long storage (nitrite levels can increase during refrigeration). This is especially important for babies under eight months, as their stomach acid is too low to properly break down the nitrites.

NUTRITION FACTS

Serving Size 1 cup
Calories 170
Calories from Fat 5
Total Fat 0.5g
Saturated Fat 0g
Trans Fat 0g
Cholesterol 0mg
Sodium 80mg
Total Carbohydrate 41g
Dietary Fiber 3g
Sugars 30g
Protein 2g

petit
appetit

EAT, DRINK,
AND
BE MERRY

Papaya Slurpie

This is cool and refreshing on a hot day. Be sure your blender is able to grind the ice in this recipe, or your child will be surprised by cold chunks, which can also be a choking hazard.

MAKES ABOUT 1¾ CUPS

¼ cup organic unfiltered apple juice
½ cup sparkling mineral water
1 cup frozen papaya chunks
½ cup ice chips or pieces

Pour the apple juice and water into a blender and process until combined.

Add the frozen papaya and ice and process until a slushy consistency is reached and the ice is incorporated. You may have to pulse to move the ice and papaya around so everything reaches the blades.

TIP

Ripeness. Ripen papayas at room temperature and never store a papaya that is less than half ripe in the refrigerator. Cooler temperatures permanently shut off the ripening process.

NUTRITION FACTS

Serving Size about ¾ cup
Calories 50
Calories from Fat 0
Total Fat 0g
Saturated Fat 0g
Trans Fat 0g
Cholesterol 0mg
Sodium 5mg
Total Carbohydrate 12g
Dietary Fiber 1g
Sugars 9g
Protein 1g

Drink:
Beverages

Strawberry-Banana Shake

This is a quick and easy shake to whip up for a breakfast or an afternoon snack. The frozen berries give cold without the need for ice, while the banana gives a smooth and creamy texture. Any leftovers? If so, freeze in ice-pop molds or in a freezer-safe container for a frozen treat later.

MAKES 2 CUPS

1 cup frozen organic strawberries
½ cup organic whole milk
1 banana, quartered

Put strawberries, milk, and banana into a blender and blend until smooth and creamy.

Go Green! During nonpeak berry season, stock up on frozen organic berries for easy smoothies and shakes anytime. You'll also skip the high price, reduced flavor, and pesticides of conventionally grown fresh berries grown and sold out of season.

NUTRITION FACTS

Serving Size 1 cup (204g)
Calories 110
Calories from Fat 5
Total Fat 0g
Saturated Fat 0g
Trans Fat 0g
Cholesterol 0mg
Sodium 30mg
Total Carbohydrate 25g
Dietary Fiber 3g
Sugars 15g
Protein 3g

petit
appetit

EAT, DRINK,
AND
BE MERRY

Choco-Banana Shake

When I was a student at UC Davis, there was an amazing chocolate-banana shake served at Murder Burger. It brings back fond memories just thinking about it. I'm sure they made theirs with chocolate ice cream; however, this version captures that wonderful taste without the extra fat and calories.

MAKES 2 CUPS

1 large banana, frozen (see Tip, page 113)
1 cup ice cubes
1 cup organic chocolate soy milk
1 tablespoon organic unsweetened cocoa powder
1 tablespoon honey (see Note, page 46)

Cut frozen banana into same-size chunks. Place all ingredients into a blender and process until smooth.

NUTRITION FACTS

Serving Size 1 cup (330g)
Calories 170
Calories from Fat 25
Total Fat 3g
Saturated Fat 0g
Trans Fat 0g
Cholesterol 0mg
Sodium 20mg
Total Carbohydrate 35g
Dietary Fiber 4g
Sugars 24g
Protein 5g

Drink:
Beverages

Raspberry-Kiwi Smoothie

Recent studies have shown that ounce for ounce kiwifruit's nutritional value is higher than any other fruit, with a high level of antioxidants, potassium, and vitamins C and E. Raspberries add a boost of potassium, vitamin K, and fiber. Serve immediately and freeze any leftover smoothie in an ice-pop tray to enjoy later.

MAKES 3¾ CUPS

1 cup organic unfiltered apple juice
8 ounces organic plain whole-milk yogurt
2 kiwifruit, peeled and chopped (about ¾ cup)
12 ounces frozen organic unsweetened raspberries
1 tablespoon organic berry fruit spread

Combine apple juice, yogurt, and kiwifruit in blender and blend until smooth. Add raspberries and fruit spread and blend again until smooth and thick.

Go Green! Raspberries are delicate and difficult to wash. Buying organic will eliminate any concern of pesticides on these tasty gems.

petit
appetit

EAT, DRINK,
AND
BE MERRY

Great Grape Slush

This is a healthy improvement over the brightly colored slushies with fake flavors and colorings from fast-food restaurants and convenience stores. You can add ice cubes for older children, which will increase the yield.

MAKES 1 ½ CUPS

¾ cup frozen organic seedless purple grapes
1 organic apple, peeled, cored, and chopped
½ cup organic unfiltered apple juice

Add all ingredients to a blender and blend until slushy.

TIP

Freeze these. Spread individual grapes on a pan and freeze. Transfer to a freezer bag or container to have available for kids to eat alone as a frosty snack, or make this tasty slush.

NUTRITION FACTS

Serving Size 1 ½ cups
Calories 170
Calories from Fat 5
Total Fat 0g
Saturated Fat 0g
Trans Fat 0g
Cholesterol 0mg
Sodium 0mg
Total Carbohydrate 43g
Dietary Fiber 3g
Sugars 37g
Protein 1g

Drink:
Beverages

Creamy: Milks and Alternatives

Rice Milk

For those with dairy intolerances or potential milk allergies, there are beverage alternatives. Rice milk can be purchased in grocery stores. However, if you have leftover rice and want to make it yourself without added sweeteners and flavorings, here's how to do it at home. This recipe is adapted from *The Kid-Friendly ADHD & Autism Cookbook* by Pamela Compart, MD, and Dana Laake, RDH, MS, LDN. This is easiest to make if both the water and rice are warm.

MAKES 4 TO 4½ CUPS

4 cups warm water
1 cup cooked rice
1 teaspoon pure vanilla extract

Place all ingredients in a blender and blend on medium until smooth, about 1 minute. Let the milk sit for about 30 minutes. You will see the liquid, or milk, is at the top and the rice solids are on the bottom. Pour the milk steadily into another container (a glass jar works well), leaving most of the sediment in the blender pitcher.

Milk can be stored in the refrigerator for up to 5 days.

petit
appetit

EAT, DRINK,
AND
BE MERRY

Almond Milk

There are many milk alternatives, some of which call for soaking, blanching, and peeling of nuts. I find it easiest to purchase raw slivered nuts without skins, found easily in natural food stores and specialty grocers. This recipe is unsweetened, so you can add your own favorite sweetener, if desired; agave nectar, honey, or maple syrup are good choices to avoid refined sugar (see Note, page 46). Milk can be stored in refrigerator for two to three days.

MAKES ABOUT 2 CUPS

1 cup raw slivered almonds
3 cups warm water

Place almonds in a pitcher or large bowl and add water. Allow to soak for at least 4 hours.

Transfer water and almonds to a blender and blend on medium until nuts are completely blended, 1 to 2 minutes.

Strain the milk through a cheesecloth or fine-mesh colander 2 times to remove sediment and solids.

NUTRITION FACTS

Serving Size 1 cup (227g)
Calories 330
Calories from Fat 250
Total Fat 28g
Saturated Fat 2.5g
Trans Fat 0g
Cholesterol 0mg
Sodium 5mg
Total Carbohydrate 10g
Dietary Fiber 6g
Sugars 1g
Protein 11g

Drink:
Beverages

Strawberry Milk

Milk is such an important part of a child's diet due to calcium needs. While the individual flavored milks from the grocery store and coffee bars are convenient, they are also high in sugar. But you can make your own quick strawberry-flavored milks at home without the refined sugars. Combining ingredients using a blender makes these drinks fun and frothy, too.

MAKES ¾ CUP

½ cup organic whole milk
¼ cup fresh or frozen organic strawberries (about 6)
¼ teaspoon pure vanilla extract
¼ teaspoon agave nectar (optional; see Note, page 46)

Place all ingredients in a blender and process until combined.

NUTRITION FACTS

Serving Size ¾ cup
Calories 70
Calories from Fat 10
Total Fat 1.5g
Saturated Fat 1g
Trans Fat 0g
Cholesterol 5mg
Sodium 55mg
Total Carbohydrate 11g
Dietary Fiber 1g
Sugars 10g
Protein 4g

petit
appetit

EAT, DRINK,
AND
BE MERRY

Vanilla Milk

Using a blender to combine ingredients makes drinks fun and frothy. While flavored milks from the grocery store and coffee bars are convenient, they are also high in sugar.

MAKES ½ CUP

½ cup organic whole milk
¼ teaspoon pure vanilla extract
¼ teaspoon agave nectar (see Note, page 46)

Place all ingredients in a blender and process until combined. Or simply mix in a glass with a spoon.

Go Green! According to the *Journal of Dairy Science*, initial research has found that on average organic milk contains more omega-3 fatty acids (essential for heart, brain, and cardiovascular health) when compared to conventional milk.

NUTRITION FACTS

Serving Size ½ cup (125g)
Calories 60
Calories from Fat 10
Total Fat 1g
Saturated Fat 1g
Trans Fat 0g
Cholesterol 5mg
Sodium 55mg
Total Carbohydrate 7g
Dietary Fiber 0g
Sugars 7g
Protein 4g

Drink:
Beverages

Coolers: Sparklers, Spritzers, and Teas

Watermelon Spritzers

If you're worried your kids can't eat an entire watermelon—don't. This is a great way to enjoy watermelon on a hot summer day. This is a refreshing and sweet blend for all ages.

MAKES ABOUT 2 CUPS

2 cups cubed watermelon (about half of a medium melon)
½ cup sparkling water
1 tablespoon freshly squeezed organic lime juice (about ½ lime)

Combine all ingredients in a blender and blend on high until liquid.

KIDS KORNER

When giving my seventeen-month-old daughter a taste test, she kept excitedly giving the sign language sign for "More, more!"

petit
appetit

EAT, DRINK,
AND
BE MERRY

Juice Sparkler

This is a fun and healthy way for children to join in on a New Year's Eve toast with a sparkling drink of their own. This recipe is really simple and can be made with any kind of fresh, organic juice such as orange, pear, or apple. At holiday time I like pomegranate juice because of the bright and festive color. Pomegranates are a rich source of antioxidants and flavonoids. The juice can be found year-round in the fresh refrigerated juice section of most supermarkets.

MAKES 1 CUP

¾ cup sparkling mineral water
¼ cup fresh pomegranate juice

Combine water and juice in a glass.

VARIATION

If serving a crowd, combine three parts sparkling mineral water with one part fresh pomegranate juice in a pitcher. Serve over ice cube cuties (see page 142) for older children and adults.

KIDS KORNER

For a really festive drink, add a few cranberry ice cubes and a straw. You'll be surprised how much those touches will excite your child.

NUTRITION FACTS

Serving Size 1 cup
Calories 35
Calories from Fat 0
Total Fat 0g
Saturated Fat 0g
Trans Fat 0g
Cholesterol 0mg
Sodium 15mg
Total Carbohydrate 9g
Dietary Fiber 0g
Sugars 8g
Protein 0g

Drink:
Beverages

Kiddie Kocktail

Growing up, I remember how special it was to get a Shirley Temple when going out to a fancy dinner with my parents. It was very grown up and sweet, with a lovely ruby color. I forgot all about those drinks until my son was in a wedding and the bartender made him a boy version of my girlie classic. Here's one that skips the grenadine and substitutes cranberry for the bright hue. Sparkling water lends the bubbles instead of a soda.

MAKES ABOUT 3 CUPS

2 cups sparkling water
1 cup unsweetened cranberry juice
¼ cup Simple Syrup (page 110)

Combine all ingredients in a pitcher, stir, and pour over ice.

TIP

Maraschino cherries. Do maraschino cherries grow on a tree? Certainly not. A maraschino cherry is a sweet cherry preserved and sweetened in a brine solution (originally maraschino liqueur), then soaked in a suspension of food coloring, sugar syrup, artificial and natural flavors, and other components. Yikes!

For a healthier touch, add a few frozen pitted cherries to the bottom of the glass. Yum!

petit
appetit

EAT, DRINK,
AND
BE MERRY

Ginger Soda

Besides helping upset tummies, ginger has such a pleasant aroma and taste. Here's a natural and refreshing ginger ale drink without any of the high-fructose corn syrups and added colorings of store-bought varieties.

MAKES ⅔ CUP GINGER SYRUP; 3 ½ CUPS SODA

Ginger Syrup
½ cup light agave nectar (see Note, page 46)
1 (3-inch) piece fresh ginger, peeled and finely chopped
1 cup water

Ginger Soda
½ cup Ginger Syrup
3 cups sparkling water
Ice cubes

Make the syrup: Place agave nectar, ginger, and water in a small saucepan and bring to a boil over medium-high heat. Reduce heat to simmer, cover, and cook until ginger aroma and flavor is strong, about 1 hour. Let cool. Strain and refrigerate for up to 1 week.

Make the soda: In a pitcher, combine ½ cup syrup with the water. Pour over ice to serve.

TIP

Choosing ginger. Good-quality fresh ginger should have smooth, light brown skin with a light sheen and white flesh. Pick the roots with the least number of knots and/or branching.

NUTRITION FACTS

Serving Size 1 cup
Calories 35
Calories from Fat 0
Total Fat 0g
Saturated Fat 0g
Trans Fat 0g
Cholesterol 0mg
Sodium 5mg
Total Carbohydrate 10g
Dietary Fiber 0g
Sugars 10g
Protein 0g

Drink:
Beverages

Mint Syrup

The symbol of hospitality, mint has been used for scores of culinary and medicinal purposes over the centuries. This simple mint syrup can be added as a sweetener to hot and cold teas, as well as lemonade and plain water.

MAKES 2 CUPS SYRUP

¾ cup turbinado sugar
2 cups water
2 cups fresh mint (1 bunch), torn into 2-inch pieces

In a small saucepan, combine sugar, water, and mint. Bring to a boil over medium heat and cook until sugar has dissolved, about 1 minute. Remove from heat and let stand for at least 30 minutes.

Pour though a fine-mesh strainer set over a bowl or pitcher and discard mint.

Store in an airtight container in the refrigerator for up to 1 month.

NUTRITION FACTS

Serving Size 1 tablespoon (14g)
Calories 10
Calories from Fat 0
Total Fat 0g
Saturated Fat 0g
Trans Fat 0g
Cholesterol 0mg
Sodium 0mg
Total Carbohydrate 3g
Dietary Fiber 0g
Sugars 3g
Protein 0g

petit
appetit

EAT, DRINK,
AND
BE MERRY

Sparkling Mint Soda

Here's how to make your own version of fancy restaurant herb soda at home, for a fraction of the cost.

MAKES ABOUT 1 CUP

1 cup sparkling water
3 tablespoons Mint Syrup (opposite page)

Mix together in a glass and serve cold or over ice.

TIP

Herb snacks. When my son was about two years old, he learned what mint and rosemary plants looked like. Enjoying the smell and flavor, he still takes a leaf and has a taste whenever the opportunity strikes.

NUTRITION FACTS

Serving Size 1 cup
Calories 35
Calories from Fat 0
Total Fat 0g
Saturated Fat 0g
Trans Fat 0g
Cholesterol 0mg
Sodium 0mg
Total Carbohydrate 10g
Dietary Fiber 0g
Sugars 9g
Protein 0g

Drink:
Beverages

Bloody Good Iced Tea

Make your own version of the latest popular premade iced teas with better ingredients, more choices, no high-fructose corn syrups, and less cost. The tea choices and flavors seem almost endless to create new tastes with every pitcher. While blood oranges are a sweet option when making this in winter, feel free to substitute regular oranges to enjoy this any time of the year.

MAKES 2 QUARTS

8 cups water
8 bags decaffeinated white tea
Juice of 4 blood oranges (about ¾ cup)
4 teaspoons agave nectar (see Note, page 46)

Bring water to a boil in a saucepan. Remove from heat, add tea bags, and let steep for 5 minutes. Carefully squeeze tea bags and discard. Let cool.

Pour tea into a pitcher and stir in orange juice and agave nectar. Serve chilled over ice.

NUTRITION FACTS

Serving Size 1 cup
Calories 20
Calories from Fat 0
Total Fat 0g
Saturated Fat 0g
Trans Fat 0g
Cholesterol 0mg
Sodium 0mg
Total Carbohydrate 5g
Dietary Fiber 0g
Sugars 4g
Protein 0g

petit
appetit

EAT, DRINK,
AND
BE MERRY

Pear White Tea

There are many colors and subtle flavors of decaffeinated tea available. For other flavor variations, this can be made with white tea or green or black. The mild flavor of white tea is enhanced by the pear juice, yet the color remains golden. If you like sweeter tea, add agave nectar (see Note, page 46).

MAKES 6 CUPS

4 cups water
4 bags decaffeinated white tea
2 cups organic pear juice

Bring water to a boil in a saucepan. Remove from heat, add tea bags, and let steep for 5 minutes. Carefully squeeze tea bags and discard. Let cool.

Pour tea into a glass pitcher and add pear juice. Serve over ice. Keep cold in refrigerator.

NUTRITION FACTS

Serving Size 1 cup
Calories 40
Calories from Fat 0
Total Fat 0g
Saturated Fat 0g
Trans Fat 0g
Cholesterol 0mg
Sodium 0mg
Total Carbohydrate 10g
Dietary Fiber 0g
Sugars 6g
Protein 0g

Drink:
Beverages

Minty Iced Green Tea

This is the standard and favorite "iced tea" in my family's refrigerator. The mint syrup sweetens the sometimes bitter taste of green tea. Despite the name, this tea will not be green in color—much to my son's dismay.

MAKES 4½ CUPS

4 cups water
4 bags green tea
½ cup Mint Syrup (page 130)

Bring water to a boil in a saucepan. Remove from heat, add tea bags, cover, and let steep for 5 minutes. Carefully squeeze tea bags and discard. Let cool.

Pour tea into a glass pitcher and add syrup. Serve over ice.

NUTRITION FACTS

Serving Size about 1 cup
Calories 20
Calories from Fat 0
Total Fat 0g
Saturated Fat 0g
Trans Fat 0g
Cholesterol 0mg
Sodium 5mg
Total Carbohydrate 6g
Dietary Fiber 0g
Sugars 5g
Protein 0g

petit
appetit

EAT, DRINK,
AND
BE MERRY

Warmers: Hot Ciders, Chocolates, Teas, and Broths

The Spanish ladies of the New World are madly addicted to chocolate, to such a point that, not content to drink it several times each day, they even have it served to them in church.

—JEAN-ANTHELEME BRILLAT-SAVARIN (1755–1826)

Hot Cocoa

There really is a difference between hot chocolate and hot cocoa. Because cocoa powder is made by removing most of the cocoa butter and grinding the nibs, it is lower in fat than bar chocolate. This version is made with cocoa and evaporated cane juice. It's similar to the sweetness of the processed packaged powder versions but without the additives and preservatives.

MAKES 1 CUP

1 tablespoon plus 1 teaspoon unsweetened organic cocoa powder
1 tablespoon plus 1 teaspoon evaporated cane juice
¼ teaspoon pure vanilla extract
1 cup organic nonfat milk

Heat all ingredients in a small saucepan over medium-low heat, whisking constantly. Heat until hot and bubbles form around edge of pot, about 5 minutes. Do not boil. Serve warm.

NUTRITION FACTS

Serving Size 1 cup
Calories 190
Calories from Fat 10
Total Fat 1g
Saturated Fat 0g
Trans Fat 0g
Cholesterol 5mg
Sodium 105mg
Total Carbohydrate 36g
Dietary Fiber 1g
Sugars 32g
Protein 10g

Drink:
Beverages

Mexican Hot Chocolate

This is perfect after a day playing outside in the winter. Nothing warms both children and adults after splashing in puddles like a cup of hot chocolate. Use the best-quality unsweetened cocoa for the richest chocolate flavor without the addition of too much sweetener. This recipe can be sweetened with agave nectar or honey; both blend well in beverages.

MAKES ABOUT 4 CUPS

½ cup water
⅓ cup agave nectar (see Note, page 46)
5 tablespoons organic unsweetened cocoa powder
½ teaspoon ground cinnamon
⅛ teaspoon freshly ground nutmeg
⅛ teaspoon salt
3 cups organic nonfat milk
½ teaspoon pure vanilla extract

Combine the water, agave nectar, cocoa, cinnamon, nutmeg, and salt in a medium saucepan. Heat over medium heat, stirring with a whisk to combine, until it comes to a boil, about 4 to 5 minutes. Slowly add milk and vanilla while whisking. Heat until tiny bubbles form around the edge of the pan, whisking occasionally, about 8 minutes. Be careful not to boil. Remove from heat and ladle into mugs.

KIDS KORNER
My son is averse to hot foods, so he has to practice patience and wait until his hot chocolate is cool, more like spicy chocolate milk. He says, "I like my hot chocolate cold."

NUTRITION FACTS

Serving Size 1 cup
Calories 170
Calories from Fat 5
Total Fat 1g
Saturated Fat 0g
Trans Fat 0g
Cholesterol 5mg
Sodium 150mg
Total Carbohydrate 34g
Dietary Fiber 1g
Sugars 30g
Protein 7g

petit
appetit

EAT, DRINK,
AND
BE MERRY

Calientito

Calientito means "little hot one," and this drink is a spiced cider made with spices and fruit. You can use just about any fruit and fruit juice combination here. This is good for the kids at a party when serving adults mulled wine. The name sounds appropriate for my feisty daughter.

MAKES 5 CUPS; 5 SERVINGS

2 cups organic unfiltered apple juice
2 cups pomegranate juice
1 cup water
1 cinnamon stick
½ cup orange segments
½ cup chopped pear
1 tablespoon organic raisins
1 teaspoon pure vanilla extract

In a large saucepan, combine all ingredients and simmer over medium heat for 15 to 20 minutes. Discard cinnamon stick. Serve hot or wait to cool for younger, sensitive mouths. If serving to younger children, strain before serving to prevent choking.

NUTRITION FACTS

Serving Size 1 cup
Calories 130
Calories from Fat 0
Total Fat 0g
Saturated Fat 0g
Trans Fat 0g
Cholesterol 0mg
Sodium 15mg
Total Carbohydrate 33g
Dietary Fiber 1g
Sugars 30g
Protein 1g

Drink:
Beverages

Mint Chamomile Tea

A cup of chamomile tea can be soothing for a child on a cold day or with a cold inside. The added mint syrup lends a bit of sweet and spice. Most children don't like drinks and food to be too hot; keep temperature on warm or lukewarm.

MAKES 1 CUP

1 cup water
1 bag chamomile tea
2 teaspoons Mint Syrup (page 130)

Bring water to a boil in a saucepan. Add tea bag and let steep for 3 to 5 minutes. Carefully squeeze tea bag and discard. Add syrup and stir.

TIP

Tea for two and more. Tea is the most popular drink in the world.

NUTRITION FACTS

Serving Size 1 cup
Calories 5
Calories from Fat 0
Total Fat 0g
Saturated Fat 0g
Trans Fat 0g
Cholesterol 0mg
Sodium 5mg
Total Carbohydrate 2g
Dietary Fiber 0g
Sugars 1g
Protein 0g

petit
appetit

EAT, DRINK,
AND
BE MERRY

Little Lattes

Everyone likes the warmth and comfort of a warm drink on a cold day. Having a frother on hand is great for making quick foam from any kind of hot milk. When making steamed milk for my latte one day, I discovered my son really enjoyed the foam on the top. I poured him a glass of the warm milk and he loved it. I laughed at his cute milk-foam mustache.

MAKES 1 CUP

¾ cup organic vanilla soy milk

Heat milk in a small saucepan over medium-low heat until just under boiling, 5 to 6 minutes. Pour milk into a frother and froth until foam becomes thick but can still be poured.

KIDS KORNER
Serve steamed milk with a shaker each of cinnamon and chocolate and let kids top their lattes with something special, like the grown-ups do.

NUTRITION FACTS

Serving Size about 1 cup
Calories 110
Calories from Fat 25
Total Fat 3g
Saturated Fat 0g
Trans Fat 0g
Cholesterol 0mg
Sodium 105mg
Total Carbohydrate 16g
Dietary Fiber 0g
Sugars 10g
Protein 5g

Drink:
Beverages

Dried Fruit Broth

If constipation is a problem and your pediatrician suggests juice, here's a way to make your own broth. It's not as sweet as store juice and not as strong for young taste buds or their systems. This is much easier to swallow than full-force commercially packaged prune juice, but will still have some of the laxative benefits.

MAKES 1 CUP BROTH

½ cup dried organic prunes, peaches, or apricots
2 cups water

Put dried fruit and water in a small saucepan and bring to a boil over medium-high heat. Cover, reduce heat to low, and simmer for 40 minutes. Broth will be reduced, darker in color, and have sweet fruit flavor. Strain through a strainer into a bowl.

TIP

Want more laxative? Puree the remaining cooked fruit in a food processor or blender and mix with plain yogurt or spread on toast. The fruit can even be enjoyed alone, as it will be soft but lighter in flavor.

petit
appetit

EAT, DRINK,
AND
BE MERRY

Very Veggie Broth

This is a favorite recipe from *The Petit Appetit Cookbook*, as it is a basic broth recipe for a baby's bottle or sippy cup. It delivers a punch of calcium and vitamin C for a child (or any age) needing a liquid diet or vitamin pick-me-up. Serve warm or cool in a cup or bottle for baby. This broth also freezes well in ice cube trays for later use.

MAKES ABOUT 3 CUPS; 6 SERVINGS

1 quart cold water
1 cup organic cauliflower flowerets (about 3 to 4 ounces)
1 cup organic broccoli florets (about 2 to 3 ounces)
1 cup organic collard or dandelion greens, rinsed and roughly chopped
1 cup rounds organic carrots (about 3 to 4 ounces)

Place water in a medium pot with a lid. Add vegetables and bring to a boil over high heat. Reduce heat to simmer and cover pot. Cook for 1 hour.

Strain broth and reserve vegetables. These can be pureed or mashed for baby.

TIP

Not just baby broth. This is a great broth for many ages and uses. It can be a liquid meal for someone under the weather, a calcium-rich soup for baby, or a flavorful liquid for poaching meats and fish. Always having broth cubes in the freezer means lots of cooking options for you and your family.

NUTRITION FACTS

Serving Size ½ cup
Calories 10
Calories from Fat 0
Total Fat 0g
Saturated Fat 0g
Cholesterol 0mg
Sodium 15mg
Total Carbohydrate 1g
Dietary Fiber 0g
Sugars 1g
Protein 0g

Drink:
Beverages

Berry Cube Cuties

No need to make plain ice cubes if you have something fun and tasty to add to your drinks! There are a variety of shapes and molds for ice cubes as well. Be careful when serving these to preschoolers and older, as the whole berries could cause a choking risk once the ice melts and berries are floating in the drink.

MAKES 12 CUBES

24 to 36 berries (cranberries, blueberries, or mixture)
1½ cups water

Let children drop berries in an empty ice cube tray, 2 to 3 per cube. Carefully pour water over berries in trays. Berries may float to top. Freeze in freezer like regular ice cubes. Once frozen, pop out and place in sparkling water for a fruity and colorful surprise.

VARIATIONS

Minty Cube Cuties: Let children place 1 to 2 mint leaves in an empty ice cube tray. Carefully pour water over mint in trays. Mint may float to top.

Juicy Cube Cuties: Carefully pour 1 ½ cups juice (any flavor) into an empty ice tray. Freeze in freezer like regular ice cubes.

petit
appetit

EAT, DRINK,
AND
BE MERRY

142

CHAPTER 8

Be Merry: Foods for Special Occasions and Everyday Celebrations

*T*HIS CHAPTER OF PARTY PLEASING RECIPES helps families mark milestones and celebrate special events with healthy, delicious recipes and simple tips for party planning. Food is an important part of celebrations of all kinds. Many of our memories are shaped by the colors, smells, and tastes of the things we enjoy and associate with holidays, being with friends and family, and having fun. Planning, making, and decorating your own unique food creations is so much more memorable and fun than going to a mega store for something premade and ordinary.

REMEMBER IT!

Everyone remembers what foods were part of their holidays and traditions growing up. It may be a special cookie you baked with your mom for giving the neighbors at Christmastime, or the fancy eggs you dyed with cousins at Easter. Pay homage to your parents and grandparents by sharing stories and recipes with your child about childhood holidays and special days when you were growing up and what made them special.

> *We always ate Alaskan King crab legs. I loved it because it was special food, but the table was not formal. We would have to get all messy to get to the crabmeat and we would always show off a particularly large chunk of meat we harvested from the shell with a variety of kitchen tools.*
>
> LESLIE PAVE, private chef and food writer, on her Christmas Eve tradition

CREATE IT!

Of course, some people only want to stick to tradition and do it how their parents taught them. Others look forward to creating new recipes and building new traditions with their own children. Most families I know try to do both.

In creating new celebrations with your own family, look outside the traditional holidays and determine what suits you and your kids. It also celebrates the uniqueness of your children and shows them how special you think they are. Taking the time and energy to consider their interests encourages children to celebrate "everyday." So ask them what makes the day special and how they want to mark changes, seasons, and occasions.

The recipes in this section celebrate some kid favorites for traditional holidays such as Christmas, Hannukah, and Halloween, and also focus on new reasons for celebrations. How about marking a half birthday with half a cake? Or document the first day of school with a special lunch box treat. Enjoy the first day of snow by making the perfect cup of cocoa.

CELEBRATING AT SCHOOL

Because you are a parent, you're now part of a bigger community through your child's school. There are new expectations for potlucks and picnics. There are recipes here that are perfect for packing and sharing for school functions, whether you sign up to bring a dessert or main dish. Here are some helpful tips for a successful dish to share at school:

- ◆ **Remember school guidelines** when choosing a dish. If it's nut-free or kosher at lunchtime, remember that for events.

petit
appetit

EAT, DRINK,
AND
BE MERRY

144

- **Respect the party rules.** Many preschool and elementary schools have banned the grocery store cakes and cupcakes with the "mile-high" frosting (as it read in my son's preschool bulletin).

> *Teachers usually start out telling parents to send in healthy snacks. At first, parents send in something healthy for a class party, like a banana muffin. But then moms try to outdo one another. Then, it's chocolate cupcakes, then bigger chocolate cupcakes. Pretty soon, you have parents sending in goody bags filled with candy, and the situation is out of control.*
>
> HARRIET WOROBEY, director, Nutrition Department of Rutgers University

- **Write down all the ingredients** used in your dish on a card and display it in plain view so those with allergies don't have to wonder and ask.

- **Be aware of potential choking hazards** such as raisins, nuts, grapes, etc. Even if your child's class can handle all foods, there may be younger siblings in attendance who may have trouble.

- **Get your child's opinion** and make something that he'll enjoy and be proud to help make and bring to share.

- **Bring something individual** such as cupcakes or muffins for a birthday, rather than a cake, as there is less mess, less waste (no plates or even forks) and no cutting necessary. This is much easier on teachers.

Some schools have a special birthday box with partyware, balloons, and streamers ready for each child's birthday. Many of these baskets are even "green," stocked with dishes to wash, reusable party hats, and cloth napkins. Other teachers choose to mark the birthday with a special craft project like making a birthday crown or baking muffins with the class rather than overindulging in birthday cake.

CELEBRATING AT HOME

Looks Count

Party planner Monica Matheny always uses a theme and tries to think of interesting connections to foods. She says, "Partly the food is used as decoration and partly

Be Merry:
Foods for
Special Occasions
and Everyday
Celebrations

145

it's used to feed the guests." Even when it's not a full-blown party and the "guests" are your own family, you can add some creative or decorative elements such as adding a special happy face of raisins on Sunday morning pancakes. Putting a few little thoughtfully placed skeletons around the bowl of trail mix can go a long way toward making a child smile.

Party Foods Are Not Created Equal

There are many ways to create healthier versions of party foods your child sees at other celebrations. Kids like colored icing on cookies. They won't care that you used cranberry juice rather than chemical food dye for pink. A pizza party is even better when the dough is kneaded and hand-shaped by the partiers rather than a frozen-food manufacturer.

TIPS FOR A GREEN AND KID-FRIENDLY TABLE

◆ For a special (and greener) party atmosphere, you can also be creative with décor and tableware. Have children pick flowers, leaves, pinecones, and other natural objects to decorate the table.

◆ Minimize time and cleanup by purchasing disposable partyware made from renewable resources such as bamboo or corn waste.

◆ Buy cloth napkins instead of paper. The colors and patterns are endless for festive options all year long.

◆ Reduce waste by using your own dishes and utensils (borrow more if you need them) that can be washed. For a list of resources of festive partyware, see the Resources (page 258).

◆ Offer appropriate-size utensils. Adult-size forks and spoons make for bigger messes and more frustration for little ones who have a hard time grasping and maneuvering foods from plate to mouth. Buy small metal children's sets or coffee teaspoons for children.

◆ Allow children to use "real" dishes. Children like to feel special, and using grown-up plates lends an air of excitement—whether it's Thanksgiving or simply Tuesday.

petit
appetit

EAT, DRINK,
AND
BE MERRY

146

I know many moms, myself included, who use ramekins to feed our babies, because they stay put and don't tip over like a plastic cup or bowl. And once older, kids then use the same dish set as my husband and I, just the smaller butter or salad-size plates. Recently there has also been the scare of recalled children's dinnerware and utensils due to lead paint and unhealthful plastics. Besides avoiding a health risk, I want my children to feel included and know I trust and have confidence in their eating skills. I don't want to set up the expectation that I think they will break or throw something.

Don't Forget the Candles

For celebrations and special nights, my son asks for candles to be lit, and he likes to turn down the lights. Creating this more grown-up atmosphere makes him feel special and can even lead to better table manners both at home and when eating out. Best options include odorless soy or beeswax candles for a clean, long-lasting burn.

WHEN TO INDULGE

I want a feast. I want a bean feast. Cupcakes and doughnuts, so good you could go nuts. Give it to me now!

VERUCA SALT, from *Willy Wonka & the Chocolate Factory*

All ages feel parties and special occasions are time for indulging, which can often lead to overdoing. The combination of excitement, family, friends, gifts, decorations, and sugar overload can lead to disaster and tears. The holiday parties and get-togethers only get more frequent as children get older, attend school, make new friends, and become little citizens of the community. City and community events can create tension between parents and children, as these venues sometimes offer candy and "treats" at parades, egg hunts, haunted houses, and open houses.

I couldn't believe the city had candy in the Easter eggs for 0- to 2-year-olds. There're plenty of years ahead for candy. I was going around like a crazy person removing all the candy from the eggs within my son's reach.

MOTHER OF A ONE-YEAR-OLD who attended a city-sponsored Easter Egg hunt

Then there is the awkward moment of seeing the grocery store cake with the mile-high frosting and drink boxes at a party. You don't want to alienate your child and not let him indulge, yet you cringe (okay, *I* cringe) with each bite of shocking blue frosting. Plus when it's over you don't want your child proclaiming, "I want a [insert character name] cake like that for my birthday, too!"

Limiting Overindulgence

- **Attend only those events** that your child really wants to go to and knows the child hosting.

> We went to a few parties for my son's classmates where I felt like we were just exchanging a piece of cake for a gift. My son didn't even recognize the birthday boy. Not very heartfelt either way.
>
> SIX-YEAR-OLD LIAM'S mom

- **Remind your child** that he can make his own choices if you make the party foods and cake at home together. Then he's not limited to what's at the store. Just be prepared if he wants to make a space shuttle–shaped cake!

- **Bring your child's favorite "treat" foods** to enjoy at festivals, events, and holiday celebrations, in case there are no healthy choices. This is especially good for small children who may be tempted by foods that are not age- or diet-appropriate.

- **Have fun** making the party food with your child. Let her help and she'll feel more a part of things, and also proud to share her creations.

- **Make children's favorites** with a healthy twist. The kids won't know your chocolate cupcakes also contain bran and are trans fat free.

- **Create new "treats"** for traditional celebrations such as Halloween and Easter. Young children who receive dried fruit bags and stickers for Halloween don't miss the sugars and cavities in big bags of candy.

- **Talk to your teacher** and school about guidelines to limit sugars and processed foods. They will appreciate your concern and be happy to lower the sugar rush in the class as well.

petit
appetit

EAT, DRINK,
AND
BE MERRY

148

- **Share your food concerns** with other parents at school, day-care, community center, and sports activities. You'd be surprised how many like-minded parents are uncomfortable as well. Together you can come up with some solutions that make all families happy.

- **Establish limits** ahead of time. Children need your expectations before going to an event or celebration so there are no misunderstandings and added stress. For instance, my son knows on Halloween he gets to choose three pieces of candy to eat, then the remainder of what's gathered gets traded in for a toy of my son's choosing and the candy goes to those who are not able to go out trick or treating (maybe a sick friend—which is usually a euphemism for the garbage).

> *Don't people know a ten-month-old should not have a lollipop? The clown at the spring festival handed my son a lollipop. Luckily he didn't know what it was for and I was able to get it.*
>
> ELEVEN-MONTH-OLD LUKE'S mom

CATER TO SPECIAL NEEDS

Parties, festivals, and holidays are much tougher for a child who has allergies or intolerances that do not allow him to participate in the festive foods due to health reasons. Those allergic to gluten and wheat can't usually have a piece of the birthday cake. Here are the best ways to make your child feel part of the festivities:

- **Let him pick** his own special treats to bring and enjoy with everyone else. (Everyone else may wish they had his.)

> *Cassi always looks forward to school birthday parties because she gets her special pink (gluten-free) cookies that her mom makes and brings in, since she can't have the usual cupcakes.*
>
> FOUR-YEAR-OLD CASSI'S teacher

- **Ask the host** ahead of time and see what they are serving or making and ask if you can help bring something. Usually a host will appreciate the help and you can provide something everyone can enjoy. You'll want to know of any special issues when it's your turn to host.

◆ **Tell the hostess** of any concerns ahead of time so your child is not accidentally served a problematic or protentially dangerous food.

CELEBRATING HOLIDAYS WITH CHILDREN

Often with the traditional holiday season families go overboard with decorations and wanting to make everything "perfect," whether it's the table setting for Christmas or your daughter's first birthday cake. When the focus is on perfection and how it will look in the pictures, people tend to keep children out of the kitchen and away from participating because they're pressed for time and getting ready for "people" to come over. We need to remind ourselves that these "people" are our friends and relatives. They enjoy seeing happy faces (yours and your kids) rather than stressed-out parents and disappointed children.

> *When I make the effort to step back and slow down the pace for my daughter, Maylee, we cook together. Whether it's making dinner or baking cookies, I'm always amazed at how time stops and it's just the two of us. We laugh, we make a mess, we talk about nonsense, and we have fun. For us, cooking is not just about good nutrition, but it's a way to escape the clock, even if just for a few hours.*
>
> MAXINE WOLF, mother, and CEO, and publisher of *Kiwi Magazine*

The holiday season is a wonderful opportunity to allow your children to help and celebrate together as a family. Keep children entertained and occupied with a fun and educational activity that incorporates a range of skills and senses, such as counting, measuring, reading, touching, listening, planning, smelling, tasting, and creativity. Task allocation depends largely on the age and dexterity of the child. Here's a list of festive holiday ideas for the petit partygoers at your holiday gathering:

◆ **Ask children** for their ideas when planning the holiday menu. "Would you like to serve your friends mini sandwiches or mini meatballs?" "Gingerbread or carrot cake?"

◆ **Take kids** to the store and farmers' market to help choose ingredients. Be sure to point out seasonal items such as cranberries for Thanksgiving and eggs for Easter.

petit
appetit

EAT, DRINK,
AND
BE MERRY

150

- **Decorate holiday cookies** (see page 214) or cupcakes (page 155). Set up a special kids decorating party at a designated table. Decoration ideas include: colored sugars, cookie cutters, frosting, edible flowers, dried fruits, and coconut.

- **Set up a crafts table** where kids can decorate their own placemat or draw pictures and names for holiday place cards.

- **Go outside** for a treasure hunt to look for items to decorate the holiday table. Branches, pinecones, small stones, and flowers can become a beautiful, inexpensive, one-of-a-kind, "green" centerpiece.

- **Enlist your child** as the "official taste tester," passing a spoon to him for critiquing and approval before food is served.

The goal of any get-together is to make all ages of guests feel welcome and have a good time. Traditional holidays can blend past memories and traditions with new recipes and activities to please everyone. For creating special everyday celebrations, look to your child for suggestions and inspiration. S'mores at a father-son camping trip can be just as special and memorable (if not more so) to your child as the big Thanksgiving dinner. Knowing your audience and keeping things simple and fun leads to lots of laughter and smiles.

Be Merry:
Foods for
Special Occasions
and Everyday
Celebrations

151

Birthdays

*L*et your child blow out the candles with these options for celebrating at home or a party elsewhere. There are a range of flavors and shapes of cakes and suggestions for even the smallest celebrant to mark her first year. Looking for a way to mark a six-month milestone? Cut cakes or cupcakes in half and serve one side only. Halves are important to kids. When asked their age, kids will always add enthusiastically, "And a half!"

Angel Food Cake

This is a yummy, light, and airy cake for celebrating just about anything. It is a lighter alternative to chocolate cakes with heavy frosting. The fun part for kids and adults is letting them choose their own toppings and décor for their piece. Set out fresh raspberries, strawberries, and blueberries; whip up some cream; and maybe have some chocolate sauce for a truly decadent treat. Let children create their own special pieces.

MAKES 12 SERVINGS

1 cup cake flour, sifted
1 ⅓ cups evaporated cane juice
12 large cage-free organic egg whites, at room temperature
½ teaspoon cream of tartar
¼ teaspoon salt
1 teaspoon pure vanilla extract
½ teaspoon almond extract

Preheat oven to 325°F. Grease and flour a 10-inch Bundt pan or tube pan and set aside.

petit
appetit

EAT, DRINK,
AND
BE MERRY

152

Mix cake flour and evaporated cane juice together in a bowl. Beat egg whites and the cream of tartar with an electric mixer on high until stiff peaks form, about 5 minutes. Sift ⅓ cup of the flour mixture into the egg whites and gently fold in. Repeat by sifting another ⅓ cup of flour and finally the last ⅓ cup until all is combined. Fold in salt and vanilla and almond extracts until combined.

Pour or spoon batter into prepared pan. It will fill the pan. Bake for 45 to 55 minutes, until top is golden brown and batter does not shake. Remove pan from oven and completely cool in pan on a wire rack, about 1 hour. When cool, place plate over top of pan and carefully turn over. If cake does not come out, slide a knife around the edges of the pan to loosen cake.

NUTRITION FACTS

Serving Size 1 slice (69g)
Calories 160
Calories from Fat 0
Total Fat 0g
Saturated Fat 0g
Trans Fat 0g
Cholesterol 0mg
Sodium 105mg
Total Carbohydrate 33g
Dietary Fiber 0g
Sugars 24g
Protein 5g

Be Merry:
Foods for
Special Occasions
and Everyday
Celebrations

Chocolate Whipped Cream

This was new to me. But once I discovered this, it became my staple for dressing up cakes, cupcakes, and even fruit. It is light with a subtle chocolate flavor, with less sugar than store-bought whipped cream.

MAKES ABOUT 5 SERVINGS

½ cup heavy cream
2 tablespoons confectioners' sugar
1 tablespoon organic unsweetened cocoa powder
½ teaspoon pure vanilla extract

Using a stand or hand mixer set on high, whip the cream in a stainless steel bowl until thick and cream has reached desired thickness, 2 to 3 minutes. Add the sugar, cocoa, and vanilla and mix until the cream is fluffy and light. Cover and chill until ready to use.

petit
appetit

EAT, DRINK,
AND
BE MERRY

Carrot Cupcakes

These cupcakes are perfect for celebrating baby's first year. They have no nuts or raisins for potentially allergic little revelers. This versatile batter can be baked in mini cupcake/muffin pans, regular pans, or mini Bundt pans. Happy Birthday, baby!

MAKES 24 MINI CUPCAKES, 12 CUPCAKES, OR 6 MINI BUNDT CAKES

1 cup packed brown sugar
1¼ cups expeller-pressed canola oil or sunflower oil
4 large cage-free organic eggs
2 cups unbleached all-purpose flour
1 cup whole wheat pastry flour
1½ teaspoons baking soda
2 teaspoons ground cinnamon
½ teaspoon freshly grated nutmeg
½ teaspoon salt
2 teaspoons grated organic orange zest (see Go Green! page 156)
12 ounces organic carrots, peeled and grated (3 cups)

Frosting
8 ounces organic light cream cheese
2 cups organic confectioners' sugar
1 tablespoon freshly squeezed lime juice
2 teaspoons grated organic orange zest

Preheat oven to 400°F. Line 24 mini muffin cups or 12 standard muffin cups with paper cups. Or grease and flour 6 mini Bundt pans and set aside.

Beat sugar and oil together until combined. Beat in eggs, one at a time. Add flours, baking soda, cinnamon, nutmeg, salt, and zest and beat until combined. Fold in carrots.

Spoon batter into prepared pans, filling cups half full. Bake for 10 to 12 minutes (15 to 20 minutes for standard muffin cups or 20 to 25 minutes for Bundt pans), until a wooden pick inserted in centers comes out clean. Cool cupcakes on rack while making frosting.

Be Merry:
Foods for
Special Occasions
and Everyday
Celebrations

Prepare the frosting: Beat cream cheese in a medium bowl until smooth and creamy. Sift sugar over cream cheese and beat until combined. Add lime juice and beat until creamy.

Once cupcakes are cool, top each cupcake with frosting and smooth using a dull knife or metal spatula. These do not have to be perfect. Top each cupcake center with a few sprinkles of orange zest.

Go Green! While orange is not on the Dirty Dozen list as potentially harmful, we've suggested organic because we're using the zest (outside peel) where pesticides can be heavy.

petit
appetit
EAT, DRINK,
AND
BE MERRY

156

Baby Bundt Cakes

These little cakes were inspired from a recipe in Nigella Lawson's *How to Be a Domestic Goddess* cookbook. My sister gave me an adorable mini Bundt pan set, so I adapted this recipe for my daughter's first birthday. I made a few changes, mostly to serve more hungry mouths. These easy but elegant cakes are perfect for a celebration or gathering. They can be dressed up with frosting and berries or enjoyed on their own. My son said, "Wow! I get a whole cake?!"

MAKES 12 (4-INCH) MINI BUNDT CAKES

½ cup organic plain whole-milk yogurt

¾ cup organic unsalted butter, melted

4 large cage-free organic eggs

2 teaspoons grated organic lemon zest (about ½ lemon)
(see Go Green! opposite page)

2 cups unbleached all-purpose flour

1 tablespoon baking soda

⅛ teaspoon salt

¾ cup plus 2 tablespoons evaporated cane juice

Icing

1 ⅓ cups confectioners' sugar

2 tablespoons freshly squeezed lemon juice (about 1 lemon)

Preheat oven to 325°F. Grease 12 mini Bundt pans and set aside.

In a small bowl, beat together yogurt, butter, eggs, and lemon zest. In a large bowl, combine flour, baking soda, salt, and evaporated cane juice. Make a well in the center of the flour mixture and fold in the yogurt mixture with a rubber spatula. Fill each Bundt pan half full. Bake for 25 to 30 minutes, until a wooden pick inserted in centers of cakes comes out clean. Remove pans from oven and let cool about 5 minutes. Carefully turn out cakes on wire racks to cool completely.

Make icing: Sift the confectioners' sugar into a small bowl. Stir in enough lemon juice to make a thick icing that can be drizzled down the

NUTRITION FACTS

Serving Size 1 mini cake (93g)

Calories 310

Calories from Fat 120

Total Fat 14g

Saturated Fat 8g

Trans Fat 0g

Cholesterol 100mg

Sodium 380mg

Total Carbohydrate 44g

Dietary Fiber 1g

Sugars 27g

Protein 5g

Be Merry:
Foods for
Special Occasions
and Everyday
Celebrations

tops of the cakes. (Be sure the cakes are cool before icing, otherwise icing will disappear into cake—still tasty but not as pretty.)

TIP
Baby's bundt and beyond. This makes a good birthday cake for ages 1, 11, 21, and 101. If you want to make a wish, fill the center with berries to lend support for the candle.

petit
appetit

EAT, DRINK,
AND
BE MERRY

158

Better Brownie Cupcakes

I call these cupcakes "better" because they are better for you than the usual chocolate cupcakes found at the grocer or bakery. And children (or adults) won't believe these are wheat-free. Who knew potato flour, brown rice flour, and oat bran could make such a yummy brownie dessert? As my husband says, "It still has chocolate in it. Anything tastes good with chocolate." These are great for packing and sharing—they don't need any frosting, so they're less messy and easy to tote.

MAKES 9 STANDARD-SIZE CUPCAKES OR 18 MINI CUPCAKES

6 tablespoons organic unsalted butter
4 ounces (½ cup) organic semisweet chocolate, chips or chopped
½ cup evaporated cane juice
⅛ teaspoon salt
2 large cage-free organic eggs
1 teaspoon pure vanilla extract
½ cup brown rice flour
2 teaspoons potato flour
¼ cup oat bran

Preheat oven to 350°F. Line 9 standard muffin cups or 18 mini muffin cups with paper liners and set aside.

In a double boiler or microwave, melt butter and chocolate together until smooth and combined. Remove from heat and let cool slightly.

Stir evaporated cane juice, salt, eggs, and vanilla into chocolate mixture and mix well. Stir in rice flour, potato flour, and bran. Scoop by tablespoonful into muffin cups (about ¼ cup for standard muffins and 2 tablespoons for mini).

Bake for 18 minutes for standard muffins and 12 minutes for mini, until puffed but gooey in center. Let cool in pan for 10 minutes, then transfer to a wire rack. Store in the refrigerator for fudge-like texture.

KIDS KORNER
My seventeen-year-old cousin, after hearing what was in the cupcakes, said, "Wow, these taste like real brownies." In healthy cooking, that's about as good a compliment as you can get.

NUTRITION FACTS
Serving Size 1 standard cupcake (46g)
Calories 190
Calories from Fat 110
Total Fat 12g
Saturated Fat 7g
Trans Fat 0g
Cholesterol 65mg
Sodium 50mg
Total Carbohydrate 18g
Dietary Fiber 2g
Sugars 7g
Protein 3g

Be Merry:
Foods for
Special Occasions
and Everyday
Celebrations

Little Devil's Cake

This is not a true devil's food cake because it does not contain melted chocolate in addition to cocoa. However, your little devil will be happy to indulge in this tasty cake. The drizzle of frosting is especially pretty and lends moisture to the cake.

MAKES 1 (8-INCH-ROUND) CAKE; 8 SERVINGS

5 tablespoons organic unsalted butter, melted
½ cup organic unsweetened cocoa powder
½ cup organic applesauce
½ cup packed brown sugar
2 large cage-free organic eggs
1½ teaspoons pure vanilla extract
½ teaspoon baking soda
¼ teaspoon salt
¾ cup unbleached all-purpose flour
¼ cup hot water

Icing
1 cup sifted confectioners' sugar
¼ teaspoon pure vanilla extract
1 tablespoon organic milk, plus additional if needed

Preheat oven to 350°F. Grease and flour an 8-inch-round cake pan and set aside.

In a small bowl, whisk together butter and cocoa. Stir in applesauce and brown sugar until combined. Beat in eggs, one at a time, beating well after each addition. Stir in vanilla, baking soda, and salt.

Gradually add flour to cocoa mixture, stirring just until blended but do not over mix. Stir in hot water, just until blended.

Pour batter into prepared pan and bake for 25 minutes, until a wooden pick inserted in center comes out clean. Cool for 10 minutes in pan on a wire rack. Gently turn out cake and cool completely on wire rack before icing.

petit
appetit

EAT, DRINK,
AND
BE MERRY

160

Make icing: Combine all icing ingredients in a small bowl. Using a fork, drizzle icing over cake. To serve, cut into 8 wedges.

TIP

Disappearing icing. We made this for my son's half birthday. The next day my son wanted a piece and noticed the icing was gone. He wondered what happened. I explained it was magic and that it just sunk into the cake. He asked, "If I say abracadabra, will it reappear?"

NUTRITION FACTS

Serving Size 1 wedge (93g)
Calories 260
Calories from Fat 80
Total Fat 9g
Saturated Fat 5g
Trans Fat 0g
Cholesterol 70mg
Sodium 180mg
Total Carbohydrate 42g
Dietary Fiber 1g
Sugars 30g
Protein 4g

Be Merry:
Foods for
Special Occasions
and Everyday
Celebrations

PIZZA PARTY: DO-IT-YOURSELF PIZZA BAR

$\int$here's no other kitchen activity that's more fun for kids than creating their own personal pizzas. This birthday party suggestion makes pizza making and cooking an easy and unique theme for boys and girls of all ages. Kids love to knead dough and choose their own toppings. It is not necessary to have perfect pies, so get everyone's hands in there. Make dough, prep toppings, and set the work surface with tablecloths, rolling pins, and flour before the little pizza makers arrive so everything is ready and goes smoothly. The best part is after they've finished the pizza-making activity, the little chefs can eat.

Presto Pizza Dough

A favorite from *The Petit Appetit Cookbook,* this dough is so versatile and makes pizza, bread sticks, and teething biscuits. For a new twist (or roll) on the typical pie, try this dough with Pizza Pinwheels (page 164).

MAKES 1 (12- TO 14-INCH) PIZZA; 12 SERVINGS

1 tablespoon active dry yeast (1-ounce package)
½ cup plus 2 tablespoons warm water
¾ cup whole wheat flour
¾ cup unbleached all-purpose flour
¼ cup extra-virgin olive oil
½ teaspoon salt

In a large bowl, dissolve yeast in warm water. Let stand until foamy. Add remaining ingredients to yeast and water. Mix together and knead

petit
appetit

EAT, DRINK,
AND
BE MERRY

162

by hand until dough is smooth, about 3 minutes. Make dough into a ball and return to bowl; cover with plastic wrap. Let rise until doubled, about 30 minutes.

Make pizza: Preheat oven to 425°F. Place dough on a greased baking or pizza pan and press with your fingers to spread into desired shape. Add desired sauce and toppings and bake for 15 to 20 minutes, until crust is brown on the edges.

TIP

Double time. Double all the ingredients to make a thick-crust pizza. Or simply make one pizza now and save the second dough ball in the freezer for the next time your little ones ask for pizza.

NUTRITION FACTS

Serving Size 1/12 of pizza crust (without toppings) (26g)
Servings 12
Calories 70
Calories from Fat 0
Total Fat 0g
Saturated Fat 0g
Cholesterol 0mg
Sodium 100mg
Total Carbohydrate 13g
Dietary Fiber 2g
Sugars 0g
Protein 3g

Be Merry:
Foods for
Special Occasions
and Everyday
Celebrations

Pizza Pinwheels

This idea should be credited to *Parents* magazine. However, we've made a healthier version of their Twirly Whirly Pizza (September 2007) by making our own crust rather than heading to the freezer section for premade pizza dough. Of course you can let your imagination fly when choosing "toppings," although they will be a surprise on the inside rather than the outside.

MAKES 8 SERVINGS

Presto Pizza Dough (page 162) or 1 pound whole wheat pizza dough
½ to ¾ cup Tot's Tomato Sauce (page 63) or favorite jarred organic brand
¾ cup shredded mozzarella cheese (rBGH-free)
½ cup fresh organic baby spinach leaves
2 tablespoons chopped black olives

Preheat oven to 400°F. Grease an 8-inch-round metal baking pan and set aside.

Roll dough out into a 10 × 12-inch rectangle. Spread sauce on top. Sprinkle with half the cheese. Top with spinach leaves (kids can help arrange) and sprinkle with olives.

Starting with shorter end, roll dough into a tube, with all sauce and toppings inside. Carefully transfer roll to a cutting board. Using a sharp knife, make hard, quick crosswise cuts to slice through dough, preventing dough from mashing and sauce from spilling out. Cut log in half, then each half in half, then each quarter in half again, so you have 8 equal pieces.

Reshape dough wheels and arrange in prepared baking pan, leaving about ½ to 1 inch between each wheel, so they can expand and rise and push into each other when they bake. Sprinkle wheels with remaining cheese. Bake for 22 to 25 minutes, until golden brown and dough is cooked. Carefully remove each wheel from the pan with a spatula or pie server.

petit
appetit

EAT, DRINK,
AND
BE MERRY

164

KIDS KORNER

My son helped make these the first time and seemed excited while we made the dough and cut the pizza wheels/rolls. However, he was not as pleased when I put one on his plate. He asked, "What happened to the regular pizza? I want the flat kind." However, when I explained this is what we were making and there was no other pizza, he reluctantly tried. After eating two whole wheels, he stated, "Let's have this kind every time! Okay?"

Go Green! Spinach is on the Dirty Dozen list (see page 15) and is also high in nitrites. Reduce your family's exposure by buying organic.

NUTRITION FACTS

Serving Size 1 pinwheel (53g)

Calories 130
Calories from Fat 60
Total Fat 6g
Saturated Fat 1.5g
Trans Fat 0g
Cholesterol 5mg
Sodium 210mg
Total Carbohydrate 13g
Dietary Fiber 1g
Sugars 1g
Protein 4g

Be Merry:
Foods for
Special Occasions
and Everyday
Celebrations

GROUP PLEASERS

PERFECT FOR PACKING

VEGETARIAN

A Berry-Sweet Pizza

A sweet (but not too sweet) ending to a pizza party, the ricotta cheese is creamy and gives this pizza a boost of protein and calcium. The berries lend an added touch of flavor and color.

MAKES 8 SERVINGS

Crust

1 tablespoon active dry yeast (1-ounce package)
½ cup plus 2 tablespoons warm water
¾ cup unbleached all-purpose flour
¼ cup extra-virgin olive oil
½ teaspoon salt
½ teaspoon evaporated cane juice

Topping

1 cup smooth ricotta cheese (rBGH-free)
1 teaspoon freshly squeezed organic lemon juice
2 teaspoons honey (see Note, page 46)
1 teaspoon grated organic lemon zest (see Go Green! page 46)
1 cup organic raspberries

Preheat oven to 425° F. Line a large baking pan with parchment paper and set aside.

Make the crust: In a large bowl, dissolve yeast in warm water. Let stand until foamy. Add remaining ingredients to yeast and water. Mix together and knead by hand until dough is smooth, about 3 minutes. Form dough into a ball and return to bowl; cover with plastic wrap. Let rise at room temperature until doubled, about 30 minutes.

Knead dough for about 2 to 3 minutes and divide in half. Divide each half in half again so you have 4 equal balls. Roll out each ball into a 5-inch circle.

Place pizzas on prepared baking sheet. Bake for 12 to 15 minutes, until golden brown.

petit
appetit

EAT, DRINK,
AND
BE MERRY

166

Make the topping: Combine all topping ingredients, except raspberries, in a small bowl. Spread each pizza with cheese mixture (about ¼ cup each).

Arrange raspberries on top of cheese mixture. Cut into 8 pieces.

KIDS KORNER
Kids can spread the cheese as well as decorate the pizzas with berry patterns and faces.

Be Merry:
Foods for
Special Occasions
and Everyday
Celebrations

petit
appetit

EAT, DRINK,
AND
BE MERRY

TEDDY BEAR TEA PARTY

*C*reate an entire at-home birthday tea party with these finger sandwiches (below), plus scones (page 195), cookies (page 170), and of course tea (page 133). Invite friends and teddy bears (they won't eat much). You can choose to make a single tea sandwich or a variety for pleasing adults and children. Children's event designer Monica Matheny says tea sandwiches (crusts removed) are the most enjoyed food (besides cake!) at children's parties. Most popular is standard peanut butter and fruit spread.

Tiny Tea Sandwiches

My mom, sister, and I go to tea at least once a year when we get together. Sometimes it's for the holidays, a celebration shower, or just a girl's day. However, our ladies' tea has a new party crasher—my four-and-a-half-year-old son. He loves to sip tea and enjoy sandwiches and sweets with the ladies.

Turkey and Prosciutto Tea Sandwiches

MAKES 24 (2-INCH) SANDWICHES

24 (¼-inch-thick) slices whole wheat bread or 48 (2½-inch) slices cocktail bread
6 ounces goat cheese (rBGH-free)
6 ounces thinly sliced organic turkey
6 ounces thinly sliced prosciutto

Cut desired shapes in sandwich bread using cookie cutter, or simply trim crusts and cut squares, triangles, or rectangles with a knife. You'll get 2 pieces per slice.

Lay half of the bread slices on a work surface. Spread the goat cheese on bread. Cut or fold the turkey and prosciutto slices to fit the sandwich size and shapes. Layer one slice on each bread slice. Then top with second piece of bread.

Salmon Tea Sandwiches

MAKES 24 (2-INCH) SANDWICHES

24 (¼-inch-thick) slices whole wheat bread or 48 (2½-inch) slices
    cocktail bread
4 ounces organic unsalted butter
8 ounces thinly sliced smoked salmon

Cut desired shapes in sandwich bread using cookie cutters, or simply trim crusts and cut squares, triangles, or rectangles with knife.
You'll get 2 pieces per slice.

Lay half of bread slices on a work surface. Spread butter on bread.
Cut or fold the salmon slices to fit the sandwich size and shapes. Layer
one slice on each bread slice. Then top with second piece of bread.

VARIATIONS

Use 1 teaspoon per 2-inch sandwich of the following: Egg and Olive Salad (page 192)
or Tuna Waldorf Salad (page 71).

TIP

Tea for three. My husband was pleasantly surprised when I talked him into taking his
grandmother to a fancy hotel tea. We three had a lovely day, and my husband discov
ered there's more to tea than just drinking tea, as he enjoyed the sandwiches, scones,
sweets, tea (and champagne).

NUTRITION FACTS

Serving Size 1 sandwich
(40g)
Calories 90
Calories from Fat 25
Total Fat 3g
Saturated Fat 1.5g
Trans Fat 0g
Cholesterol 10mg
Sodium 380mg
Total Carbohydrate 8g
Dietary Fiber 1g
Sugars 1g
Protein 7g

Be Merry:
Foods for
Special Occasions
and Everyday
Celebrations

Peanut Butter Truffle Cookies

This is a yummy recipe from *The Kid-Friendly ADHD & Autism Cookbook* by Pamela Compart and Dana Laake, which stresses a gluten-free, casein-free diet. This is a rich peanut butter and chocolate treat for those children who do not eat wheat, gluten, or milk. If you are not concerned about gluten or milk, then feel free to substitute regular semisweet chocolate chips. These cookies are quite light and fragile. Watch for crumbs!

MAKES ABOUT 36 COOKIES

1 cup organic creamy peanut butter
1 cup packed brown sugar
1 large cage-free organic egg
1 teaspoon baking soda
½ cup gluten-free, casein-free semisweet chocolate chips

Preheat oven to 350°F. Line a baking sheet with parchment paper and set aside.

In a large bowl, cream together all ingredients except the chocolate chips with a wooden spoon. Add chocolate chips and stir to combine.

Drop by rounded teaspoonfuls onto prepared pan. Bake for 9 to 10 minutes. Allow cookies to cool completely on pan or they will crumble apart.

NUTRITION FACTS

Serving Size 1 cookie (18g)
Calories 80
Calories from Fat 40
Total Fat 4.5g
Saturated Fat 1.5g
Trans Fat 0g
Cholesterol 5mg
Sodium 70mg
Total Carbohydrate 9g
Dietary Fiber 1g
Sugars 8g
Protein 2g

petit
appetit

EAT, DRINK,
AND
BE MERRY

PARTY HOSTING AT HOME

Having friends and relatives over to celebrate your child's birthday or other milestone doesn't have to be stressful. Choose a few simple dishes to feed all ages that can be prepped or made ahead of time so you can enjoy the party, too.

Mac and Cheese to Please

Macaroni and cheese is a favorite for any age. This is much tastier and healthier (with lots of calcium, vitamin D, and protein) than the box version, and takes just a few minutes more. Children always want their "own," so serving in individual ramekins at a party is a fun way for children to enjoy. Just be sure to make these before guests arrive so they are completely cool before handling.

MAKES 6 CUPS

8 ounces elbow macaroni (egg-free for those under one year)
1 cup organic whole milk
3 cups (about 12 ounces) shredded sharp white Cheddar cheese (rBGH-free)
Salt, to taste
¼ teaspoon freshly ground black pepper
3 tablespoons freshly grated Parmesan cheese (rBGH-free)

Preheat oven to 350°F. Bring a pot of water to a boil over high heat. Reduce heat to medium and add macaroni. Simmer until macaroni is tender, 7 to 10 minutes. Drain pasta and return to cooking pot.

In a small saucepan, heat milk over low heat until hot. Add Cheddar cheese and hot milk to macaroni and toss. Season with salt and pepper, and stir to combine.

NUTRITION FACTS
Serving Size about 1 cup
(175g)
Calories 370
Calories from Fat 190
Total Fat 21g
Saturated Fat 11g
Trans Fat 0g
Cholesterol 65mg
Sodium 440mg
Total Carbohydrate 27g
Dietary Fiber 1g
Sugars 2g
Protein 21g

Be Merry:
Foods for
Special Occasions
and Everyday
Celebrations

Divide mixture into 6 (4-inch) ramekins. Sprinkle Parmesan cheese over top and bake for 10 minutes, until bubbling. Allow to cool completely before serving.

TIP

No time for homemade? Even the boxed brands' macaroni needs to be cooked, so there isn't much difference in cooking time. However, if you like the convenience of the boxed, pre-measured ingredients, buy pre-shredded cheese.

> *My twins love to eat wagon wheel pasta with just about any sauce and veggie on top. The kids spend the whole meal saying, 'Wheels! Wheels! Wheels!' while cramming their mouths full.*
>
> TWO-YEAR-OLD IMOGIN'S and PAUL'S mom

petit
appetit

EAT, DRINK,
AND
BE MERRY

172

Veggie Tempura

Kids like crispy food and dips, so here's a fun way to present a variety of colors and flavors of veggies. Get creative and pick your family's favorites such as broccoli, zucchini, mushrooms, and sliced bell peppers. A bonus is that you can even eat with your fingers. Try this at your next playdate or gathering and watch these crunchy veggies disappear. Serve with Mustard-Honey Sauce (page 66).

MAKES ABOUT 6 SERVINGS

1½ cups panko crumbs
¼ teaspoon salt
3 large cage-free organic eggs
8 ounces green beans
1 large yellow onion, cut into ½-inch-thick rings
1 large (12-ounce) organic sweet potato, sliced into ½-inch rounds
2 tablespoons brown rice flour

Preheat oven to 450°F. Line 2 baking sheets with aluminum foil. Grease foil, and set pans aside.

In a shallow bowl, combine panko crumbs and salt. Set aside. In a medium bowl, beat eggs slightly. Set aside.

In a large bowl, toss vegetables in flour. Shake off excess flour and dip each veggie piece into eggs, then press into panko crumbs to coat. Be sure to wash fingers every so often, as the batter sticks and gets lumpy.

Place green beans and onion in a single layer on one prepared baking sheet. Arrange sweet potato slices in a single layer on second baking sheet. Brush or spray veggies lightly with cooking oil. Bake for 12 to 15 minutes for onion and beans and 16 to 18 minutes for sweet potatoes. Veggies should be fork-tender but crunchy and brown on the outside.

TIP

If using many different types of vegetables, I suggest cooking each type on their own baking sheets so they are cooked evenly and can be removed separately before overcooking.

NUTRITION FACTS

Serving Size about ¾ cup
(167g)
Calories 180
Calories from Fat 30
Total Fat 3g
Saturated Fat 1g
Trans Fat 0g
Cholesterol 105mg
Sodium 240mg
Total Carbohydrate 34g
Dietary Fiber 4g
Sugars 5g
Protein 7g

Be Merry:
Foods for
Special Occasions
and Everyday
Celebrations

Tortellini Treats

This is so simple, yet so exciting for children. It works at home for a birthday buffet or playdate as well as packed in a school lunch bag or for a day at the park. This satisfies dippers (my daughter) and non-dippers (my son). Before having a four-year-old, I thought the flat wooden sticks only came from eating lots of Popsicles and washing the sticks—not so. Craft and discount stores sell flat wooden sticks by the bagful.

MAKES 8 TO 10 (4-INCH) SKEWERS (6 TORTELLINI PER SKEWER)

1 (10-ounce) package cheese-filled whole wheat tortellini
1 cup Tot's Tomato Sauce (page 63)

Prepare tortellini according to package directions. Drain.

When cool enough to handle, thread tortellini on flat wooden sticks. Serve with sauce.

Go Green! Be sure to wash and recycle kebob sticks for gluing, building, and creating all kinds of art projects with your children.

NUTRITION FACTS

Serving Size 2 skewers plus sauce
Calories 240
Calories from Fat 50
Total Fat 6g
Saturated Fat 2.5g
Trans Fat 0g
Cholesterol 30mg
Sodium 470mg
Total Carbohydrate 38g
Dietary Fiber 2g
Sugars 2g
Protein 11g

petit
appetit

EAT, DRINK,
AND
BE MERRY

Holidays

Traditional celebrations with kids can sometimes be a challenge. Whether it be a too-early bedtime, dietary restrictions, or age-inappropriate expectations, parents need to recognize and embrace the limitations of the holidays with children. Give the old a new twist that your family can call their own and is unique and special—like your children.

NEW YEAR'S EVE AT 9:00 P.M.

How about a party to celebrate the New Year on East Coast time or Australian time, no matter where you live? Plan for everyone to be awake and able to celebrate with sparkling drinks and party snack foods. Record a ball drop or get crafty and create one of your own for a kids' countdown.

Kids' Crab Cakes

Just because "kids" is part of the title, don't be hesitant to share these with adults, too. They are simply shapes for smaller mouths, or a single hors d'oeuvre bite for Mom and Dad. These are festive and special for a holiday appetizer, and made healthier than the usual crab cakes with yogurt substituting for mayonnaise. My family likes to ring in the New Year with crab cakes and sparkling drinks (pages 126–129).

MAKES 16 TO 18 (1½-INCH) CRAB CAKES

1 large cage-free organic egg
1 tablespoon organic plain yogurt

Be Merry:
Foods for
Special Occasions
and Everyday
Celebrations

1 teaspoon Dijon mustard

1 tablespoon fresh dill or 1 teaspoon dried dill

½ teaspoon grated yellow onion

⅛ teaspoon freshly ground black pepper

1 cup soft bread crumbs

8 ounces fresh or canned lump crabmeat

3 tablespoons dry bread crumbs or panko

2 teaspoons expeller-pressed canola oil

NUTRITION FACTS

Serving Size 1 crab cake
(23g)
Calories 35
Calories from Fat 10
Total Fat 1.5g
Saturated Fat 0g
Trans Fat 0g
Cholesterol 25mg
Sodium 90mg
Total Carbohydrate 2g
Dietary Fiber 0g
Sugars 0g
Protein 4g

Preheat oven to 450°F. Line a large baking sheet or jelly roll pan with parchment paper and set aside.

In a medium bowl, whisk together egg, yogurt, mustard, dill, onion, and pepper. Stir in soft bread crumbs until combined. Stir in crabmeat until combined but do not overmix.

In a small bowl, combine dry bread crumbs and oil. Set aside.

Using your fingers, shape heaping tablespoonfuls of the crab mixture into 1½-inch rounds and flatten. Press each side of cake into dry bread crumb mixture to stick.

Arrange on prepared baking sheet. Bake for 12 to 15 minutes, until golden on bottom and cooked through.

TIPS

Homemade bread crumbs. To make soft bread crumbs, trim crust from one-quarter of a 1-pound rustic country or white loaf, such as *pugliese*, and roughly break into chunks. Put center bread in food processor and process for 10 or 12 seconds. Alternatively, you can use 1½ pieces of trimmed sourdough or white sandwich bread.

To make fine dry bread crumbs, take 1 cup of ½-inch bread pieces and arrange in a single layer on a baking sheet. Bake in a 300°F oven for 10 to 15 minutes, until dry, stirring twice during cooking. Let cool. Process in a food processor and blend into fine crumbs, about 30 seconds. One slice yields about ¼ cup crumbs.

petit
appetit

EAT, DRINK,
AND
BE MERRY

176

Baked Mini Meatballs

The oat bran takes the place of the traditional bread crumbs for added moisture and nutrition. For a Swedish variation, serve these with lingonberries. Feel free to substitute your family's favorite spices for variety. Serve with rounded toothpicks for easy dipping and eating.

MAKES 45 TO 50 MINI MEATBALLS; 6 SERVINGS

½ cup oat bran
¼ cup organic milk
1 pound lean ground organic beef
1 tablespoon dried dill
⅛ teaspoon freshly grated nutmeg
¼ teaspoon salt
¼ teaspoon freshly ground black pepper
1 clove garlic, minced
1 large cage-free organic egg

Preheat oven to 400°F. Line 2 baking sheets with aluminum foil. Grease foil, and set pans aside.

In a large bowl, combine oat bran and milk. Add beef, dill, nutmeg, salt, pepper, garlic, and egg. Using your hands, combine ingredients just until blended. Be careful not to overmix. Spoon out rounded teaspoons of beef mixture, roll into mini meatballs, and set on prepared pans.

Bake for 10 to 12 minutes, until browned and cooked through.

NUTRITION FACTS

Serving Size about 8 mini meatballs (103g)
Calories 130
Calories from Fat 45
Total Fat 5g
Saturated Fat 1.5g
Trans Fat 0g
Cholesterol 75mg
Sodium 160mg
Total Carbohydrate 6g
Dietary Fiber 1g
Sugars 1g
Protein 18g

Be Merry:
Foods for
Special Occasions
and Everyday
Celebrations

VALENTINE'S DAY
SWEETS AND TREATS

Wondering how to keep the processed candy away from your little one, but want him to feel the Valentine love? Make your own treats and sweets to share with family and school Valentines.

Fruity Bonbons

These are classic candies that are made simply by pressing together dried fruits and spices. Known as "sweetmeats" by the British, they look lovely and whimsical on a party table, especially when rolled in raw sugar and coconut.

MAKES 16 TO 18 (1-INCH-DIAMETER) BONBONS

1 cup dried whole apricots
⅛ teaspoon ground allspice
½ teaspoon ground cinnamon
1 tablespoon organic unfiltered apple juice

For rolling (optional)
2 tablespoons turbinado sugar
2 tablespoons unsweetened finely shredded coconut

Line a mini muffin pan with mini muffin or truffle papers, and set pan aside.

Place dried apricots into a small bowl and cover with about ½ cup hot water. Let soak for 5 minutes to reconstitute. Drain off water and put apricots into a food processor fitted with a steel blade. Pulse until apricots are in small bits. Add spices and pulse to combine. Add apple juice while processing to bring mixture together.

petit
appetit

EAT, DRINK,
AND
BE MERRY

178

Spread out sugar and coconut (if using) on separate plates. Using a melon baller or teaspoon, scoop rounded teaspoonfuls of apricot mixture and roll into a ball with wet fingertips. Roll balls into desired coating. Place bonbons in mini muffin cups. Place in the refrigerator to keep firm until serving.

KIDS KORNER

Kids love to line the muffin cups with papers and place each bonbon in its own space. Older children can help shape and roll in sugar.

NUTRITION FACTS

Serving Size 1 bonbon (15g)
Calories 35
Calories from Fat 0
Total Fat 0g
Saturated Fat 0g
Trans Fat 0g
Cholesterol 0mg
Sodium 10mg
Total Carbohydrate 9g
Dietary Fiber 1g
Sugars 6g
Protein 0g

Be Merry:
Foods for
Special Occasions
and Everyday
Celebrations

Hearty Oatmeal Cut-Outs

This was inspired by my son's *Great Big Backyard* animal magazine, with a few changes in sugars and flours and the addition of naturally pink-colored (thanks to cranberry juice) frosting. My son brought these to share with his preschool class to represent the letter "H" for hearts. Feel free to use other shapes, but those with less detail (circle, heart, star) work the best because of the oatmeal chunks.

MAKES 35 (3-INCH) HEARTS

ICING YIELDS ⅓ CUP

1¼ cups whole wheat pastry flour
1 cup rolled oats
1 teaspoon baking soda
½ teaspoon freshly grated nutmeg
½ teaspoon ground cinnamon
½ teaspoon salt
1 cup turbinado sugar
½ cup (1 stick) organic unsalted butter, melted
⅔ cup organic milk

Icing
1 cup confectioners' sugar, sifted
¼ teaspoon pure vanilla extract
1 tablespoon cranberry juice
1 teaspoon organic milk

In a large bowl, combine flour, oats, baking soda, spices, and salt. Stir in sugar, butter, and milk until well mixed. (You may need to knead the dough together.) Form into a ball and refrigerate for 1 hour.

Preheat oven to 350°F. Line 2 baking sheets with parchment paper and set aside.

Place dough on a lightly floured surface and roll out with a rolling pin until ¼-inch thickness. Cut out shapes with cookie cutters and arrange on prepared baking sheet about 1½ inches apart. Bake for 10 to 12 minutes, until golden on bottoms.

petit
appetit

EAT, DRINK,
AND
BE MERRY

180

Using a metal spatula, carefully transfer cookies to a wire rack to cool completely before icing.

Prepare icing: Combine all icing ingredients in a small bowl. Using a small spreader or squeeze bottle, ice the hearts with stripes, dots, outlines, or cover the tops completely.

KIDS KORNER

I brought these cookies to my son's preschool to have the children decorate for Valentine's Day. The children loved playing with the squeeze bottles of icing. Used to condiments in such bottles, they kept asking, "Please, pass the mustard!"

NUTRITION FACTS

Serving Size 1 cookie (24g)
Calories 90
Calories from Fat 25
Total Fat 3g
Saturated Fat 1.5g
Trans Fat 0g
Cholesterol 5mg
Sodium 70mg
Total Carbohydrate 14g
Dietary Fiber 1g
Sugars 9g
Protein 1g

Be Merry:
Foods for
Special Occasions
and Everyday
Celebrations

CHINESE NEW YEAR

Chinese New Year brings luck and hope as well as colorful lion dancers and firecrackers. Ring in the New Year with symbolic foods and ingredients to teach children about the culture.

> *The Chinese New Year meal has become a new tradition in our home. It's difficult to prepare the whole meal, so I buy some of it in Chinatown and then make a few dishes myself. I am learning more each year. This year we tried to get most of the symbols and décor on the table.*
>
> FOUR-YEAR-OLD MICAH'S AND EIGHTEEN-MONTH-OLD SELAH'S mom

Tangerine Granita

This recipe was inspired by pastry chef Andrea Mautner of Restaurant TWO in San Francisco. While attending a cooking class, she prepared a wonderful dessert with this as one of the "elements." I thought this simple, icy treat would be perfect for a Chinese New Year celebration. One of the symbols for luck is tangerines, which are given to children during the holiday.

MAKES 8 (½-CUP) SERVINGS

Juice of 5 to 6 tangerines (about 1½ cups)
¾ cup Simple Syrup (page 110)
¼ cup water

Combine tangerine juice, simple syrup, and water in a bowl. Pour into an 8-inch glass baking dish or pie dish. Freeze for about 2 to 3 hours, until frozen.

Once fully frozen, scrape granita into flakes with a fork. They may melt easily and be a bit slushy. Granita can be eaten as a slushy now, or

petit
appetit

EAT, DRINK,
AND
BE MERRY

182

refreeze for another hour. It will become icier. Spoon into tall, old-fashioned ice cream glasses or mini ramekins. Serve immediately or return to freezer until ready to serve. Fluff with a fork again before serving.

TIP

Clear the freezer. Be sure you have a level space to set the granita to harden before walking over to the freezer with the liquid.

KIDS KORNER

This will melt quickly. If kids aren't eating it fast enough, serve along with straws to get all of the juice. Or, spoon over vanilla ice cream or frozen yogurt for an old-time Creamsicle reminder.

NUTRITION FACTS

Serving Size ½ cup (73g)
Calories 100
Calories from Fat 0
Total Fat 0g
Saturated Fat 0g
Trans Fat 0g
Cholesterol 0mg
Sodium 15mg
Total Carbohydrate 26g
Dietary Fiber 0g
Sugars 25g
Protein 0g

Be Merry:
Foods for
Special Occasions
and Everyday
Celebrations

MILK FREE

GROUP PLEASERS

PERFECT FOR PACKING

VEGETARIAN

Long-Life Noodles

Fireworks, lantern festivals, dragon dances, parades, and lots of food are all part of this special occasion. Both symbolic and delicious, noodles make a great food for sharing during Chinese New Year. There are many options for noodles that could work besides rice noodles; try Chinese egg noodles, udon, or soba for a variation. The peanut butter lends a bit of sweetness your child will enjoy.

MAKES 8 TO 10 (1-CUP) SERVINGS

8 ounces rice noodles
2 teaspoons expeller-pressed canola oil
1 teaspoon minced garlic
1 teaspoon minced fresh ginger or ½ teaspoon ground ginger
1 cup julienned organic carrot (1 large)
1 cup julienned organic red bell pepper (1 large or 4 mini)
¼ cup chopped scallions (about 3)
2 tablespoons gluten-free tamari
1 tablespoon peanut butter
½ cup organic vegetable broth
1 teaspoon freshly squeezed lime juice

Prepare the noodles according to package directions. Drain and set aside.

Heat 1 teaspoon of the oil in a medium pot over medium heat. Add the garlic and ginger and cook until fragrant and soft, about 1 minute. Add the carrot and bell pepper and cover. Cook until vegetables are tender but not soft, 5 to 7 minutes.

Add remaining 1 teaspoon oil, scallions, tamari, peanut butter, broth, and lime juice and bring to a boil. Add the noodles and heat until hot, stirring to combine with vegetables and sauce.

NUTRITION FACTS

Serving size 1 cup
Calories 100
Calories from Fat 20
Total Fat 2.5g
Saturated Fat 0g
Trans Fat 0g
Cholesterol 0mg
Sodium 290mg
Total Carbohydrate 18g
Dietary Fiber 2g
Sugars 2g
Protein 2g

petit
appetit

EAT, DRINK,
AND
BE MERRY

Beef-Filled Lettuce Cups

Lettuce cups are a fun excuse for kids to eat with their hands. If you're looking for the flavor without the mess, you can simply have children eat the beef mixture out of a bowl with a spoon or fork. This also works as a salad when entertaining by shredding the lettuce and mixing with the beef to be enjoyed with chop sticks out of individual Chinese take-out boxes. For vegetarians, substitute diced firm tofu for the beef.

MAKES 3 CUPS BEEF MIXTURE OR 16 TO 18 FILLED LETTUCE CUPS

2 teaspoons expeller-pressed canola oil

2 tablespoons minced organic red bell pepper

1 tablespoon minced shallot

1 teaspoon minced garlic

1 pound organic lean beef

¼ cup fresh organic mushrooms (portobello, crimini, or shiitake), chopped

3 tablespoons minced fresh cilantro leaves

2 teaspoons organic low-sodium tamari

1½ teaspoons ground allspice

1 teaspoon ground ginger

1 teaspoon freshly squeezed lime juice

16 to 18 organic butter lettuce leaves

2 tablespoons prepared plum sauce (optional)

In a large frying pan or wok, heat oil over medium-high heat. Add bell pepper, shallot, and garlic and stir-fry for 1 minute. Add beef, breaking apart and stirring, until starting to brown, about 5 minutes. Drain off excess fat and liquid from mixture.

Stir in the mushrooms, cilantro, tamari, allspice, ginger, and lime juice and cook until beef is cooked and mushrooms are tender, about 2 minutes.

NUTRITION FACTS

Serving Size 3 filled lettuce cups (112g)
Calories 110
Calories from Fat 40
Total Fat 4.5g
Saturated Fat 1g
Trans Fat 0g
Cholesterol 40mg
Sodium 160mg
Total Carbohydrate 2g
Dietary Fiber 1g
Sugars 1g
Protein 15g

Be Merry:
Foods for
Special Occasions
and Everyday
Celebrations

Serve beef mixture in a large bowl alongside lettuce leaves. To eat, spoon beef mixture into leaves then top with ½ teaspoon plum sauce (if using).

TIP

Pack perfectly. To pack and take to a family dinner or potluck, put beef mixture in one container and layer crisp lettuce leaves in another.

petit
appetit

EAT, DRINK,
AND
BE MERRY

186

ST. PATRICK'S DAY

Laughter is brightest where food is best.
—IRISH PROVERB

Everyone is Irish on St. Patrick's Day. When I was a kid, my mom and grandfather would "surprise" my sister and me on St. Patrick's Day morning with green milk and pancakes. Here I've skipped the fake colors and dyes and used natural green foods for your little leprechaun.

Spinach Hummus

Is your family ho hum for hummus? Try this variation using spinach. This is a quick and easy dish to perk up a crudité plate for a play group, or simply to pack with pita points in your child's lunch box.

MAKES 1½ CUPS

8 ounces canned chickpeas, drained and rinsed (¾ cup)
1 clove garlic
1 cup packed organic spinach leaves
1 tablespoon freshly squeezed lemon juice
½ teaspoon ground cumin
1 teaspoon kosher salt
½ teaspoon freshly ground black pepper
¼ cup extra-virgin olive oil
Pita points or vegetable sticks, to serve

In a blender or food processor, combine chickpeas and garlic, and puree until smooth. Add spinach, lemon juice, cumin, salt, and pepper. Blend thoroughly. With motor running, gradually add olive oil and process until smooth and creamy. Taste and adjust seasoning as needed.

Serve with pita points.

Go Green! To make the task even easier, purchase prepackaged organic spinach or baby spinach leaves, but still remember to wash.

NUTRITION FACTS

Serving Size 2 tablespoons (28g)

Calories 80
Calories from Fat 45
Total Fat 5g
Saturated Fat 0.5g
Trans Fat 0g
Cholesterol 0mg
Sodium 160mg
Total Carbohydrate 6g
Dietary Fiber 2g
Sugars 1g
Protein 2g

Be Merry:
Foods for
Special Occasions
and Everyday
Celebrations

Irish Wheaten Soda Bread

This is the easiest and quickest bread I have ever made: no rising, no kneading, no bread machine, and no mixer required. It is the perfect accompaniment to soups and salads. The bread will be a bit flat, so it's best suited for tea sandwiches or spread open-face with Pumpkin Butter (page 65). It was inspired by *Heartlands Cooking: Breads* by Frances Towner Giedt (Reader's Digest, 1996), with a few adjustments.

MAKES 8-INCH-ROUND LOAF; 12 SERVINGS

2¾ cups whole wheat flour, plus more for sprinkling
½ teaspoon salt
1 teaspoon baking soda
1¼ cups organic whole milk
1 tablespoon white wine vinegar
1 large cage-free organic egg
2 tablespoons honey (see Note, page 46)

Preheat oven to 375°F. Line a baking sheet with parchment paper and set aside.

In a large bowl, combine flour, salt, and baking soda. In a medium bowl, whisk together milk, vinegar, egg, and honey. Make a well in the flour mixture and pour in milk mixture. Stir with a rubber spatula or wooden spoon until everything is moist and combined. Do not over-mix. Dough will be very sticky.

Sprinkle flour on top of dough and lift out with hands onto pre-pared baking sheet. Plop dough on center of sheet. It will settle in a mound (and you'll think this will never work). Try to round as best as possible. Bake for 20 to 25 minutes, until it is nicely browned and makes a hollow sound underneath when tapped. Cool on a rack for 10 minutes before slicing.

TIP

Rise above it. Because this dough has no yeast, it will not rise as high as a typical loaf. However, the ugly-looking mound of dough on the baking sheet will turn into a love-ly and delicious free-form round loaf. Trust me.

NUTRITION FACTS

Serving Size 1 slice (62g)
Calories 130
Calories from Fat 15
Total Fat 1.5g
Saturated Fat 0.5g
Trans Fat 0g
Cholesterol 20mg
Sodium 220mg
Total Carbohydrate 25g
Dietary Fiber 4g
Sugars 5g
Protein 5g

petit
appetit

EAT, DRINK,
AND
BE MERRY

EASTER EGGING

$\mathcal{E}$ggs have been served since ancient times because they symbolize spring and rebirth. During April they are served at a Passover seder meal as well as dyed and decorated for Easter traditions. Here are some natural ways to color the perfectly hard-cooked eggs, as well as how to enjoy them (before they spoil in your basket).

A Good Egg: Hard-Cooked Eggs

Most pediatricians recommend feeding only egg yolks during the first year, as the whites are especially allergenic. Hard-cooking is the best way to separate an egg for a baby who cannot yet have whites. Note that even with a careful separation of white and yolk, some white may remain on the yolk. If allergies run in your family, you may wish to wait to introduce any egg until after one year, or as recommended by your pediatrician. Following is a way to ensure the perfect hard-cooked egg.

6 large cage-free organic eggs

Place eggs in a pot with a lid. Add enough water to cover eggs. Put pot over medium-high heat. When water comes to a rolling boil, cover pan, and turn off heat. Leave pot on burner, covered, for 18 minutes.

Drain and rinse eggs under cold running water.

To peel: Tap the egg all over to break shell. Egg shells peel easiest from the rounder end (where there is an air space). Eggs should have bright yellow centers. If gray or green color appears, the eggs have been overcooked.

Unpeeled eggs keep in the refrigerator for up to 1 week. If you're dyeing eggs and plan to eat them later, they must be stored in the refrigerator, not at room temperature in a basket.

Be Merry:
Foods for
Special Occasions
and Everyday
Celebrations

Egg Decorating Tips

Here're some fun tips for decorating eggs with children.

DYEING

◆ Start by layering a table with newspapers to mop up any spills or drips.

◆ Use empty egg cartons as drying racks for the eggs once dyed.

◆ Keep paper towels handy to blot any dye that collects under eggs.

◆ Use individual containers for each color. I find ramekins to work well. Containers should be sturdy enough to hold liquid and egg, and allow for fingers or spoons to lift eggs in and out. Don't use anything too tall or plastic, which can tip. Be sure to rinse contain ers of dyes so there are no stains.

◆ Use plastic utensils or wooden sticks to stir each color. This makes cleanup a breeze, and there's no risk of stained utensils.

◆ Let children create their own masterpieces, even if all the eggs come out blue. Be patient.

Go Green! If you do not want to use the prepackaged dyes and colors, you can make your own natural dyes by boiling common ingredients in water with a tablespoon of vinegar until desired shade is reached. Be sure to strain to remove solids. Here are the color options and what to add to the water:

YELLOW: Turmeric or yellow onion skins

ORANGE: Make yellow and add beet juice

PINK: Cranberry juice concentrate

BLUE: Grape juice concentrate, red cabbage

RED: Beets, paprika

GREEN: Spinach or kale

petit
appetit

EAT, DRINK,
AND
BE MERRY

OTHER OPTIONS

Some children are too small, or you may not be up to the challenge or mess of working with dyes. Other ideas include:

- Stickers: Your child's favorite stickers can transform an ordinary egg without mess or stained fingers.

- Collage: Using a glue stick or craft glue, add sequins, beads, ribbons, feathers, or anything else your child can dream up.

- Drawing/Coloring: Bring out the crayons, markers, and pens for children to draw and color on eggs (warn them not to push too hard).

Be Merry:
Foods for
Special Occasions
and Everyday
Celebrations

191

Egg and Olive Salad

Run out of ideas for all those hard-cooked eggs after Easter? Many adults think of egg salad and olive spread as comforting foods from their childhood. This recipe combines the best of both. The lemon and yogurt give this spread a new fresh taste and a healthy alternative to the standard mayonnaise flavor, which many children do not like. Serve before the kids' Easter egg hunt, with the chocolate eggs and jelly beans.

MAKES 15 (2-TABLESPOON) SERVINGS

2 hard-cooked eggs (page 189)
⅓ cup pitted black olives (about 10 whole), chopped
1 tablespoon freshly squeezed lemon juice
1 tablespoon organic plain whole-milk yogurt
Salt and freshly ground black pepper, to taste

Chop eggs finely using an egg slicer or knife. Mix all ingredients together in a small bowl until combined.

VARIATION

Stuff this spread into pita bread with arugula or roll it up in spinach leaves.

petit
appetit

EAT, DRINK,
AND
BE MERRY

CINCO DE MAYO

Dust off your sombreros and get into the fifth of May by celebrating the culture and experiences of Americans of Mexican ancestry. Like St. Patrick's Day, this holiday is observed by many Americans regardless of ethnic origins, to pay homage through special music, drinks, and of course food.

Fantastic Fajitas

Fajitas can be made to suit just about every appetite. The chicken can easily be substituted with beef, pork, shrimp, or grilled veggies.

MAKES 6 SERVINGS

3 tablespoons extra-virgin olive oil
½ teaspoon ground cumin
⅛ teaspoon chili powder
½ teaspoon dried oregano
3 large organic free-range chicken breasts (1 to 1½ pounds total), cut into 1-inch-wide strips
1 medium onion, sliced
1 clove garlic, minced
1 large organic red bell pepper, sliced

Accompaniments
6 corn or flour tortillas or 12 mini tortillas, warmed
Silly Salsa (page 88)
Oscar Dip (page 62)

Combine 2 tablespoons of the oil, spices, and chicken in a glass dish and marinate for up to 1 hour.

NUTRITION FACTS
Serving Size 1 (6-inch) tortilla with chicken and toppings (155g)
Calories 260
Calories from Fat 100
Total Fat 11g
Saturated Fat 2g
Trans Fat 0g
Cholesterol 65mg
Sodium 70mg
Total Carbohydrate 15g
Dietary Fiber 3g
Sugars 2g
Protein 25g

Be Merry:
Foods for
Special Occasions
and Everyday
Celebrations

Heat remaining 1 tablespoon of oil in a large skillet over medium-high heat. Add onion and garlic and sauté for 1 to 2 minutes. Add bell pepper and cook until bell pepper and onion are soft, about 5 minutes. Remove vegetables and set aside.

Add chicken and marinade to skillet and cook, stirring occasionally, until chicken is cooked through and no longer pink, 5 to 7 minutes. Add vegetables to skillet and cook until hot, about 1 minute.

Present fajitas with warm tortillas, salsa, and dip, and allow kids and adults to assemble them.

Go Green! Be sure to buy organic corn tortillas to reduce the possibility of genetically modified ingredients.

petit
appetit

EAT, DRINK,
AND
BE MERRY

194

MOTHER'S DAY BRUNCH

Are the kids too young or active for a leisurely brunch to celebrate Mom? Maybe you're hosting and toasting your mom or your spouse is surprising you (and the kids) with breakfast in bed. Here're a few simple recipes for keeping the celebration easy and light—for a welcome change.

Dried Cherry Scones

These little scones are perfect for sharing at a family brunch gathering. Using the food processor to mix and combine dough makes this a very quick and easy recipe. If you do not have a processor, you may use a rubber spatula and your hands to combine and knead the dough together. Besides brunch, these little scones would be welcome at the children's tea, too (pages 168–169).

MAKES 30 (2-INCH) SCONES

½ cup chopped organic dried cherries or cranberries

2 cups whole wheat pastry flour

3 tablespoons brown sugar

2 teaspoons baking powder

½ teaspoon baking soda

½ teaspoon salt

¼ cup organic unsalted butter, cut into pieces

1 teaspoon grated organic lemon zest (see Go Green! page 64)

1 large cage-free organic egg yolk, lightly beaten

1 (6-ounce) carton organic plain yogurt

 Preheat oven to 400°F. Line a large baking sheet with parchment paper and set aside.

 In a small bowl, combine cherries and hot water to cover. Let stand for 5 minutes and drain off water.

NUTRITION FACTS

Serving Size 1 scone (20g)
Calories 60
Calories from Fat 20
Total Fat 2g
Saturated Fat 1g
Trans Fat 0g
Cholesterol 10mg
Sodium 90 mg
Total Carbohydrate 9g
Dietary Fiber 1g
Sugars 3g
Protein 1g

Be Merry:
Foods for
Special Occasions
and Everyday
Celebrations

In a food processor, pulse flour, brown sugar, baking powder, baking soda, and salt until combined. Add butter and process until crumb-like texture forms. Add cherries and zest and pulse to combine.

In a small bowl, combine egg yolk and yogurt. Add egg mixture to flour in processor, and pulse just until combined, about 20 pulses.

Turn dough out onto a lightly floured surface and knead dough until smooth, 10 to 12 strokes. Pat dough with your fingers into a rectangle shape. Roll dough into a rectangle about 10 × 12 inches. Using a knife, cut dough into 2-inch strips. Cut each strip diagonally into 2-inch triangles.

Place scones on prepared pan and bake for 5 to 7 minutes, until light brown. Remove from sheet with a metal spatula and cool on a wire rack.

KIDS KORNER

Turn on the zoom-zoom. When my children were younger, it seemed odd to refer to using the "processor" and stand mixer so I talked about the sound. Plus I always had to warn them there was going to be a loud noise, in case they weren't ready. Now they each ask, "Can I turn on the zoom-zoom?"

petit
appetit

EAT, DRINK,
AND
BE MERRY

196

Picnic Eggs

Deviled eggs are a picnic and family brunch favorite. It's such a classic, there are even specific dishes designed to hold and serve them.

MAKES 12 EGG HALVES; 6 SERVINGS

6 hard-cooked eggs (page 189)
1½ tablespoons mayonnaise
1½ tablespoons organic plain whole-milk yogurt
1 teaspoon prepared mustard
1 teaspoon cider vinegar
2 teaspoons chopped fresh flat-leaf parsley
⅛ teaspoon kosher salt
Sweet paprika

Halve eggs lengthwise and press the yolks from the whites. Set whites aside, hole sides up, on a plate.

Mash yolks with mayonnaise, yogurt, mustard, vinegar, parsley, and salt in a medium bowl until the mixture is smooth and light.

Using a teaspoon or melon baller, drop egg yolk mixture into the hole of each egg half. Sprinkle each egg half with paprika.

TIP

Fancy pants. If you're looking for a fancier presentation, you can pipe egg yolk mixture into egg white halves with a pastry bag or plastic bag with a tip cut in one end.

NUTRITION FACTS

Serving Size 2 egg halves (60g)
Calories 100
Calories from Fat 70
Total Fat 8g
Saturated Fat 2g
Trans Fat 0g
Cholesterol 215mg
Sodium 140mg
Total Carbohydrate 1g
Dietary Fiber 0g
Sugars 1g
Protein 6g

Be Merry:
Foods for
Special Occasions
and Everyday
Celebrations

Yogurt Parfait

This simple parfait can be made with just about any fresh or dried fruit for color and sweetness, and a favorite cereal topping for added crunch. Let the kids assemble these for a snack, breakfast, or dessert. Serving parfaits in a tall clear glass or old-fashioned ice cream dish makes it special and festive for all ages.

MAKES ABOUT 8 CUPS

1 pint organic fresh strawberries
1 quart organic plain or vanilla whole-milk yogurt
1 cup favorite low-sugar granola or cereal
1 pint fresh blueberries

In a medium glass bowl or individual bowls, layer strawberries on bottom, then add yogurt and granola; top with blueberries.

petit
appetit

EAT, DRINK,
AND
BE MERRY

FATHER'S DAY BARBECUE

Dads and grills are a natural pairing. Gather the family outside for a salute to Dad with some kids' favorite foods and games in the sun. Be sure to make the Frozen Lemonade, too (page 110).

Super Slider Mini Burgers

This was inspired by a beautiful mini burger brought to my son at the Napa Valley Grille in Yountville, California. The circle of toast on top was the perfect size to complement the round patty. He of course ate it all separately anyway, but he thought it was pretty. These are simple to make for a crowd and easy for children and adults to hold. Be sure to serve with lots of condiments and topping options for all ages to build their own burger.

MAKES 15 TO 16 (2-INCH) BURGERS

1¼ pounds organic ground beef
10 to 12 slices whole wheat sandwich bread
Salt and freshly ground black pepper, to taste

Heat oven to 350°F. Line a jelly roll pan with aluminum foil. Grease foil, and set pan aside.

Put beef into a large bowl and season with salt and pepper. Using a 2-inch round cookie cutter or ring mold, break off meat by tablespoons and press to fit (2 inches by ½ inch high) in mold. Repeat until beef is gone.

Place each burger on the prepared pan. Bake for 8 to 10 minutes, until cooked through and juices run clear.

Using a cookie cutter, cut bread pieces to fit burgers. You should get 2 to 3 rounds per slice. Toast bread in 325°F oven on a baking sheet or in toaster oven.

Sandwich burgers between pieces of toasted rounds.

Serve with a variety of condiments such as mustard, ketchup, aioli, barbecue sauce, cheese, and anything else your child can dream up.

Go Green! Organic ketchup contains 83 percent more cancer-fighting lycopene than conventional ketchup.

NUTRITION FACTS

Serving Size 1 burger without condiments (56g)
Calories 90
Calories from Fat 20
Total Fat 2g
Saturated Fat 0.5g
Trans Fat 0g
Cholesterol 20mg
Sodium 110mg
Total Carbohydrate 8g
Dietary Fiber 1g
Sugars 1g
Protein 10g

Be Merry:
Foods for
Special Occasions
and Everyday
Celebrations

Berry-Yogurt Pops

Yogurt pops are simple to make at home and work for an afterschool treat or party pleasure at a backyard barbecue. You can buy a variety of inexpensive frozen pop molds in markets and kitchen stores. They usually make eight pops with ¼ to ⅓ cup liquid in each.

MAKES 8 (¼-CUP) POPS

1½ cups organic plain low-fat yogurt
¾ cup fresh or frozen organic berries, thawed
1 tablespoon honey (see Note, page 46)

Combine all ingredients in a blender or processor and process until smooth.

Carefully spoon mixture into ice-pop molds, filling almost to the top. Gently bang molds 2 to 3 times to burst any air bubbles inside. Put tops on and transfer to the freezer on a flat shelf to freeze until solid, about 3 hours.

To remove pops from the mold, stand mold in a bowl of cold water (or run water under one, to release only one pop) for 1 to 2 minutes until the pops lift out.

TIP

Berry good. Got too many berries? Freeze them for later. First trim away any green leaves or stems and gently rinse under cool water. Do not soak, as too much liquid will be absorbed. Place berries on a clean kitchen towel and allow to air-dry completely. Arrange berries in a single layer on a baking sheet and place in the freezer for about 1 hour. When firm to touch, transfer to an airtight container or self-sealing bag and freeze to have on hand anytime.

NUTRITION FACTS

Serving Size 1 pop (59g)
Calories 40
Calories from Fat 5
Total Fat 0.5g
Saturated Fat 0g
Trans Fat 0g
Cholesterol 5mg
Sodium 30mg
Total Carbohydrate 6g
Dietary Fiber 1g
Sugars 6g
Protein 2g

petit
appetit

EAT, DRINK,
AND
BE MERRY

HALLOWEEN

A Halloween-night party is a fun way to get friends with small children together and show off costumes. All ages enjoy opening the door for the big-kid trick-or-treaters, and everyone will enjoy these warm, festive recipes on a cool fall night. If you have trick-or-treaters in your family, serve these healthy and filling recipes before they head out to collect (and eat) all the candy.

White Bean and Chicken Chili

The origin of this recipe is *San Francisco Flavors*, by the San Francisco Junior League. The original is great, but not many parents with small children have two hours to allow a stew to cook, let alone remember to soak dried beans overnight. The prep time is reduced in this recipe by using canned beans and sautéing the cooked chicken in the spices to soak up additional flavor. You can reduce your time further if you have leftover chicken on hand or buy precooked chicken and preshredded cheese. This version for busy families takes only thirty-five to forty minutes from start to finish.

MAKES 12 CUPS

1 tablespoon extra-virgin olive oil

1 yellow onion, chopped

4 cloves garlic, minced

½ (4-ounce) can chopped mild green chilies, or 2 fresh chilies, roasted, seeded, and chopped

2 teaspoons ground cumin

1 teaspoon dried oregano

¼ teaspoon ground cloves

¼ teaspoon red pepper flakes

2 pounds cooked boneless, skinless, organic free-range chicken (can be leftover or purchased precooked)

Be Merry:
Foods for
Special Occasions
and Everyday
Celebrations

201

2 (15-ounce) cans cannellini beans, drained and rinsed
4 cups organic low-sodium chicken broth
2 tablespoons cornstarch mixed with 2 tablespoons water
2 cups shredded Monterey jack or mozzarella cheese (rBGH-free)
Salt and freshly ground black pepper, to taste

In a large stock pot over medium heat, heat oil. Add onion and sauté until soft, about 5 to 7 minutes. Add garlic, chilies, cumin, oregano, cloves, and red pepper flakes and sauté until fragrant, about 2 minutes. Mix in chicken and cook for 2 minutes. Add beans and broth. Bring to a boil, reduce heat to low, and cover. Simmer for 20 minutes, stirring once or twice.

Transfer 1 cup of the broth to a small bowl and whisk in cornstarch mixture. Stir cornstarch mixture back into pot, cover, and cook another 5 minutes, stirring, to thicken.

Add 1 cup of the cheese to the pot and stir until melted. Season with salt and pepper. Serve with remaining cheese.

petit
appetit

EAT, DRINK,
AND
BE MERRY

Roasted Pumpkin Seeds

Each person has his own technique and recipe for toasting pumpkin seeds. For a fun-tasting party at school, have each family bring in their own for children to sample and vote for their favorites. Incorporate extra seeds into trail mixes for a seasonal surprise.

MAKES 8 SERVINGS PER 1 CUP SEEDS

1 whole pumpkin

For each 1 cup pumpkin seeds
1 teaspoon extra-virgin olive oil
½ teaspoon salt
½ teaspoon curry powder or ½ teaspoon sugar and ½ teaspoon ground cinnamon

Heat oven to 300°F. Line a baking sheet with aluminum foil and set aside.

Cut off top of pumpkin and scoop out insides. Separate out as much of the pumpkin strings and flesh from the seeds as possible. Some of the slime and strings you can't remove will provide a crisp coating on the seeds.

In a small bowl, combine seeds, oil, and seasonings. Stir until coated. Spread out seeds in a single layer on prepared baking sheet. Roast for about 40 minutes, until golden brown and dry, stirring with a spatula every 10 minutes during cooking. Let cool on paper towels and store in an airtight container for up to 1 week.

KIDS KORNER
My favorite part about carving a pumpkin at Halloween is getting my hands into the pumpkin to pull out the seeds and stringy goop. However, my son, like many children, does not share the enthusiasm for the slimy, gooey mess. And my daughter just wants to eat the goop and seeds right out of the pumpkin.

NUTRITION FACTS
Serving Size 2 tablespoons (28g)
Calories 150
Calories from Fat 120
Total Fat 13g
Saturated Fat 2.5g
Trans Fat 0g
Cholesterol 0mg
Sodium 230mg
Total Carbohydrate 5g
Dietary Fiber 1g
Sugars 0g
Protein 7g

Be Merry: Foods for Special Occasions and Everyday Celebrations

Go Green! Heading to a pumpkin patch is a real treat for kids and adults. Skip the fake "patches" at the mall or roadside where pumpkins are trucked in, and visit a real pumpkin patch and farm. Every year we go to a wonderful dairy farm that grows organic pumpkins, corn, and potatoes. We pet goats, milk cows, dig potatoes, cut our own pumpkin, and ride on a tractor. That certainly beats a jack-o'-lantern bounce house any day.

petit
appetit

EAT, DRINK,
AND
BE MERRY

204

THANKSGIVING FAMILY DINNER

This is the big one. The pressure's on to get all the right foods and recipes. The turkey, stuffing, and gravy are a given (and you don't want to offend your own mother), but here are a few twists for quick and easy sides and snacks for the day that complement the traditional fare.

Leaf Us Alone Brussels Sprouts

Although they are one of my favorites, I realize Brussels sprouts are not welcome by many. I think they get a bad rap because they are usually boiled, bland, and still rock-hard in the center. Peeling the leaves and discarding the center core makes for an entirely different taste and texture. And yes, you and your kids may even have a new green favorite. Note that this recipe takes time and patience, but little hands make great peelers.

MAKES 6 SERVINGS

1 pound Brussels sprouts
¼ cup extra-virgin olive oil
1 teaspoon freshly squeezed lemon juice
⅛ teaspoon salt
⅛ teaspoon freshly ground black pepper

Preheat oven to 375°F. Line a jelly roll pan with aluminum foil.

Cut off bottom stem or core of each sprout. Carefully peel away the leaves until it becomes too hard to peel. Cut off bottom core again and peel more layers. Continue cutting and peeling until it is too difficult to peel apart.

Place leaves in a large mixing bowl. Drizzle with olive oil and lemon juice and stir until all leaves are coated. Sprinkle with salt and pepper and stir again.

Be Merry:
Foods for
Special Occasions
and Everyday
Celebrations

Spread leaves onto prepared baking pan in a single layer. Roast for 10 to 12 minutes, until leaves are cooked and start to crisp with golden edges.

KIDS KORNER
I brought these to the table to peel while my children were having a snack. It must have looked interesting, as both my four-year-old and eighteen-month-old starting peeling, too. I told them they were Brussels Buddies. My son just kept telling his dad, "We're only eating the skins."

NUTRITION FACTS

Serving Size about ½ cup (77g)
Calories 35
Calories from Fat 5
Total Fat 0g
Saturated Fat 0g
Trans Fat 0g
Cholesterol 0mg
Sodium 65mg
Total Carbohydrate 7g
Dietary Fiber 3g
Sugars 2g
Protein 3g

petit
appetit

EAT, DRINK,
AND
BE MERRY

Pumpkin Tarts

These are a hit at holiday time, as everyone gets their own pie. The crust is a traditional graham cracker recipe with a creamy pumpkin cheesecake–like filling. These are something to be thankful for!

MAKES 8 (3½-INCH) TARTS

Crust

14 natural graham crackers (such as Whole Foods)
3 tablespoons evaporated cane juice
8 tablespoons organic unsalted butter, melted

Filling

½ cup canned pumpkin puree
½ cup organic Neufchâtel cheese
3 tablespoons confectioners' sugar
¼ teaspoon ground cinnamon
⅛ teaspoon ground allspice
⅛ teaspoon freshly grated nutmeg

Preheat oven to 350°F. Coat 8 (3½-inch) tartlet molds or ramekins with cooking spray or oil and set aside.

Make crusts: In a medium bowl or food processor, mix all crust ingredients together. Press mixture into bottoms and sides of tartlet molds or ramekins. Bake crusts for 8 to 10 minutes, until golden brown. Remove and let cool on a wire rack.

Make filling: In a medium bowl, beat together all ingredients until smooth. Spoon 1 heaping tablespoon of filling into each crust. Refrigerate for 1 hour.

These can be eaten right out of the mold or ramekin. Or slide a knife around crust and carefully remove tart from dish.

NUTRITION FACTS

Serving Size 1 tart (64g)
Calories 220
Calories from Fat 130
Total Fat 15g
Saturated Fat 9g
Trans Fat 0g
Cholesterol 40mg
Sodium 150mg
Total Carbohydrate 19g
Dietary Fiber 1g
Sugars 12g
Protein 3g

Be Merry:
Foods for
Special Occasions
and Everyday
Celebrations

HANUKKAH, O HANUKKAH

The celebration of Hanukkah is marked by the symbol of light (candles) and oil (for cooking). There is a custom of eating foods fried or baked in oil, as the original miracle of the Hanukkah menorah involved the discovery of a small flask of oil, which was only supposed to last one day and instead it lasted eight. Enjoy a little Calientito (page 137) while sharing blessings and songs.

Potato Latkes

Wanting to reduce the amount of oil and frying in traditional latkes, I developed a version that's finished in the oven to add crispness without extra fat and grease. These are great accompanied by Applesauce (page 68) and Yogurt-Herb Dip (page 61).

MAKES 12 SERVINGS

1½ pounds (about 2) organic russet potatoes, scrubbed and shredded (4 cups)
1 medium yellow onion, shredded (½ cup)
2 medium shallots, minced (1 tablespoon)
1 teaspoon kosher salt
1 large cage-free organic egg
2 (6-inch squares) whole wheat matzo, broken into pieces
Freshly ground black pepper, to taste
1 tablespoon extra-virgin olive oil

Toss potatoes, onion, shallots, and salt together in a medium bowl. Transfer to a sieve set over a large bowl and let drain for about 15 minutes. Squeeze potato mixture by handfuls over a glass bowl to release excess moisture (some moisture should remain) and put potato mix-

petit
appetit

EAT, DRINK,
AND
BE MERRY

208

ture in a separate bowl. Potato liquid will have a pasty-white sediment (starch) in the bottom of the glass bowl. Carefully pour off and discard top liquid and add starchy portion to the potato mixture. Stir in egg.

Put matzo pieces into a food processor and process to coarse crumbs. Sprinkle crumbs and pepper over potato mixture and toss to combine. Cover and refrigerate until matzo is softened, 15 to 20 minutes.

Preheat oven to 425°F. Coat a baking sheet with oil and set aside.

Heat olive oil in a large nonstick skillet over medium heat. Stir the potato mixture. Using a ¼-cup measuring cup, scoop potato mixture and add to pan without crowding. Press with a spatula to flatten each to about a 3-inch cake. Cook until crispy and golden, about 2 to 3 minutes per side. Transfer the latkes to prepared baking sheet. Continue cooking, using additional oil to prevent sticking, if needed. Once all are cooked and on baking sheet, transfer to the oven and warm until heated through, about 10 minutes.

TIP
Kids' help vs. processor. Instead of using the processor to make matzo crumbs, put matzo in a plastic bag and have kids roll with a rolling pin to break and crumble. Of course the project takes longer, but it's more fun.

NUTRITION FACTS
Serving Size 1 latke (81 g)
Calories 90
Calories from Fat 15
Total Fat 1.5g
Saturated Fat 0g
Trans Fat 0g
Cholesterol 20mg
Sodium 170mg
Total Carbohydrate 17g
Dietary Fiber 1g
Sugars 1g
Protein 3g

Be Merry:
Foods for
Special Occasions
and Everyday
Celebrations

Matzo Brei

Holiday foods are a great way to introduce different customs, cultures, and traditions to your children. The first time I made this my son exclaimed, "Wow, a giant pancake!" Matzo is packaged in a box and found in the ethnic sections of grocery stores and is a large wheat cracker, made with only wheat flour and water. Commonly served for breakfast, snack, or side dish, it can be made both savory or sweet. This version is sweetened with the addition of powdered sugar, cinnamon, and fresh berries.

MAKES 1 (8- TO 10-INCH) PANCAKE; 8 SERVINGS

6 (6-inch squares) whole wheat matzo
1 cup boiling water
2 cage-free organic eggs
¼ teaspoon kosher salt
2 tablespoons organic unsalted butter
2 teaspoons confectioners' sugar
2 teaspoons ground cinnamon
1 cup fresh organic berries (raspberries, blackberries, blueberries, or combination)

In a large mixing bowl, break matzo into small (1-inch) pieces. Pour water over matzo and allow to soften for 1 minute.

In a small bowl, whisk eggs and salt together and mix into matzo mixture.

In a medium skillet, melt the butter over medium-high heat. When the foam subsides, transfer the matzo mixture to pan and flatten with a spatula. Fry until crisp and golden, about 4 minutes. Carefully flip over with a spatula to fry the other side for another 4 minutes.

Slide matzo brei onto a large plate and sprinkle with the powdered sugar and cinnamon. Top with berries and serve.

KIDS KORNER
Kids have a great time decorating and choosing their own toppings. Putting sugars and cinnamon in shakers is easy for children, with less waste and mess for adults.

NUTRITION FACTS

Serving Size ⅛ of pancake plus topping (84g)
Calories 140
Calories from Fat 35
Total Fat 4g
Saturated Fat 2g
Trans Fat 0g
Cholesterol 60mg
Sodium 80mg
Total Carbohydrate 21g
Dietary Fiber 0g
Sugars 1g
Protein 4g

petit
appetit

EAT, DRINK,
AND
BE MERRY

CHRISTMAS TREE–TRIMMING GET-TOGETHER

Children love to decorate for the holidays. Instead of spending all your time and energy on the actual day, spread it out. Organize get-togethers beforehand when times aren't so rushed and you can enjoy the seasonal, simple pleasures with your children. An afternoon of holiday tree-trimming is a fun way to spend time with children and family.

Gingerbread

The smell of gingerbread in a house full of decorations means the season has begun. This is a simple make-ahead recipe that will feed a crowd of tree trimmers during the holidays. Besides being delicious, the addition of molasses is a good way to get iron into some children's diets.

MAKES 16 SERVINGS

1½ cups unbleached all-purpose flour
¼ cup packed brown sugar
1 teaspoon ground cinnamon
1 teaspoon ground ginger
½ teaspoon baking powder
½ teaspoon baking soda
½ cup mild or light molasses
¼ cup expeller-pressed canola oil
1 large cage-free organic egg
½ cup water

Preheat oven to 350°F. Lightly grease and flour an 8-inch-square glass baking dish and set aside.

In a large bowl, combine flour, brown sugar, cinnamon, ginger, baking powder, and baking soda. Add the molasses, oil, egg, and water and beat on low speed until combined. Increase speed to high and beat for 2 minutes.

Be Merry:
Foods for
Special Occasions
and Everyday
Celebrations

Pour into prepared dish and bake for 30 minutes, until a wooden pick comes out clean. Cool on rack for 10 minutes before cutting into 2-inch squares. Serve warm with yogurt or whipped cream.

Go Green! Why not double the recipe and give to neighbors and friends packaged in pretty recycled tins or a glass plate? Children will love helping with wrap and special delivery.

petit
appetit

EAT, DRINK,
AND
BE MERRY

Minty Chocolate Pudding

This is a creamy treat for all ages that uses real mint rather than fake flavoring you'd find in processed puddings. This is not a quick and instant pudding; it requires lots of whisking (the key to its smooth texture), but it is worth the effort for the home-made flavor and to avoid artificial sweeteners and additives. These can be served and enjoyed out of large or small ramekins depending on the gathering and party size. A little goes a long way in terms of richness, but that doesn't mean your child won't ask for more.

MAKES 4½ CUPS

3 cups organic nonfat milk
½ cup packed fresh mint leaves (about ½ ounce)
⅔ cup evaporated cane juice
¼ cup cornstarch
3 tablespoons organic unsweetened cocoa powder
⅛ teaspoon salt
3 large cage-free organic egg yolks, lightly beaten
½ teaspoon pure vanilla extract
2 ounces organic semisweet chocolate chips or pieces

Heat milk over medium-high heat in a medium-heavy saucepan until tiny bubbles form around edge. Be careful not to boil. Remove from heat and add mint. Let steep for 15 minutes. Strain milk through a sieve over a bowl. Return milk to pan. Discard mint solids.

In a small bowl, whisk together evaporated cane juice, cornstarch, cocoa, and salt; add to milk. Over medium heat, bring milk mixture to a boil, stirring constantly with a whisk until mixture thickens, about 5 minutes.

Place egg yolks in a medium bowl and gradually add half of hot milk mixture, stirring constantly with a whisk. Add egg mixture to pan and bring to a boil, stirring constantly. Cook until thickened, about 1 minute. Remove from heat and add vanilla and chocolate chips, stirring until chocolate is melted. Pour pudding into ramekins; cover surface of pudding with plastic wrap. Chill in refrigerator for 1 hour.

Be Merry:
Foods for
Special Occasions
and Everyday
Celebrations

Everyday Celebrations

KIDS' COOKIES WITH MOM

When I asked parents, kids, doctors, nutritionists, chefs, and others about a favorite food memory or first recipe they made as a child, making and decorating cookies with Mom was the answer more than 80 percent of the time. Whether it's to cheer up a child after a bad day at school or to create something special for Grandma and Grandpa's visit, making cookies makes a lasting impression.

Sugar Cookie Cut-Outs

Adapted from the standard *New Cook Book from Better Homes and Gardens* (2002), this is a classic sugar cookie recipe and one that works for all seasons. Kids can help dump the measured ingredients into the mixing bowl and turn on and off the electric mixer to help make the dough. Of course, the fun really begins with the help of choosing and cutting shapes and icing and decorating at the end.

MAKES ABOUT 35 (2½-INCH) COOKIES

⅔ cup organic unsalted butter, at room temperature
¾ cup sugar
1 teaspoon baking powder
¼ teaspoon salt
1 large cage-free organic egg
1 tablespoon organic milk
1 teaspoon pure vanilla extract
2 cups unbleached all-purpose flour

petit
appetit

EAT, DRINK,
AND
BE MERRY

In a large mixing bowl, beat butter with an electric mixer on medium speed for 30 seconds. Add sugar, baking powder, and salt and beat until combined. Beat in egg, milk, and vanilla until combined. Beat in the flour, ¼ cup at a time, until all is incorporated.

Cover and chill dough for at least 30 minutes. Preheat oven to 375°F. Line 2 baking sheets with parchment paper and set aside.

On a lightly floured surface and using a floured rolling pin, roll dough out to ⅛-inch thickness. Cut into desired shapes. Place 1 inch apart on prepared baking sheets.

Bake for 7 to 9 minutes, until edges are firm and bottoms are very lightly browned. Transfer to a wire rack to cool.

KIDS KORNER

Once completely cool, these can be frosted with your child's favorite royal icing or powdered sugar icing. For easy frosting, set out small spreaders and squeeze bottles so frosting decorates the cookies and not your child, the floor, and the table. Add sprinkles to wet frosting for even more fun (and mess). Allow frosting to completely dry before stacking and packing.

TIP

Party! Cookies are easier to transport than cake and cupcakes. For a beach birthday party, I made starfish- and crab-shaped cookies with royal icing, which packed and stacked beautifully. Plus, I didn't have to worry about sand blowing into cake frosting.

NUTRITION FACTS

Serving Size 2 cookies (34g)
Calories 160
Calories from Fat 60
Total Fat 7g
Saturated Fat 4.5g
Trans Fat 0g
Cholesterol 30mg
Sodium 115mg
Total Carbohydrate 19g
Dietary Fiber 0g
Sugars 8g
Protein 2g

Be Merry:
Foods for
Special Occasions
and Everyday
Celebrations

FIRST DAY OF SNOW

*I*t doesn't matter how cold it is outside, children love to see falling snowflakes, especially the first snow of the season. Spending an afternoon catching snowflakes on your tongue, making snowballs, and sledding makes for the perfect winter day. To complete the picture, invite the kids in to warm up and enjoy chocolate cookies and Little Lattes (page 139).

Chocolatey Sliced Cookies

This rich chocolate cookie is made even better with a hint of spice. Great on their own with a cup of milk or hot cocoa, these cookies also make tasty ice cream sandwiches with vanilla or mint middles.

MAKES ABOUT 28 (2½-INCH) COOKIES

1½ cups whole wheat pastry flour
½ cup organic unsweetened cocoa powder
¼ teaspoon baking soda
¼ teaspoon ground cinnamon
½ cup packed brown sugar
½ cup turbinado sugar
4 tablespoons organic unsalted butter, melted
¼ cup Applesauce (page 68) or jarred organic unsweetened applesauce
1 teaspoon pure vanilla extract
1 large cage-free organic egg

In a medium bowl, combine flour, cocoa, baking soda, and cinnamon; set aside. In a large bowl, beat sugars and butter until creamy. Beat in the applesauce, vanilla, and egg. Blend in the flour mixture until just combined.

Transfer dough to one end of a large piece of waxed paper. Fold paper over dough completely and roll into a 12-inch log. Freeze for at least 1 hour.

petit
appetit

EAT, DRINK,
AND
BE MERRY

216

Preheat oven to 350°F. Line two baking sheets with parchment paper and set aside.

Unwrap dough and slice crosswise into ½-inch-thick rounds. Lay rounds 1 inch apart on prepared pans. Bake for 10 to 12 minutes, until no longer soggy when touched. Transfer to a wire rack to cool.

Go Green! According to the Fair Trade Labeling Organizations International, in October 2006, more than 1.5 million disadvantaged producers worldwide were directly benefiting from fair trade while an additional 5 million benefited from fair trade–funded infrastructure and community development projects. Buying fair trade cocoa, coffee, bananas, sugar, and other foods and crafts supports this movement and its participants.

NUTRITION FACTS

Serving Size 1 cookie (21g)
Calories 80
Calories from Fat 20
Total Fat 2g
Saturated Fat 1g
Trans Fat 0g
Cholesterol 10mg
Sodium 15mg
Total Carbohydrate 13g
Dietary Fiber 1g
Sugars 7g
Protein 1g

Be Merry:
Foods for
Special Occasions
and Everyday
Celebrations

PICNIC IN THE PARK

Any day can be made a little more special for children by eating outdoors. My son will ask if we can eat outside even if it's 50 degrees and sprinkling rain. There's something about the freedom of being able to chase a pigeon, have a bug buzz your ear, and give crumbs to a blackbird that makes eating outside exciting to children. With a little careful planning and packing, a picnic in the park can be a real breeze.

Baked "Fried" Chicken

This is a healthy and less messy way to enjoy crispy chicken, similar to fried. Panko are light, crispy bread crumbs most often used in tempura dishes. They yield a crunchier texture than typical bread crumbs, which can become soggy. Panko can be purchased at most specialty grocers alongside the bread crumbs or in the Asian specialty section. Serve this with Mustard-Honey Sauce (page 66).

MAKES 8 PIECES

4 boneless, skinless, organic free-range chicken breasts (about 2 to 3 pounds total)
½ cup panko crumbs
½ teaspoon sweet paprika
⅛ teaspoon freshly ground black pepper
1 large cage-free organic egg
½ teaspoon salt

Preheat oven to 425°F. Line a baking sheet with aluminum foil. Grease foil, and set baking sheet aside.

Cut each chicken breast in half lengthwise for a total of 8 similar-size strips.

petit
appetit

EAT, DRINK,
AND
BE MERRY

218

Combine the panko, paprika, and pepper on a flat plate. In a small bowl, lightly beat the egg with the salt. Dip each chicken piece in the egg mixture then press into the panko mixture to coat all sides.

Place chicken on prepared baking sheet. Bake for 30 minutes, turning once halfway through cooking time, until coating is brown and chicken juices run clear when pierced with a fork.

TIP

Packing. Allow foods to cool completely before wrapping and storing to go. You'll reduce moisture build up in the food and containers and keep food fresher longer.

Go Green! Pack reusable or renewable (bamboo) plates, cups, and silverware and cloth napkins instead of plastic and paper. Or simply cut bite-size pieces of foods and pack for children to eat with their hands; they're used to that.

NUTRITION FACTS

Serving Size 1 piece (156g)
Calories 270
Calories from Fat 50
Total Fat 6g
Saturated Fat 1.5g
Trans Fat 0g
Cholesterol 145mg
Sodium 290mg
Total Carbohydrate 6g
Dietary Fiber 0g
Sugars 0g
Protein 45g

Be Merry:
Foods for
Special Occasions
and Everyday
Celebrations

Confetti Slaw

Here the produce takes center stage with a bright, vitamin-rich mix of colors and flavors that will entice children and adults alike. For the most nutritional benefit, choose organic apples and zucchini and leave the skins intact. A word to the wise parent of a toddler: Shredding fruits and vegetables with a box grater is a great way to slip extra vegetables into dishes such as quesadillas and pasta sauces.

MAKES 4 CUPS

1 tablespoon freshly squeezed orange juice
1 teaspoon balsamic vinegar
1 teaspoon extra-virgin olive oil
1 large zucchini, shredded
1 medium organic red or orange bell pepper, diced
1 small organic Fuji apple, shredded

In a medium bowl, whisk together orange juice, vinegar, and olive oil. Add zucchini, bell pepper, and apple, and toss together to combine.

KIDS KORNER

Older children can carefully grate veggies using a box grater, with supervision to watch little knuckles.

NUTRITION FACTS

Serving Size 1 cup (177g)
Calories 50
Calories from Fat 15
Total Fat 1.5g
Saturated Fat 0g
Trans Fat 0g
Cholesterol 0mg
Sodium 15mg
Total Carbohydrate 10g
Dietary Fiber 2g
Sugars 7g
Protein 2g

petit
appetit

EAT, DRINK,
AND
BE MERRY

FIRST LOST/PULLED TOOTH

It's a big moment when your child loses a tooth, either by accident or naturally. He has a new grin, a new bite, and a new space. If the dentist pulls a tooth, like she did for my son, she advises to have something cold, but no straws the first day. This cherry sorbet is a sweet treat that requires no teeth or straws to enjoy, and very little time or effort to make. Basil Flaxseed Pesto (page 222) with pasta is great for testing out that new gap.

Cherry Sorbet

Making pureed cherries to add to baby cereal, I stumbled upon the discovery that frozen cherries make an instant sorbet. This is dark and creamy and very yummy for any and every age. It's a sweet treat with no added sugars and little effort (just cherries and the push of a button).

MAKES ABOUT 1¾ CUPS PUREE

1 (16-ounce) bag frozen organic dark sweet cherries

Put the cherries in a food processor fitted with the steel blade. Process the cherries until smooth, stopping occasionally to scrape down sides and incorporate cherry pieces. The mixture will be very thick. Spoon into serving bowls.

Go Green! Cherries have a short peak season and are on the Dirty Dozen list (see page 15). But you can have them all year long without pesticides by buying frozen organic ones.

NUTRITION FACTS

Serving Size ½ cup (151g)
Calories 130
Calories from Fat 0
Total Fat 0g
Saturated Fat 0g
Trans Fat 0g
Cholesterol 0mg
Sodium 0mg
Total Carbohydrate 33g
Dietary Fiber 1g
Sugars 32g
Protein 2g

Be Merry:
Foods for
Special Occasions
and Everyday
Celebrations

petit
appetit

EAT, DRINK,
AND
BE MERRY

Basil Flaxseed Pesto

Your child is curious and now wants to try all the tricks with the new gap in his grin. Slurping spaghetti noodles was never so exciting before a missing front tooth. This is a new and improved version of the usual basil pesto. This version has no nuts, but it has a "nutty" texture from flaxseeds. The flax also provides a dose of heart-healthy lignans and omega-3 fatty acids. Slurp away over spaghetti, or make ahead for a sauce or dip for veggies and bread sticks.

MAKES ABOUT ¾ CUP

3 cups packed basil leaves
2 tablespoons flaxseeds
1 medium clove garlic, minced
½ teaspoon salt
¼ teaspoon freshly ground black pepper
⅓ cup extra-virgin olive oil
⅓ cup freshly grated Parmesan cheese (rBGH-free)

Place the basil, flaxseeds, garlic, salt, and pepper in a food processor fitted with the steel blade. Process until chopped and combined. With motor running, add oil in a steady stream and process until smooth (but with seeds), about 45 seconds. Scrape down halfway through processing. Add cheese and process just until blended. (If making ahead, it's best to freeze pesto before adding the cheese. When ready to use, simply defrost and add cheese before serving.)

To serve with pasta, cook 8 ounces spaghetti according to manufacturer's instructions and drain. Stir in sauce to coat noodles.

TIP

Party planning! To serve pesto pasta outdoors, pack in small Chinese take-out boxes. Little hands can spoon or fork noodles with ease and less mess and cleanup.

FAMILY GAME NIGHT

Yummy bites and a competitive, fun spirit make for a night of laughs with family and friends over favorite games. Our house favorites are Sorry!, Trouble, and Candy Land. Challenge the genders, the neighbors, or your best friends to come over for a game and a tasty snack.

Grilled Cheese Bites

Who doesn't love grilled cheese sandwiches? Little and big gamers will like the small bite-size cocktail bread. Sold in the deli or cheese department of most grocery stores, the cocktail bread makes the perfect size for adult appetizers and children's snacks, without the time and bread wasted from cutting sandwich-size shapes. There are many variations and additions to this classic sandwich. Besides surprise additions, you can also create variety (in color and flavor) with different bread and cheese choices. Serve with Mustard-Honey Sauce (page 66) for dippers.

MAKES 12 (2½-INCH) SANDWICH BITES

½ (1 pound) loaf sliced cocktail pumpernickel bread
6 ounces sharp Cheddar cheese (rBGH-free), thinly sliced
12 thin slices organic apple (optional)
About ½ cup dried currants (optional)
12 thin slices tomatoes (optional)
2 tablespoons organic butter, melted

Lay 12 slices of cocktail bread on a work surface. Layer each piece of bread with cheese, folding or cutting cheese to fit. Add toppings (if using). Top with second slices of cocktail bread.

Brush butter on top of each sandwich. Heat large griddle or grill pan over medium heat. Brush pan with butter.

Be Merry:
Foods for
Special Occasions
and Everyday
Celebrations

Using a spatula, transfer sandwiches to the hot griddle with the nonbuttered side down. Cook for 2 minutes or until cheese starts to melt and bottom is slightly crisp and brown. Flip using spatula and cook other side for about 2 minutes, until cheese has melted and bread is crisp.

TIP

No cocktail bread? Simply cut desired shapes in your child's favorite sandwich bread. For a party, you may even want to have a variety of breads.

KIDS KORNER

Kids can create their own grilled cheese masterpiece. Put ingredients out in small bowls for little hands to layer and return to the kitchen for Mom or Dad to grill.

petit appetit

EAT, DRINK, AND BE MERRY

Vegetable Fritters

Crispy on the outside and soft and moist on the inside, this preparation will induce even the choosiest toddler to not only eat, but enjoy, their veggies. Serve with yogurt or Mustard-Honey Sauce (page 66) for small hands to dip.

MAKES 15 (2-INCH) FRITTERS

1 cup grated sweet potato (1 medium)
1 cup grated unpeeled zucchini (1 medium)
1 cup organic corn flour
½ teaspoon baking powder
⅛ teaspoon salt
⅛ teaspoon freshly ground black pepper
1 large cage-free organic egg, lightly beaten
¼ cup organic whole milk
2 tablespoons expeller-pressed canola oil

Preheat oven to 250°F.

Wrap grated vegetables in a clean kitchen towel or paper towels and gently squeeze to extract as much liquid as possible. Transfer to a medium mixing bowl.

In a small bowl, combine corn flour, baking powder, salt, and pepper. In a separate bowl, whisk together egg and milk. Stir flour mixture into vegetables. Add egg mixture and stir until just combined.

Heat oil in a large skillet over medium-high heat. Scoop out large tablespoonfuls of batter, form into rounded balls with wet fingertips, and flatten into cakes. In batches, cook cakes over medium heat until brown, turning once, 2 to 3 minutes. Drain on paper towels and place on baking sheet in oven to keep warm until all fritters are made.

NUTRITION FACTS

Serving Size 1 fritter (28g)
Calories 60
Calories from Fat 25
Total Fat 2.5g
Saturated Fat 0g
Trans Fat 0g
Cholesterol 15mg
Sodium 40mg
Total Carbohydrate 8g
Dietary Fiber 1g
Sugars 1g
Protein 1g

Be Merry:
Foods for
Special Occasions
and Everyday
Celebrations

Baked Chicken and Apple Bites

Kids like the round, easy-to-handle shape of meatballs. Here's a twist on the usual beef meatballs using chicken and a touch of sweetness from apples. Serve these with rounded toothpicks and a variety of sauces such as Mustard-Honey Sauce (page 66) or barbecue sauce for dipping, or skewer together with chunks of cheese and pineapple.

MAKES 28 TO 30 (1½-INCH) BALLS

1 organic green apple, such as Granny Smith or Delicious, peeled, cored, and grated
½ pound ground organic free-range chicken
3 green onions, minced (about 3 tablespoons)
1 tablespoon minced fresh parsley
¾ cup dry whole wheat bread crumbs (see Tips, page 176)
¼ teaspoon salt
⅛ teaspoon freshly ground black pepper
1 teaspoon balsamic vinegar

Preheat oven to 400°F. Line a baking sheet with parchment paper and set aside.

Squeeze out excess liquid from grated apple using paper or clean kitchen towels.

Put all ingredients into a food processor and pulse until blended.

Using a melon baller or tablespoon, spoon out a heaping tablespoonful of chicken mixture and roll into a ball using your hands. Repeat until all mixture is used. Place chicken balls on prepared pan. Bake for 10 minutes, until cooked through and brown on bottom.

TIP

Grating or shredding is easiest with a food processor, but can also be done on a box grater. Be sure to squeeze out any excess liquid before adding to mixture.

petit
appetit

EAT, DRINK,
AND
BE MERRY

BAKE SALE

Undoubtedly, your child's school or club will have bake sales. These fruit and veggie breads and spice bars give something unique in a sea of the usual brownies and crispy treats. The breads can bring in higher dollars if presented whole. Or do individual bars and slices for single (i.e., "I want to eat it now!") sales.

Banana Bread

Banana bread is a good treat for sharing. This one is unique in that it doesn't have nuts for those with allergies, and uses date sugar rather than using traditional brown or white sugar. Date sugar is a healthier substitute for sugar in many baked goods, as it is similar in texture, but simply made from dried dates. This is a great do-ahead bread and is even better the next day. If you're looking to make it really special, slice and toast and add sliced bananas, nut butter, or honey on top.

MAKES 1 (8 × 4-INCH) LOAF

1 cup unbleached all-purpose flour
¾ cup whole wheat pastry flour
⅔ cup date sugar
2 teaspoons baking powder
½ teaspoon baking soda
½ teaspoon ground cinnamon
½ teaspoon freshly grated nutmeg
¼ teaspoon salt
2 large ripe bananas, mashed (about 1 cup)
¾ cup orange juice
2 large cage-free organic eggs
4 tablespoons expeller-pressed canola oil

Be Merry:
Foods for
Special Occasions
and Everyday
Celebrations

227

Preheat oven to 350°F. Lightly grease and flour an 8 x 4-inch loaf pan and set aside.

In a mixing bowl, combine flours, date sugar, baking powder, baking soda, spices, and salt.

In a separate bowl, combine the bananas, orange juice, eggs, and oil. Pour into flour mixture. Mix on low speed until combined, then beat on high speed for 2 minutes.

Spoon batter into prepared pan. Bake for 1 hour, until a wooden skewer inserted in the center comes out clean.

Let cool in pan on a wire rack for 20 minutes. Turn out on wire rack to cool completely. If bread does not come out, insert a sharp knife around the edges to loosen. Cut into 15 slices.

Go Green! Think of unique ways to package and present bake sale and food gift items. Recycled tins, mismatched glass plates, bamboo boxes, cheesecloth or fabric wraps, and flower pots all make unique, creative, and reusable packing options.

Young children need some elbow room in the kitchen. Use a several-sizes-larger-than-you'd-think mixing bowl. It can make all the difference in your child's confidence.

MOLLIE KATZEN, bestselling cookbook author and mom of Sam, twenty-one, and Eve, fourteen

---

petit
appetit

EAT, DRINK,
AND
BE MERRY

"Kini" Bread

Add a little green to your child's diet without them realizing their food contains nutritious veggies. The recipe was inspired by my cousin Karen, who made it for a family brunch gathering. My son loved this bread that he called "kini" bread, rather than thinking of zucchini.

MAKES 1 (8 × 4-INCH) LOAF

1½ cups grated unpeeled zucchini
2 cups whole wheat pastry flour
½ teaspoon salt
1 teaspoon baking powder
½ teaspoon baking soda
½ teaspoon ground cinnamon
2 large cage-free organic eggs
1 cup evaporated cane juice
½ cup expeller-pressed canola oil
1 teaspoon pure vanilla extract
½ teaspoon grated organic orange zest (see Go Green! page 156)

Preheat oven to 350°F. Grease an 8 × 4-inch loaf pan and set aside.

Combine the zucchini, flour, salt, baking powder, baking soda, and cinnamon in a large bowl. In a medium bowl, beat the eggs, evaporated cane juice, oil, vanilla, and zest. Make a well in the center of the zucchini mixture. Pour the egg mixture into the well and combine with a rubber spatula.

Pour dough into prepared baking pan. Bake for 1 hour, until a wooden skewer inserted in the center comes out clean.

Let cool in pan on a wire rack for 20 minutes. Turn out on wire rack to cool completely. Cut into 15 slices.

TIP

Double time. Since you're making the recipe anyway, consider doubling to save time and effort. The second loaf can go in your freezer, be shared with the school or neighbors, or made for a gathering. Check to be sure you have enough ingredients before you get started.

NUTRITION FACTS

Serving Size 1 slice (57g)
Calories 190
Calories from Fat 80
Total Fat 8g
Saturated Fat 0.5g
Trans Fat 0g
Cholesterol 30mg
Sodium 170mg
Total Carbohydrate 25g
Dietary Fiber 2g
Sugars 13g
Protein 3g

Be Merry:
Foods for
Special Occasions
and Everyday
Celebrations

Raisin-Spice Bars

This is a very quick and easy treat that makes a large amount for a bake sale, school function, or everyday party. They have a rich color and flavor due to the molasses. Helpful children can add ingredients and stir away.

MAKES 24 BARS

1 cup whole wheat flour
1 cup unbleached all-purpose flour
⅔ cup packed brown sugar
2 teaspoons ground cinnamon
1½ teaspoons ground ginger
½ teaspoon baking soda
½ teaspoon salt
2 large cage-free organic eggs
⅔ cup mild molasses
6 tablespoons organic unsalted butter, melted
2 teaspoons pure vanilla extract
¾ cup organic raisins

Preheat oven to 375°F. Grease a 13 x 9-inch baking pan and set aside.

In a large bowl, stir flours, sugar, cinnamon, ginger, baking soda, and salt with a wooden spoon or rubber spatula until combined. In a medium bowl, whisk together the eggs, molasses, butter, and vanilla. Pour the egg mixture into flour mixture and stir just until blended. Stir in raisins.

Pour batter into prepared pan. Bake for 17 to 20 minutes, until brown on edges; bars should be moist. Cool completely in pan on wire rack. When cool, cut lengthwise into 6 strips then cut each strip crosswise into 4 pieces.

TIP

"Slow as molasses in January" is an adage in American English for someone or something that is very slow. Speed up the molasses and prevent sticking when measuring by first lightly spraying the measuring cup with cooking spray.

petit
appetit

EAT, DRINK,
AND
BE MERRY

SLEEPOVER

There's not much sleeping at a sleepover, but here're a few ways to help celebrate this rite of passage and fortify kids with energy to stay up all night (and morning).

Chicks in the Covers

This is my version of pigs in a blanket, but I felt my improved recipe needed a newer and cuter name. This recipe uses the versatile pizza dough recipe instead of the processed biscuit or rolls from the supermarket. Of course, you can put any favorite sausage, tofu, or beef hot dog in these covers. Here we've used the mini chicken apple sausage because they're already a perfect fit. However, you can cut your favorite sausage into whichever size you'd like for variation. For a crowd of friends, you could even do a variety of meat and vegetarian options and serve with dipping sauces such as Mustard-Honey Sauce (page 66) and organic ketchup.

MAKES 36 (3-PIECE) SERVINGS

Presto Pizza Dough (page 162) or 1 pound whole wheat pizza dough
1 (12-ounce) package precooked mini organic chicken apple sausages

Egg wash (optional)
1 large cage-free organic egg
1 tablespoon organic milk

Preheat oven to 400°F. Line a baking sheet with parchment paper and set aside.

Put dough on a lightly floured surface and flour hands. Press dough into a rectangle shape and roll to ¼-inch thickness, about 12 by 14 inches. Cut dough lengthwise into 1-inch-wide strips. Cut each strip into 4-inch-long pieces.

If using egg wash, whisk together egg and milk in a small bowl.

Be Merry:
Foods for
Special Occasions
and Everyday
Celebrations

Place 1 sausage at end of a dough strip and roll dough around sausage. Place on prepared pan, seam side down, about 1 inch apart. Brush each sausage roll with egg wash (if using). Bake for 12 to 15 minutes, until dough is cooked and heated through.

KIDS KORNER

There are many ways for children to get involved: from rolling and kneading pizza dough to counting and wrapping sausages.

NUTRITION FACTS

Serving Size 3 pieces (67g)
Calories 160
Calories from Fat 80
Total Fat 9g
Saturated Fat 2g
Trans Fat 0g
Cholesterol 45mg
Sodium 330mg
Total Carbohydrate 12g
Dietary Fiber 1g
Sugars 0g
Protein 7g

petit
appetit

EAT, DRINK,
AND
BE MERRY

Oatmeal "Bar"

Oatmeal is an easily digestible grain with a nice creamy texture that lends itself to many flavorings for children and adults alike. See the suggestions below or create your own favorites using this master recipe. This oatmeal can be made and stored in the refrigerator for up to three days. If the whole oats are too coarse for baby or if you prefer a mushy texture, grind uncooked oats in a blender or food processor for a smoother consistency and shorter cooking time.

MAKES ABOUT 2 CUPS

2 cups water
½ teaspoon ground cinnamon
1 teaspoon pure vanilla extract
1 cup rolled oats (see gluten-free icon, page 3)

Combine water, cinnamon, and vanilla in a saucepan and bring to a boil over high heat. Reduce heat to low and stir in oats.

When mixture begins to simmer, cover, turn off heat, and let stand for 15 minutes, until thick and creamy. Stir in flavor options (below) or enjoy alone.

VARIATIONS

To add flavor, color, and texture, add these to ½ cup oats: 1 tablespoon mashed banana and a sprinkle of grated shredded coconut; 1 tablespoon organic applesauce plus 1 tablespoon currants; or 1 tablespoon grated organic apple and a sprinkle of freshly grated nutmeg.

KIDS KORNER

Sundae morning. They didn't sleep, but they're hungry from talking all night. Put out bowls of currants, dried fruit, fresh fruit, honey, spices, and coconut and let the sleepyheads create their own oatmeal sundaes.

NUTRITION FACTS

Serving Size ½ cup
Calories 80
Calories from Fat 10
Total Fat 1.5g
Saturated Fat 0g
Trans Fat 0g
Cholesterol 0mg
Sodium 0mg
Total Carbohydrate 14g
Dietary Fiber 2g
Sugars 1g
Protein 4g

Be Merry:
Foods for
Special Occasions
and Everyday
Celebrations

CAMPING OUT

Whether you're on a family campout in the mountains or just out in Grandma's backyard, you can't sleep in a tent and not make s'mores. It's certainly one of the motivating factors for camping and enduring chilly nights, scary sounds, and no electricity.

S'mores

Here's a favorite graham cracker recipe from *The Petit Appetit Cookbook*. Remember to roll them thinner for crisp grahams or thicker for a cookie version. This time, we've enhanced the recipe for the outdoors. The homemade graham cracker and bittersweet chocolate elevates this snack above the typical processed variety. People (especially adults) are very particular about how they like their marshmallow cooked. Golden versus burned is always the debate around our campfires.

MAKES ABOUT 48 (2-INCH) CRACKERS OR 24 S'MORES

Greatest Graham Crackers
1 cup graham or whole wheat flour
1 cup unbleached all-purpose flour
1 teaspoon baking powder
¼ cup organic unsalted butter
½ cup honey (see Note, page 46)
¼ cup organic milk, plus 1 tablespoon extra for brushing

S'mores
48 Greatest Graham Crackers
24 organic dark chocolate squares
24 kosher marshmallows

Make crackers: Preheat oven to 400°F. Combine flours and baking powder in a medium bowl. Cut in butter until the consistency of corn-

petit
appetit

EAT, DRINK,
AND
BE MERRY

234

meal. Mix in honey; dough will still be lumpy. Mix in milk until a stiff dough comes together.

Roll dough out on a liberally floured surface to ¼-inch thickness. Cut into squares or use cookie cutters to make desired shapes. Prick each cracker with a fork and brush with milk.

Bake crackers on ungreased baking sheets for 12 to 15 minutes, until golden brown. Remove pan from oven and let crackers cool on pan, 2 minutes. Transfer to a wire rack and let cool completely.

Make S'mores: Place a cracker on a small plate. Layer with a chocolate square. Put a marshmallow on a metal skewer. Roast marshmallow until desired color, from golden brown to dark and crispy. Carefully remove marshmallow from skewer and place on chocolate square. Top marshmallow with another cracker and squeeze together. Repeat with remaining crackers, chocolate, and marshmallows.

Be Merry:
Foods for
Special Occasions
and Everyday
Celebrations

SLEEPING-IN SUNDAY

I'm told older children sleep in on weekends once they're active in sports, up late at night, and tired from the school week. Those of us with small children can only hope (and dream). Either way, most families I know like to relax on Sundays with a homemade breakfast. Whether it's at 7 a.m. or 11 a.m., your kids will be waking you for one of these breakfast choices.

French Toast Fingers

This is a crispy version of French toast that's perfect for small hands to pick up and dip in syrup or fruit puree. The crispness is provided by a healthy dose of toasted wheat germ. Remove bread crusts if desired or serve with crusts for extra crunch.

MAKES 24 (1- TO 1½-INCH) FINGERS

6 slices whole wheat bread
3 large cage-free organic eggs
⅓ cup organic whole milk
1 tablespoon freshly squeezed orange juice
1 teaspoon pure vanilla extract
½ teaspoon ground cinnamon
4 tablespoons toasted wheat germ

Preheat oven to 325°F.

Cut bread in half and then each half in half again to form 4 fingers for a total of 24 pieces.

In a shallow bowl, beat eggs, milk, orange juice, vanilla, and cinnamon together. Spread wheat germ on a flat plate.

Carefully add half of the bread fingers to egg and milk mixture to saturate (if bread breaks now, the fingers will be "bites"—still tasty but smaller). Carefully remove egg-soaked bread pieces, shaking off excess, and roll in wheat germ.

petit
appetit

EAT, DRINK,
AND
BE MERRY

236

Lightly grease a nonstick 12-inch skillet and heat over medium heat. Lay bread pieces in a single layer in skillet and cook to brown both sides, about 5 minutes, turning with a spatula.

Remove toast fingers and keep warm on a baking sheet in oven until all toast is cooked. Repeat with remaining bread and cook until golden.

TIP

Breakfast for dinner. Growing up, my mom would sometimes make "breakfast for dinner," which my sister and I thought was a real treat. Now it's fun (and easy) to make for my own kids when they ask. Getting them dressed for dinner also means a pajama party.

NUTRITION FACTS

Serving Size 4 fingers (75g)
Calories 130
Calories from Fat 40
Total Fat 4.5g
Saturated Fat 1.5g
Trans Fat 0g
Cholesterol 105mg
Sodium 170mg
Total Carbohydrate 15g
Dietary Fiber 3g
Sugars 3g
Protein 9g

Be Merry:
Foods for
Special Occasions
and Everyday
Celebrations

Pumpkin Pancakes

Pancakes are a great weekend family tradition as well as a sleepover treat for all ages. These flavorful pancakes have a healthy dose of vitamin C and beta-carotene, thanks to the pumpkin. The canned version has just as many nutrients as fresh and requires much less effort.

MAKES 15 TO 18 (4-INCH) PANCAKES

1 cup whole wheat flour
2 tablespoons turbinado sugar
2 teaspoons baking powder
1 teaspoon salt
1 teaspoon ground cinnamon
¼ teaspoon freshly grated nutmeg
1 ⅓ cups whole organic milk
1 cup canned pumpkin puree
4 large cage-free organic eggs, separated, at room temperature
½ cup organic unsalted butter, melted
1 tablespoon pure vanilla extract

Preheat oven to 200°F.

In a large mixing bowl, stir together flour, sugar, baking powder, salt, cinnamon, and nutmeg until blended.

In a medium mixing bowl, combine milk, pumpkin, egg yolks, butter, and vanilla, and beat until smooth. Pour wet mixture into dry ingredients and stir with a rubber spatula until blended.

In a clean medium mixing bowl with clean, dry beaters, beat egg whites with an electric mixer until stiff peaks form when the beaters are lifted, about 2 minutes. Gently fold egg whites into batter with a rubber spatula until just combined.

Spray a large nonstick griddle or frying pan with cooking spray and heat over medium heat. Pour batter by ¼ cupfuls into pan and cook until bubbles form on top of pancakes, 2 to 3 minutes. Flip each pan-

petit
appetit

EAT, DRINK,
AND
BE MERRY

238

cake and cook until golden, about 1 minute longer. Keep pancakes warm in the oven while cooking remaining batter.

TIP

For convenience, refrigerate any leftover cooked pancakes in an airtight container in the refrigerator for up to three days, or wrap cooked pancakes in waxed paper, seal in freezer bags, and freeze for up to one month. These are perfect for quick snacks to take to school or the park, spread with nut butters, or sandwiched with eggs.

NUTRITION FACTS

Serving Size 1 pancake (63g)

Calories 80
Calories from Fat 20
Total Fat 2.5g
Saturated Fat 1g
Trans Fat 0g
Cholesterol 60mg
Sodium 240mg
Total Carbohydrate 10g
Dietary Fiber 2g
Sugars 3g
Protein 4g

Be Merry:
Foods for
Special Occasions
and Everyday
Celebrations

MAKE FOR THE TEAM

*Y*our son invited the whole soccer team over after the game? Having a few ideas along with a stocked pantry and refrigerator (see pages 10–11) will enable you to create an impromptu get-together. You'll be saved from rushing to the store and you can be ready when the hungry boys arrive. No sweat!

French Bread Pizzas

*F*rench bread pizzas are quick and easy to prepare for a hungry crowd of kids after a practice or game. Stock your refrigerator with preshredded cheese and your prep time is even shorter. Any large, wide loaf will work, or get a variety. See below for some kid-tested favorite toppings.

Cheese Pizzas

MAKES 24 (3-INCH) PIECES

1 (1-pound) ciabatta loaf, about 14 x 7 inches
1 cup Tot's Tomato Sauce (page 63) or favorite no-sugar-added jarred
    marinara or pizza sauce
1 cup grated mozzarella cheese (rBGH-free)
1 cup grated Cheddar cheese (rBGH-free)

Preheat oven to 375°F. Line a baking sheet with aluminum foil and set aside.

Cut the bread lengthwise down the center so you have a top and bottom. Lay pieces, cut sides up, on prepared baking sheet. Spread the tomato sauce on the bread. Sprinkle cheese over sauce.

Bake for about 10 minutes, until the cheese has melted. Cut with a pizza cutter.

NUTRITION FACTS

Serving Size 2 pieces (75g)
Calories 170
Calories from Fat 40
Total Fat 4.5g
Saturated Fat 2.5g
Trans Fat 0g
Cholesterol 10mg
Sodium 470mg
Total Carbohydrate 24g
Dietary Fiber 1g
Sugars 2g
Protein 9g

petit
appetit

EAT, DRINK,
AND
BE MERRY

Veggie Pizzas

MAKES 24 (3-INCH) PIECES

1 (1-pound) ciabatta loaf, about 14 x 7 inches
1 cup Tot's Tomato Sauce (page 63) or favorite no-sugar-added
    jarred marinara or pizza sauce
2 cups grated mozzarella cheese (rBGH-free)
¼ cup sliced black olives
¼ cup sliced fresh mushrooms
½ can sliced canned water-packed artichoke hearts
1 organic red bell pepper, sliced

Preheat oven to 375°F. Line a baking sheet with aluminum foil and set aside.

Cut the bread lengthwise down the center so you have a top and bottom. Lay pieces, cut sides up, on prepared baking sheet. Spread the tomato sauce on the bread. Sprinkle cheese and toppings over sauce.

Bake for about 10 minutes, until the cheese has melted. Cut with a pizza cutter.

NUTRITION FACTS

Serving Size 2 pieces (89g)
Calories 150
Calories from Fat 15
Total Fat 2g
Saturated Fat 0g
Trans Fat 0g
Cholesterol 0mg
Sodium 550mg
Total Carbohydrate 25g
Dietary Fiber 2g
Sugars 2g
Protein 9g

Be Merry:
Foods for
Special Occasions
and Everyday
Celebrations

The Big Veggie Sandwich

When I was about eight or nine, I remember having a six-foot-long submarine sandwich at one of my birthday parties. Friends and family all came to the park and we had water balloon tosses and sack races. This isn't six feet long, but it is big. The best part is you can layer on your favorite veggie or meat combinations to come up with a single perfect sandwich or multiple tastes for your sack racers and fans.

MAKES 8 (2-INCH-WIDE) SERVINGS

1 (1-pound) ciabatta or pugliese loaf, about 14 × 7 inches
1 organic red bell pepper
1 zucchini
1 summer squash
1 portobello mushroom
3 tablespoons plus 1 teaspoon extra-virgin olive oil
1 tablespoon balsamic vinegar
1 tablespoon minced fresh thyme
1 (14-ounce) can water-packed artichoke hearts, chopped
4 ounces goat cheese (rBGH-free)

Preheat oven to 400°F. Line a baking sheet with aluminum foil. Spray a 12 × 9-inch glass baking dish with oil and set aside.

Slice vegetables lengthwise into ¼- to ⅓-inch-thick slices and layer in prepared dish.

In a small bowl, whisk together 3 tablespoons of the oil, the vinegar, and thyme. Brush vegetables with oil mixture. Bake for 25 minutes, until vegetables are tender. Remove from oven and set aside. Leave oven on.

Cut the bread lengthwise down the center so you have a top and bottom. Lay pieces, cut sides up, on a prepared baking sheet. Spread the artichoke hearts on the bottom half and goat cheese on the top half. Drizzle artichokes with 1 teaspoon of the oil. Bake for about 5 minutes, until warm.

petit
appetit

EAT, DRINK,
AND
BE MERRY

242

Layer vegetable slices on bread over artichokes and top with remaining bread, goat cheese side down. Press sandwich together and weigh down the sandwich with a baking dish or heavy plate. Let sit for 5 minutes before cutting.

TIP
Packing. If taking these for travel, be sure to wrap tightly and place toothpicks in each section to hold together. Remove picks before serving.

NUTRITION FACTS

Serving Size ⅙ of sandwich (160g)

Calories 300

Calories from Fat 110

Total Fat 12g

Saturated Fat 4.5g

Trans Fat 0g

Cholesterol 15mg

Sodium 440mg

Total Carbohydrate 36g

Dietary Fiber 3g

Sugars 4g

Protein 12g

Be Merry:
Foods for
Special Occasions
and Everyday
Celebrations

POTLUCKS

Are you the person always bringing the paper goods or the fast-food chicken to the potluck events? Make a homemade change with some healthy, easy recipes for every category from main dish, to side veggie, to salad, to dessert. Other parents and children just may ask you for your recipes!

Chicken Skewers with Tzatziki Sauce

This is a tasty chicken main dish that takes very little time, either cooked on an outside grill or indoor grill pan. The marinade will be flavorful after only ten minutes, and there's no need to let it sit more than thirty minutes. These work well for potlucks or family dinners served along with whole wheat pita bread and spinach leaves. The sauce is not as spicy as most tzatziki sauces, as it is made with green onions rather than the more flavorful red onions.

MAKES 6 (8-INCH) SKEWERS

Zest and juice of 1 organic lemon
Zest and juice of 1 organic lime
Zest and juice of 1 organic orange
¼ teaspoon ground coriander
1 clove garlic, finely chopped
2 tablespoons extra-virgin olive oil
1½ pounds free-range organic chicken breasts (about 3), cut into 1-inch cubes

Tzatziki Sauce
½ cucumber, peeled, seeded, and grated (about ¼ cup)
1 cup Greek-style yogurt
¼ cup chopped green onions (about 4)

petit
appetit

EAT, DRINK,
AND
BE MERRY

244

½ teaspoon ground coriander

Zest and juice of ½ organic lemon

Zest and juice of ½ organic lime

¼ teaspoon sea salt

⅛ teaspoon freshly ground black pepper, or more to taste

Soak 8-inch wooden skewers in water for 30 minutes or longer, or use metal skewers.

Whisk together lemon, lime, and orange zests and juices in a large bowl with coriander, garlic, and oil. Place chicken pieces in marinade and leave for a minimum of 10 minutes, but no longer than 30 minutes. Preheat grill.

Make sauce: Stir together all ingredients in a small bowl, adding pepper to taste.

Thread chicken pieces onto skewers and place on hot outdoor grill or indoor grill pan and cook until chicken is cooked through, 4 to 5 minutes on each side.

TIP

Presentation is everything. Remember to write your dish's ingredients on a card to attach to your food so people with allergies and intolerances won't have to wonder and ask. Also consider the venue; will people be sitting or standing? Can they eat this off the stick or should it be cut?

Go Green! While lemon, lime, and orange are not on the Dirty Dozen list as potentially harmful, we're suggested organic because we're using the zest (outside peel) where pesticides can be heavy.

NUTRITION FACTS

Serving Size 1 skewer with sauce (229g)

Calories 280

Calories from Fat 80

Total Fat 9g

Saturated Fat 2g

Trans Fat 0g

Cholesterol 100mg

Sodium 210mg

Total Carbohydrate 8g

Dietary Fiber 1g

Sugars 5g

Protein 38g

Be Merry:
Foods for
Special Occasions
and Everyday
Celebrations

Wheatberry and Citrus Dressing Salad

For those children who like crunch, wheatberries are an interesting, nutty, and plump option. They can be enjoyed hot or cold and with just about any dressing, veggies, or nuts. Wheatberries can be found in natural food stores and organic markets in the bulk cereal and grain section.

MAKES ABOUT 6 CUPS

2 cups wheatberries, rinsed
6 cups water
2 teaspoons fine-grain sea salt

Dressing
Grated zest and juice of 1 organic orange, about 2 teaspoons
   (see Go Green! page 156)
1 tablespoon freshly squeezed lemon juice
2 tablespoons minced green onion
½ cup extra-virgin olive oil
Salt and freshly ground black pepper, to taste

½ cup grape or cherry tomatoes, halved
½ cup kalamata olives, sliced
¼ cup shredded Parmesan cheese (rBGH-free)

Combine wheatberries, water, and salt in a large saucepan over medium-high heat. Bring to a boil, reduce heat, and cover. Simmer until plump and chewy, about 1 hour. Berries will still be al dente. Drain and transfer to a serving bowl.

Make dressing: In a small bowl, whisk together orange zest, orange and lemon juices, and onion. Whisk in olive oil and season with salt and pepper.

Mix tomatoes, olives, and cheese into wheatberries. Drizzle with dressing and toss to combine.

petit
appetit

EAT, DRINK,
AND
BE MERRY

Petit Potatoes with Sunshine Sauce

This ultra-easy side dish combines these tender little gems with a creamy calcium-rich dip full of flavor. The presentation brings families and friends together for a barbecue, potluck, or brunch.

MAKES 8 SERVINGS

2 pounds organic fingerling potatoes, the smallest you can find
    (1 to 2 inches in diameter)
2 tablespoons extra-virgin olive oil
2 teaspoons freshly squeezed lemon juice
½ teaspoon coarse sea salt

Sunshine Sauce
¼ cup organic plain whole-milk yogurt
2 tablespoons minced fresh chives
1 tablespoon prepared mustard
Salt and freshly ground black pepper, to taste

Preheat oven to 375°F. Place potatoes in a ceramic or glass baking dish.

In a small bowl, combine oil and lemon juice with a fork and drizzle over potatoes; stir to coat. Sprinkle salt over top of potatoes and stir.

Bake for 30 to 40 minutes, stirring halfway through cooking, until potatoes are fork-tender and skins are browned.

Make sauce: Stir together all ingredients in a small bowl, mixing thoroughly.

Place sauce in the middle of a warmed platter. Arrange potatoes around sauce bowl and use picks for spearing the potatoes. Serve the potatoes hot or at room temperature.

Go Green! Potatoes are the most consumed vegetable in the United States (unfortunately mostly in the form of French fries). However they are also one of the most susceptible to pesticide contamination. They are the only peeled item to make the EWG's Dirty Dozen list (see page 15).

NUTRITION FACTS

Serving Size about 1 cup
with dip (129g)
Calories 130
Calories from Fat 35
Total Fat 4g
Saturated Fat 0.5g
Trans Fat 0g
Cholesterol 0mg
Sodium 180mg
Total Carbohydrate 21g
Dietary Fiber 1g
Sugars 0g
Protein 3g

Be Merry:
Foods for
Special Occasions
and Everyday
Celebrations

Lasagna Roll-Ups

This recipe is courtesy of Michelle Stern, owner and teacher of What's Cooking, a children's cooking school in San Rafael, California. Michelle is great at getting the kids involved, both having fun and learning to cook. This recipe is also fun for a large family Sunday supper or for a team of hungry kids.

MAKES 12 SERVINGS

2 cups Tot's Tomato Sauce (page 63) or jarred pasta sauce without added sugar

12 to 14 lasagna noodles (10 × 2 inches with curled edges), boil extra to allow for breakage

2 large cage-free organic eggs

3 cups low-fat ricotta cheese (rBGH-free)

½ cup grated Parmesan cheese (rBGH-free)

2 cups shredded mozzarella cheese (rBGH-free)

1 teaspoon Italian seasoning

½ teaspoon salt

¼ teaspoon freshly ground black pepper

4 ounces fresh organic baby spinach leaves, chopped (about 3 cups)

12 cremini mushrooms, sliced (about 1½ cups)

Preheat oven to 350°F. Spread a few spoonfuls of sauce in bottom of an 8-inch-square glass or ceramic baking dish to coat bottom and set aside.

Cook lasagna noodles according to manufacturer's instructions. Drain, rinse in cold water, and lay noodles on a cutting board or work surface in a single layer until ready to use.

In a large bowl, lightly beat eggs; stir in ricotta cheese, Parmesan cheese, 1 cup mozzarella cheese, the Italian seasoning, salt, and pepper until mixed.

Place a lasagna noodle in front of you. Spread 2 to 3 tablespoons of the cheese mixture along the entire length of the noodle. Top with ¹⁄₁₂ of the spinach and ¹⁄₁₂ of the mushrooms and a little sauce, as desired.

petit
appetit

EAT, DRINK,
AND
BE MERRY

248

Carefully roll up the noodle and place it curly side up in the prepared baking dish.

Pour remaining sauce over the tops and between rolls and sprinkle with remaining mozzarella cheese.

Cover the dish with tented foil and bake for 15 minutes. Remove the foil and bake for an additional 10 to 15 minutes, until cheese is melted and noodles are heated through.

KIDS KORNER

Michelle has some good tips for empowering children to help with this recipe:
Let children use an egg slicer to slice mushrooms. With supervision, let older children snip spinach into pieces with kitchen scissors. Or tear into little pieces with clean fingers. Give children a rotary grater to grate cheese (and protect little knuckles). Have children assemble and roll lasagna rolls, and stack in the pan.

NUTRITION FACTS

Serving Size 1 roll-up (179g)
Calories 260
Calories from Fat 80
Total Fat 9g
Saturated Fat 4g
Trans Fat 0g
Cholesterol 50mg
Sodium 490mg
Total Carbohydrate 34g
Dietary Fiber 2g
Sugars 5g
Protein 15g

Be Merry:
Foods for
Special Occasions
and Everyday
Celebrations

Monica's Edamame Salad

My friend Monica brought our family a lovely dinner after I came home from the hospital when my daughter was born. The best part was this yummy and beautiful salad, and it quickly became a family favorite. Whenever I make it, my son asks, "Did Monica make this for us?" This is a very versatile and quick dish because you can use many prepackaged convenience items (such as slivered almonds), make use of leftover cooked rice, or even find precooked rice in your store. It can be made ahead for a potluck picnic or school event.

MAKES 10 CUPS

1½ cups cooked brown rice (left over or prepackaged)
1 (10-ounce) package frozen organic white corn, thawed
1 (16-ounce) package frozen organic edamame, cooked according to
    package directions
½ cup chopped organic celery
⅓ cup organic golden raisins
¼ cup chopped green onions (about 4)
½ cup julienned fresh basil leaves

Dressing
3 tablespoons seasoned rice vinegar
5 tablespoons expeller-pressed canola oil
1 tablespoon freshly squeezed lemon juice
½ teaspoon salt
½ teaspoon freshly ground black pepper

⅓ cup sliced or slivered almonds

Combine rice, corn, edamame, celery, raisins, onions, and basil in a large bowl.

Make the dressing: In a small bowl, whisk together dressing ingredients.

Pour dressing over salad and toss with a spoon until everything is coated. Sprinkle almond pieces over top.

petit
appetit

EAT, DRINK,
AND
BE MERRY

250

TIP

Picky, picky! For a choosy eater, separate out items such as raisins and edamame that make great snacks on their own, without the fight over "mixing it all together" or getting "dressing on everything."

Go Green! Bring reusable or renewable paper goods for greener dining for everyone!

NUTRITION FACTS

Serving Size 1 cup (133g)
Calories 220
Calories from Fat 100
Total Fat 11g
Saturated Fat 0.5g
Trans Fat 0g
Cholesterol 0mg
Sodium 220mg
Total Carbohydrate 23g
Dietary Fiber 4g
Sugars 6g
Protein 7g

Be Merry:
Foods for
Special Occasions
and Everyday
Celebrations

Apple-Oatmeal Cobbler

Here's a spelt flour alternative for those not eating all-purpose or whole wheat flours. This can be made with just about any ripe apples you choose, but I like the Yellow Delicious for both a sweet and tart flavor. The cobbler is gooey and will require a fork or spoon. This is great warm out of the oven with a scoop of vanilla frozen yogurt or ice cream on top.

MAKES 9 SERVINGS

7 cups sliced, peeled, cored organic apple slices (about ½ pound, about 3 to 4 apples)
⅓ cup pure maple syrup
¼ cup pineapple juice
1 tablespoon organic unsalted butter
1 teaspoon pure vanilla extract
¼ teaspoon ground cinnamon

Topping
½ cup white spelt or white whole wheat flour
½ cup packed brown sugar
¾ cup rolled oats
⅛ teaspoon sea salt
¼ teaspoon ground cinnamon
¼ cup organic unsalted butter

Preheat oven to 375°F. Grease an 8-inch-square baking dish with butter or cooking oil and set aside.

Cook apples, syrup, pineapple juice, butter, vanilla, and cinnamon in a large stockpot over medium heat until apples are tender. (The thinner the slices, the quicker they'll cook: ¼-inch thick, 5 to 6 minutes; ½-inch thick, about 10 minutes.)

Make the topping: In a large bowl, mix together flour, sugar, oats, salt, and cinnamon with a fork. Cut in butter with a pastry blender or process all together with a food processor.

Spoon apple mixture into prepared baking dish. Sprinkle with topping. Bake for 30 minutes, until golden brown. Cut into "squares" or spoon out of pan to serve.

petit
appetit

EAT, DRINK,
AND
BE MERRY

Minty Winter Fruit Salad

Hard to say the name (five times fast), but this easy and colorful salad is a break from the usual fruit salad offering at brunch or dinner gatherings. The fruit and fresh mint pair nicely together for a crisp, clean, and sweet treat at the end of a meal.

MAKES 6 SERVINGS

1 pomegranate

3 tablespoons chopped fresh mint

1 teaspoon evaporated cane juice

1 ripe pineapple, peeled, quartered, cored, and cut into bite-size pieces (about 4 cups)

1 mango, peeled, pitted, and cut into bite-size pieces (about 2 cups)

Fill a large bowl with water. Score pomegranate with a sharp knife into quarters going through the blossom end. Do not cut deeper than pith. Immerse pomegranate in water and pull apart at cuts. Continue to work under water and use fingers to pull seeds from pith. The seeds will sink to the bottom and the pith will float on top. Pour off water and pith and drain seeds.

Put mint in a mortar and grind with a pestle to release juices. Add evaporated cane juice and mash together.

Place pomegranate seeds, pineapple, and mango in a medium serving bowl. Stir in mint–cane juice mixture to combine and coat fruit. Chill in refrigerator.

KIDS KORNER

When my sister and I were little, we (mostly she) loved pomegranates. She would open them and the seeds would fly everywhere, staining her clothing and anything else in the way. I was so excited to find this trick about freeing the seeds without a mess (thank you, Lily Pulitzer). Even a child can do it.

Be Merry:
Foods for
Special Occasions
and Everyday
Celebrations

Food, Nutrition, and Shopping Resources

DOCTORS AND NUTRITIONISTS

Bernsten, Brock, MD, Town and Country Pediatrics, Mill Valley, CA

Delmonico, Sanna, MS, RD, Tiny Tummies: www.tinytummies.com

Frazee, Gianna, MD, Town and Country Pediatrics, Mill Valley, CA

Halas-Liang, Melissa, MA, RD, CDE, CNSD, Super Kids Nutrition: www.superkidsnutrition.com

Laake, Dana, RDH, MS, LDN, Dana Laake Nutrition: www.danalaake.com

Vakili, Ladan, DMD, Pediatric Dentist, Kentfield, CA

COOKING COACHES, CLASSES, AND RESTAURANTS

Andrews, Amy, kitchen coach, Amy's Food Room, food blog and original recipes: www.amysfoodroom.com

Gingrass, David, chef/owner, and Andrea Mautner, pastry chef, TWO Restaurant, San Francisco: www.two-sf.com

Lindsay, Sarah, owner, Sarah Lindsay Cakes, San Francisco: cakes, classes for kids and teens, www.sarahlindsaycakes.com

Markworth, Adrienne, director, Leah's Pantry: nonprofit nutritional education for families and children in transitional housing, www.leahspantry.org

Robertson, Ged, chef/owner, Small Shed Flatbreads, Mill Valley, CA: www.smallshed.com

Stern, Michelle, owner, What's Cooking: cooking classes and gifts for children, www.whatscooking.info

ALLERGY AND DIETARY WEBSITES

Celiac Health: info, education, and research regarding gluten-free diet and celiac disease, www.celiachealth.org

The Food Allergy and Anaphylaxis Network: info, education, research, and advocacy for those with food allergies, www.foodallergy.org

Gluten-Free Diet: info, education, and research regarding a gluten-free diet and celiac disease, www.glutenfreediet.ca

SUSTAINABLE EATING WEBSITES

100 Mile Diet: how to eat only food produced within a 100-mile radius of your home, www.100milediet.org

Eat Well Guide: www.eatwellguide.org/index.cfm

Organic Consumers Association: news, articles, research, and advocacy for organic foods and products, www.organicconsumers.org

Organictobe.org: blog of organic articles, news, and recipes, www.organictobe.org

Seafood Watch: make safe seafood choices for your local area, www.seafoodwatch.org

Sustainable Table: discover what's in season in your area, www.sustainabletable.org

ENVIRONMENTAL WEBSITES

Children's Environmental Network: www.cehn.org

Environmental Defense Fund: www.edf.org

Environmental Protection Agency: www.epa.gov

Environmental Working Group: www.ewg.org

Healthy Child Healthy World: www.healthychild.org

Institute for Children's Environmental Health: www.iceh.org

FARMERS' MARKETS AND CSA

Local Harvest: locate farmers' market or CSA (community-supported agriculture) near your home, www.localharvest.org

United State Department of Agriculture: search for wholesale and farmers' market by state, www.ams.usda.gov/farmersmarkets/map.htm

SCHOOL AND COMMUNITY PROGRAMS

Edible Schoolyard Project: organic school garden and cooking curriculum developed by Chef Alice Waters, www.edibleschoolyard.org

Farm-to-School: connecting the dots between local agriculture and school meals, www.farmtoschool.org

National Gardening Association: plant-based education through schools, communities, and backyards, www.kidsgardening.org

SPECIALTY FOOD WEBSITES

Alter Eco: fair trade chocolates, sugars, rice, teas, www.altereco-usa.com

Arrowhead Mills: organic and gluten-free whole grain products, www.arrowheadmills.com

Bob's Red Mill: organic and gluten-free whole grain flours and cereals, www.bobsredmill.com

Eden Foods: organic beans, pastas, whole grains, condiment products, www.edenfoods.com

India Tree: natural colors sugar and spice purveyor, www.indiatree.com

Maranatha Foods: organic and natural nut and seed butters, www.maranathanutbutters.com

Spectrum Organics: organic and expeller-pressed oils, www.spectrumorganics.com

Wholesome Sweeteners: organic sweeteners (molasses, agave nectar, honey, raw sugars, syrups), www.wholesomesweeteners.com

PRODUCT WEBSITES

Born Free: Bisphenol A–, PVC-, and phthalate-free bottles and cups, www.newbornfree.com

Built NY: insulated, soft baby bottle and drink carriers, www.builtny.com

Fabkins: cloth napkins for kids, www.fabkins.com

Fleurville: PVC-free lunch totes and packs, www.fleurville.com

Green to Grow: Bisphenol A–, PVC-, and phthalate-free bottles, www.greentogrow.com

Klean Kanteen: stainless steel drinking containers, www.kleankanteen.com

Laptop Lunches: bento box–style lunchbox system, www.laptoplunches.com

Lunchopolis: lead-free insulated lunchbox system, www.lunchopolis.com

Sigg: aluminum drinking containers, www.sigg.ch

Thinkbaby: Bisphenol A–, lead-, phthalate-, and nitrosamines-free bottles and cups, www.thinkbaby.com

Wrap-N-Mat: reusable sandwich wrap and placemat in one, www.wrap-n-mat.com

FOOD RETAILERS

Elephant Pharmacy: www.elephantpharmacy.com

Trader Joe's: www.traderjoes.com

Whole Foods: www.wholefoodsmarket.com

PARENTING MAGAZINES AND WEBSITES

Cookie magazine: www.cookiemagazine.com

Kiwi Magazine: www.kiwimagazine.com

Parents magazine: www.parentsmagazine.com

Real Age Parenting Center: www.realage.com/parentingcenter

Wondertime Magazine: www.wondertime.com

Books and Periodical Resources

BOOKS

Barnes, Lisa. *The Petit Appetit Cookbook.* New York: Penguin, 2005.

Better Homes and Garden Books. *New Cookbook.* Des Moines, IA: Meredith Corporation, 1989.

Collister, Linda. *Cooking with Kids.* New York: Ryland Peters & Small, Inc., 2003.

Compart, Pamela, and Dana Laake. *The Kid-Friendly ADHD & Autism Cookbook: The Ultimate Guide to the Gluten-Free, Casein-Free Diet.* Gloucester, MA: Fair Winds Press, 2006.

Eisenberg, Arlene, Heidi Murkoff, and Sandee Hathaway. *What to Expect: The Toddler Years.* New York: Workman Publishing, 1996.

Evers, Connie Liakos. *How to Teach Nutrition to Kids.* Portland, OR: 24 Carrot Press, 2006.

Hemmert, Amy, and Tammy Pelstring. *The Laptop Lunch User's Guide.* Santa Cruz, CA: Morning Run Press, 2002.

Lappe, Anna, and Bryant Terry. *Grub: Ideas for an Urban Organic Kitchen.* New York: Penguin, 2006.

Roberts, Susan B., and Melvin Heyman, *Feeding Your Child for Lifelong Health.* New York: Bantam Books, 1999.

Satter, Ellyn. *Child of Mine: Feeding with Love and Good Sense,* X edition. Boulder, CO: Bull Publishing, 2000.

Stewart, Martha. *Martha Stewart's Hors D'oeuvres Handbook,* 1st edition. New York: Clarkson N. Potter, Inc., 1999.

Stowell, Penelope. *The Greatest Potatoes.* New York: Hyperion Books for Children, 2005.

Swain, Anne, Velencia Soutter, and Robert Loblay. *Allergy-Friendly Food.* New York: Barnes and Noble Books, 2004.

Swanson, Heidi. *Super Natural Cooking.* Berkeley, CA: Celestial Arts, 2007.

Tamborlane, William, V., MD. *The Yale Guide to Children's Nutrition in Cooperation with the James Beard Foundation.* New Haven, CT: Yale University Press, 1997.

PERIODICALS AND WEBSITES

Body & Soul magazine, "Plastics and Their Use Question," online, May 10, 2007.

Cookie magazine, "A Fresh Take," Julie Alvin, February 2008.

Cookie magazine, "Green Acres," Yolanda Edwards, March/April 2006.

Delicious Living magazine, "Organic Matters," Susan Enfield Esrey, September 2007.

Kiwi Magazine, "My Organic Prescription," Alan Greene, MD, FAAP, April 2007.

The New York Times, "Some Food Additives Raise Hyperactivity, Study Finds," Elisabeth Rosenthal, September 26, 2007.

The Oregonian, "Seattle Study Shows Striking Toxicity Gulf Between Kids Who Ate Organic and Conventional Foods," online, January 30, 2008.

Organic Style, "Sweet, But Sinister," Debra Ginsberg, June 2005.

Organic Style, "Now Is the Fresh Foods Moment," Alexandra Zissu, May 2005.

Web MD—FDA News Release: Food Labels Must List Allergens, "Ingredients from Major Allergenic Foods Will Be Clearly Noted on Product Labels," Jeannie Lerch Davis, December 2005.

Wondertime Magazine, "Natural Selection," Catherine Newman, March 2008.

Index

Page numbers in **bold** indicate tables;
those in *italic* indicate icons.

Index

About the Author

LISA BARNES is the author of the iParenting Media Award–winning book *The Petit Appetit Cookbook: Easy, Organic Recipes to Nurture Your Baby and Toddler* and *Williams-Sonoma's Cooking for Baby Cookbook*. She founded Petit Appetit, a culinary service devoted to the palates and health of infants and toddlers. She started Petit Appetit because she wanted children to establish good eating habits and healthy food choices from their very first bite.

Seven years after starting Petit Appetit, and watching her own children in the kitchen and at the table, Ms. Barnes continues her passion for cooking and education. She continues to teach parents how to provide fresh, healthy, organic foods to their children through private in-home cooking classes, mothers' groups cooking demonstrations, and parenting workshops throughout Northern California. She feels it is invaluable to share recipes, feeding experiences, celebration ideas, and organic tips with other parents so they are empowered to make thoughtful and informed decisions when shopping, cooking, and eating. She also believes engaging children in this cooking process and the family meal will build confidence and enable them to make healthy eating choices when they are away from home and face outside influences of peers, family, school, and the media.

In an effort to reach a larger audience, Ms. Barnes is a frequent contributor to a variety of parenting and organic websites, including Organic to Be (www.organictobe.org), iVillage (www.ivillage.com), Organic Picks (www.organicpicks.com) and Mommy Track'd (www.mommytrackd.com). Ms. Barnes's volunteer activities focus on healthy food for all incomes, and she sits on the board of directors of Leah's Pantry, a nonprofit organization providing nutrition workshops to families, children, and seniors living in transitional and affordable housing communities.

Ms. Barnes believes healthy food should be enjoyed every day, by all ages and incomes, and should connect people to family, friends, and community. Most important, she shares her love, food, and laughter with her husband, Lee; son, Jonas; and daughter, Ellery, in Sausalito, California.